DICTIONARY OF PROVERBS

Grenville Kleiser

A.P.H. PUBLISHING CORPORATION
5, ANSARI ROAD, DARYA GANJ
NEW DELHI-110 002

Published by
S. B. Nangia
A.P.H. Publishing Corporation
5, Ansari Road, Darya Ganj
New Delhi-110 002
☎ 23274050

2005

© Author

Typesetting at
NEW APCON
20, DDA Shopping Complex
Panchsheel Park
New Delhi - 110 017
☎ 26494336, 51750865
Mobile : 9312231007

Printed in India at
Chaman Enterprises Patoudi House
Darya Ganj New Delhi-110002
☎ 23271595

PREFACE

Proverbs and idioms tell much above people's traditional ways of experiencing reality, about the proper or expected way of doing things, about values and warnings, and rules and wisdoms the elders want to impress on the minds of their young. The punch line character of proverbs — the shorter the better — makes it easy to commit them to memory for ready recall when the occasion calls for serious or humorous comment or admonition. Created by people in high and low stations, humble folk and great authors, borrowed from ancient or neighbouring cultures, proverbs have been accumulating over many centuries. Some are only locally known; many are shared around the world.

So this book will help to know the different proverbs being used alphabetically. It also has the proverbs written by the famous authors.

Grenville Kleiser

Contents

Preface v

Proverbs 1-216

    A 1
    B 26
    C 33
    D 39
    E 48
    F 54
    G 60
    H 65
    I 74
    J 115
    K 116
    L 118
    M 130
    N 138
    O 145
    P 152
    Q 158
    R 159
    S 163
    T 172
    U 186
    V 187
    W 188
    Y 207
    Z 216

Proverbs by Subjects 217

Proverbs

A baby is an alimentary canal with a loud voice at one end and no responsibility at the other.

A bank is a place that will lend you money if you can prove that you don't need it.
— *Bob Hope*

A banker is a fellow who lends you his umbrella when the sun is shining, but wants it back the minute it begins to rain.
— *Mark Twain*

A beginning is the time for taking the most delicate care that balances are correct.
— *Princess Irulan*

A Bible falling apart could only belong to a person who isn't.

A bike rest on its leg because it is too tyred.

A bird does not sing because it has an answer - it sings because it has a song.

A boaster and a liar are first cousins.

A book holds a house of gold.

A book is like a garden carried in the pocket.

A bookstore is one of the only pieces of evidence we have that people are still thinking.
— *Jerry Seinfeld*

A boy anxious to mow the lawn is too young to.

A budget is something we go without to stay within.

A camel is a horse designed by a committee.

A candidate is a person who gets money from the rich and votes from the poor to protect them from each other.

A celebrity is a person who is known for his well-knownness.

A celebrity is someone who works hard all his life to become known and then wears dark glasses to avoid being recognized.

A certain man in Texas has such a big mouth he can sing a duet by himself.

A child does not have to be taught how to be happy or the ways of love. It is fear, hatred, and prejudice that have to be taught. And from the condition of the world we can see that unfortunately there are some very good teachers.
— Javan

A child is a person who can dismantle in 5 minutes the toy it took you 5 hours to put together.

A child's life is like a piece of paper on which every person leaves a mark.

A cigarette is a pinch of tobacco, wrapped in paper, fire at one end, fool at the other.

A civilized society is one which tolerates eccentricity to the point of doubtful sanity.
— Robert Frost

A classic is something that everybody wants to have read and nobody wants to read.
— Mark Twain

A collection at a church service is one in which many take a passing interest.

A committee is a group of people who individually can do nothing, but as a group decide that nothing can be done.

A committee is a life form with six or more legs and no brain.
— Robert A. Heinlein

A common mistake that people make when trying to design something completely foolproof was to underestimate the ingenuity of complete fools.

A community is like a ship; everyone ought to be prepared to take the helm.
— Henrik Ibsen

A conclusion is simply the place where you got tired of thinking.

A conservative is a politician who wants to keep what the liberals fought for a generation ago.

A coward is incapable of exhibiting love; it is the prerogative of the brave.
— Mahatma Gandhi

A crumb from a winner's table is better than a feast from a loser's table!

Proverbs

A cynic is a person who knows the prize of everything and the value of nothing.
— Oscar Wilde

A cynic is someone who knows the price of everything and the value of nothing.

A day without sunshine is like, you know, night.

A day you waste is one you can never make up.
— George Allen

A democracy is a government in the hands of men of low birth, no property, and vulgar employments.
— Aristotle

A difference which makes no difference is not a difference.
— Mr. Spock

A diplomat is a man who always remembers a woman's birthday but never her age.
— Robert Frost

A disbelief in God does not result in a belief in nothing; disbelief in God usually results in a belief in anything.

A doctrine which is able to maintain itself not in clear light, but only in the dark, will of necessity lose its effect on mankind, with incalculable harm to human progress.
— Albert Einstein

A dog in a kennel barks at his fleas; a dog hunting does not notice them.

A dog is the only thing on earth that loves you more than he loves himself.
— Josh Billings

A dog may be the only opportunity a human has to choose a relative.
— Mordecai Siegal

A dog teaches a boy fidelity, perseverance, and to turn around three times before lying down.
— Robert Benchley

A dog thinks: Hey, these people I live with feed me, love me, provide me with a nice warm, dry house, pet me, and take good care of me. They must be Gods! A cat thinks: Hey, these people I live with feed me, love me, provide me with a nice warm, dry house, pet me, and take good care of me. I must be a God!

A dream is the mind's way of answering a question it hasn't yet figured out how to ask.
— David Duchoyny

A dreamer is one who can only find his way by moonlight, and his punishment is that he sees the dawn before the rest of the world.
— *Oscar Wilde*

A faithful friend is a medicine for life.

A faithful friend is better than gold.

A farmer who has mowed down a thousand flowers in his meadow to feed his cows should take care that on his way home he does not, in wanton pastime, switch off the head of a single flower growing at the edge of the road, for in so doing he injures life without being forced to do so by necessity.
— *Albert Schweitzer*

A father is a man who expects his children to be as good as he meant to be.

A father is someone who carried snapshots where his money used to be.

A fault which humbles a man is of more use to him than a virtue which puffs him up.

A few hours of mountain climbing turn a villain and a saint into two rather equal creature. Exhaustion is the shortest way to equality and fraternity, and liberty is added eventually by sleep.
— *Friedrich Nietzsche*

A fine is a tax for doing wrong. A tax is a fine for doing well.

A flawed concept is to elect people to rule over us, then allow them the authority to take our money.

A fly, Sir, may sting a stately horse and make him wince; but one is but an insect, and the other is a horse still.
— *Samuel Johnson*

A fool's brain digests philosophy into folly, science into superstition, and art into pedantry. Hence University education.
— *George Bernard Shaw*

A friend by your side can keep you warmer than the richest furs.

A friend cannot be known in prosperity; an enemy cannot be hidden in adversity.

A friend in power is a friend lost.

A friend is one who is there to care.

A friend is one who knows you and loves you just the same.
— *Elbert Hubbard*

Proverbs

A friend is one who walks in when the rest of the world walks out.

A friend is someone that won't begin to talk behind your back when you leave the room.

A friend is someone who can see the truth and pain in you even when you are fooling everyone else.

A friend is someone who dances with you in the sunlight and walks beside you in the shadows.

A friend is someone, who upon seeing another friend in immense pain, would rather be the one experiencing the pain than to have to watch their friend suffer.

— *Amanda Gier*

A friend is the little prize in the cereal box of life.

A friend of mine has a great attitude: When something doesn't go his way, instead of crying over spilt milk, he just milks another cow!

— *Alexander Lockhart*

A friend of mine once sent me a post card with a picture of the entire planet Earth taken from space. On the back it said, "Wish you were here."

— *Steven Wright*

A friend takes an interest in you - but not a controlling one. A friend that isn't in need is a friend indeed.

A friend to all is a friend to none.

— *Aristotle*

A friend will joyfully sing with you when you are on the mountain top, and silently walk beside you through the valley.

A friend will see you through after others see you are through.

A friend will strengthen you with his prayers, bless you with his love, and encourage you with his hope.

A friend you can buy can be bought from you.

A friendship can weather most things and thrive in thin soil, but it needs a little mulch of letters and phone calls and small, silly presents every so often — just to save it from drying out completely.

— *Pam Brown*

A garden is evidence of faith. It links us with all the misty figures of the past who also planted and were nourished by the fruits of their planting.

— *Gladys Taber*

A genius shoots at something no one else sees - and hits it!

A girl phoned me and said, "Come on over; there's nobody home." I went over. Nobody was home!

A good friend is one who can tell you all his problems - but doesn't.

A good laugh is the best medicine, whether you are sick or not.

A good many childhood ailments are cured miraculously as soon as it's too late to go to school.

A good reason to have dreams is that in dreams, you don't have to have reasons.

A good school is a community where children learn to live first and foremost as children and not as future adults.

A good sermon should have a good beginning and a good ending, and they should be as close together as possible.
— George Burns

A good way to threaten somebody is to light a stick of dynamite. Then you call the guy and hold the burning fuse up to the phone. "Hear that?" you say. "That's dynamite, baby."

A government can only rule as long as the people allow.

A great many children face the hard problem of learning good table manners without seeing any.

A great many people think they are thinking when they are merely rearranging their prejudices.
— William James

A grouch is a person who somehow can manage to find something wrong even with the good old days.

A groundless rumor often covers a lot of ground.

A hard thing about business is minding your own. A harp is a piano after taxes.

A heart only breaks if there is none to care.

A heart won't be practical until it can be made unbreakable.

A heavy snowstorm closed the schools in one town. When the children returned to school a few days later, one grade school teacher asked her students whether they had used the time away from school constructively. "I sure did, teacher," one little girl replied. "I just prayed for more snow."

A highway is a road that can make bad manners fatal.

A Hollywood celebrity recently hired two press agents to tell the world how modest he is.

Proverbs

A house is made of walls and beams; a home is built with love and dreams.

A house is who you are, not who you ought to be.

A huge part of real love is constant forgiveness.
— *Glen Close*

A human being is a part of a whole, called by us universe, a part limited in time and space. He experiences himself, his thoughts and feelings as something separated from the rest... a kind of optical delusion of his consciousness. This delusion is a kind of prison for us, restricting us to our personal desires and to affection for a few persons nearest to us. Our task must be to free ourselves from this prison by widening our circle of compassion to embrace all living creatures and the whole of nature in its beauty.
— *Albert Einstein*

A husband is what is left of the lover after the nerve has been extracted.
— *Helen Rowland*

A hypochondriac can suffer in a hundred different ways, but never in silence. A kindergarten teacher is someone who loves children and hates zippers.

A kiss is a lovely trick designed by nature to stop speech when words become superfluous.
— *Ingrid Bergman*

A laugh is worth a hundred groans in any market.

A lecture is where the notes of the professor become the notes of the student without passing through the mind of either one.

A liar is one who forgets to keep a partition between his imagination and the true facts.

A life without cause is a life without effect.
— *Barbarella*

A little boy asked his mother why the minister got a month's vacation while his dad only got two weeks. The mother answered, "Well, if he's a good minister, he needs it. If he isn't, the congregation needs it."

A little lie is like a little pregnancy; it doesn't take long before everyone knows.
— *C.S. Lewis*

A little of what you fancy does you good.

A long life may not be good enough, but a good life is long enough.
— *Benjamin Franklin*

A lot of people are willing to give God the credit, but not too many are willing to give him the cash.

A lot of people seem to have RUMORTISM.

A loyal friend is someone who sticks up for you even when you're not there.

A man can have no better epitaph than that which is inscribed in the hearts of his friends.

A man can't be too careful in the choice of his enemies.
— Oscar Wilde

A man has choice to begin love, but not to end it.
— Bon

A man is a god in ruins.
— Ralph Waldo Emerson

A man is a little soul carrying around a corpse.
— M. Aurelius

A man is not old until regrets take the place of dreams.
— John Barrymore

A man is not where he lives, but where he loves.

A man isn't really poor if he can still laugh.

A man may fulfill the object of his existence by asking a question he cannot answer, and attempting a task he cannot achieve.
— Oliver Wendall Holmes

A man never knows how to say goodbye; a woman never knows when to say it.
— Helen Rowland

A man seldom knows what he can do until he tries to undo what he did.

A man should never resign himself to fate because the resignation might be accepted. A man spends the first half of his life learning habits that shorten the other half of his life.

A man usually feels better after a few winks, especially if she winks back.

A man who does not think for himself does not think at all.
— Oscar Wilde

A man who invents himself needs someone to believe in him... Not only the need to be believed in, but the need to believe in another. You've got it: Love.
— Salman Rushdie

Proverbs

A man who throws dirt looses ground.

A man's accomplishment in business depends partly on whether he keeps his mind or his feet on the desk.

A metaphor is like a simile.

A modern miracle would be a golden wedding anniversary in Hollywood.

A mother's love never changes.

A mother's patience is like a tube of toothpaste - it's never quite gone.

A new cigarette offers coupons good for a cemetery lot.

A novel is never anything, but a philosophy put into images.
— *Albert Camus*

A path is only a path, and there is no affront, to oneself or to others, in dropping it if that is what your heart tells you. Look at every path closely and deliberately. Try it as many times as you think necessary. Then ask yourself alone, one question. Does this path have a heart? If it does, the path is good; if it doesn't it is of no use.
— *Carlos Castaneda*

A penny will hide the biggest star in the universe if you hold it close enough to your eye.

A person can survive almost everything except death.

A person is grown up not when they can take care of themself, but when they can take care of others.

A person starts to live when he can live outside himself.
— *Albert Einstein*

A person who still remembered that their ancestors had been the masters of the world would have applauded, with conscious pride, the representation of ancient freedom, if they had not long since been accustomed to prefer the solid assurance of bread to the unsubstantial visions of liberty and greatness.
— *Edward Gibbon*

A person who wraps into himself makes a small package.

A person without knowledge of his history is like a tree without roots.

A person's character and their garden both reflect the amount of weeding that was done during the growing season.

A person's faith is not judged by what he says about it, but by what he does about it.

A person's mind stretched to a new idea never goes back to its original dimensions.
— *Oliver Wendall Holmes*

A pessimist sees the difficulty in every opportunity; an optimist sees the opportunity in every difficulty.
— *Winston Churchill*

A physician can bury his mistakes, an architect can only advise his clients to plant vines.
— *Frank Lloyd Wright*

A pity beyond all telling is hid in the heart of love.
— *William Butler Yeats*

A positive attitude may not solve all your problems, but it will annoy enough people to make it worth the effort.
— *Herm Albright*

A positive mental attitude combined with definiteness of purpose is the starting point of all worthwhile achievement.
— *Napoleon Hill*

A positive mind has extra solving power!
— *Alexander Lockhart*

A professor is one who talks in someone else's sleep.
— *W.H.Auden*

A profound thought is in a constant process of becoming.
— *Albert Camus*

A promise kept pays a dividend of respect.

A proverb is a short sentence based on long experience.
— *Miguel de Cervantes*

A psychiatrist is someone who hopefully finds out what makes a person tick before they explode!
— *Alfred E. Neuman*

A real friend is one who sticks by you, even when you become successful.

A real friend never gets in your way - unless you happen to be on the way down.

A real friend warms you by his presence, trusts you with his secrets, and remembers you in his prayers.

A real patriot is the fellow who gets a parking ticket and rejoices that the system works.

A reflection of my feelings about the space program is found in a quotation from Charles A. Lindbergh's "Autobiography of Values." It reads, "Whether outwardly or inwardly, whether in space or time, the farther we penetrate the unknown, the vaster and more marvelous it becomes."

— Robert Wise

A relationship that draws on tears is not love; it is merely memories that cannot be forgotten.

— Bernard Yen

A religion that is small enough for us to understand would not be large enough for our needs.

A restaurant owner in a southern state grumbled about poor business, "If I could drop dead right now I'd be the happiest man alive."

A rock pile ceases to be a rock pile the moment a single man contemplates it, bearing within him the image of a cathedral.

— Antoine De Saint-Exupery

A ruler should love those who are ruled for love cannot cause harm.

A rumor is like a check — never endorse it till you're sure it's genuine.

A sad thing about life is meeting someone who means a lot to you, only to find out in the end that it was never bound to be and you just have to let go.

A safe but sometimes chilly way of recalling the past is to force open a crammed drawer. If you are searching for anything in particular you don't find it, but something falls out at the back that is often more interesting.

— J.M. Barrie

A scientist claims that rock music is beneficial in some cases of deafness. But, then, deafness is also beneficial in some cases of rock music.

A scientist knows more and more about less and less till he knows everything about nothing while a philosopher knows less and less about more and more till he knows nothing about everything.

A seminar on time travel will be held in two weeks ago.

A short absence quickens love, a long absence kills it.

— Charles De Saint-Evremond

A signature always reveals a man's character and sometimes even his name.

A simple lunch could be better than ten years of working relation.

— Chew Nai Chee

A simple realization that there are other points of view is the beginning of wisdom.

A single rose for the living is better than a costly wreath at the grave.

A sly rabbit will have three openings to its den.

A smile for a stranger opens many gates.

A smile is the cheapest way to improve your looks, even if your teeth are crooked.

A smile will gain you ten more years of life.

A statesman shears the sheep. A politician skins them.

A stranger to myself and to the world armed solely with a thought that negates itself as soon as it asserts, what is this condition in which I can have peace only by refusing to know...
— *Albert Camus*

A sub-clerk in the post-office is the equal of a conqueror if consciousness is common to them.
— *Albert Camus*

A synonym is a word you use when you can't spell the word you first thought of.
— *Burt Bacharach*

A teenage boy is at that akward age. He likes to park but he doesn't know exactly why.

A teenager is a person who answers the phone in the middle of the first ring.

A ton of regret never makes an ounce of difference.

A tongue four inches long can kill a man six feet tall.

A total abstainer is one who abstains from everything but abstention, and especially from inactivity in the affairs of others.
— *Ambrose Bierce*

A tragedy is the imitation of an action that is serious, with incidents arousing pity and fear, in order to accomplish the catharsis of such emotions.
— *Aristotle*

A true friend is like a good book - the inside is better than the cover.

A true friend is one who overlooks your failures and tolerates your successes.
— *United Feature Syndicate*

Proverbs

A true friend is one who sticks by you even when he gets to know you really well.

A true friend says nasty things to your face, instead of saying them behind your back.

A true friend thinks of you when all others are thinking of themselves.

A true friend walks in when the world walks out.

A valuable friend is one who'll tell you what you should be told even if it momentarily offends you.

A verbal art like poetry is reflective; it stops to think. Music is immediate, it goes on to become.
— *W.H. Auden*

A verbal contract isn't worth the paper it's written on.
— *Samuel Goldwyn*

A voice is silent only if there is no one to hear.

A vote is like a rifle; it's usefulness depends upon the character of the user.
— *Theodore Roosevelt*

A wave of enthusiasm is seldom a permanent wave.

A wide road doesn't bring the destination any closer.

A wise man once said that enthusiasm is nothing but faith with a tin can tied to its tail.

A wise man should have money in his head, but not in his heart.
— *Jonathan Swift*

A woman may very well form a friendship with a man, but for this to endure, it must be assisted by a little physical antipathy.
— *Friedrich Nietzsche*

A woman will always cherish the memory of the man who wanted to many her. A man, of the woman who he didn't.

A woman's heart is much like the moon, always changing but always has a man in it.

A wonderful realization will be the day you realize that you are unique in all the world. There is nothing that is an accident. You are a special combination for a purpose-and don't let them tell you otherwise, even if they tell you that purpose is an illusion. You are that combination so that you can do what is essential for you to do. Don't ever believe that you have nothing

to contribute. The world is an incredible unfulfilled tapestry. And only you can fulfill that tiny space that is yours.
— *Leo Buscaglia*

A word is not a crystal, transparent and unchanged; it is the skin of a living thought, and may vary greatly in color and content according to the circumstances and the time in which it is used.
— *Oliver Wendall Holmes*

A word of encouragement during failure is worth more than a whole book of praises after a success.

A word to the wise isn't as good as a word from the wise.

A youth becomes a man when the marks he wants to leave on the world have nothing to do with tires.

Ability can take you to the top, but it takes character to keep you there.

Ability is important, dependability is critical!
— *Alexander Lockhart*

Ability is what you're capable of doing. Motivation determines what you do. Attitude determines how well you do it.
— *Lou Holtz*

Ability without ambition is like a car without a motor.

Absence is to love what wind is to fire; it extinguishes the small, it enkindles the great.
— *Comte DeBussy-Rabutin*

Absence sharpens love, presence strengthens it.
— *Thomas Fuller*

Absent. Exposed to the attacks of friends and acquaintances; defamed; slandered.

Absolute freedom mocks at justice. Absolute justice denies freedom.
— *Albert Camus*

Absolute power cannot corrupt absolutely. What could corrupt the absolute?

Acceptance of what has happened is the first step to overcoming the consequences of any misfortune.
— *William James*

According to the latest official figures, 43% of all statistics are totally worthless.

Act as if what you do makes a difference. It does.
— *William James*

Proverbs

Actions are destiny's pen. The line of actions drawn today becomes tomorrow's destiny, so be sure that your pen is drawing a work of art

Active valour may often be the present of nature; but such patient diligence can be the fruit only of habit and discipline.
— *Edward Gibbon*

Adam and Eve had an ideal marriage. He didn't have to hear about all the men she could have married, and she didn't have to hear about the way his mother cooked.
— *Kimberley Broyles*

Add legs to the snake after you have finished drawing it.

Adhere to your own act, and congratulate yourself if you have done something strange and extravagant, and broken the monotony of a decorous age.
— *Ralph Waldo Emerson*

Admiration: Our polite recognition of another's resemblance to ourselves. Admitting you're wrong is like saying you're wiser today than you were yesterday.

Advice is what we ask for when we already know the answer but wish we didn't.
— *Erica Jong*

After all is said and done, more is said than done.

After three days without reading, talk becomes flavorless.

Again I tell you, it is easier for a camel to go through the eye of a needle than for someone who is rich to enter the kingdom of God.

Age is a high price to pay for maturity.

Age is like love. It cannot be hidden.

Aging is bad, but consider the alternative.

Ah, love, let us be true to one another! For the world, which seems to lie before us like a land of dreams, so various, so beautiful, so new, hath really neither joy, nor love, not light nor certitude, nor peace, nor help for pain.
— *Matthew Arnold*

Ah, mon cher, for anyone who is alone, without God and without a master, the weight of days is dreadful.
— *Albert Camus*

Aim for the highest.
— *Andrew Carnegie*

Alas! After a certain age every man is responsible for the face he has.
— Albert Camus

All animals are equal but some animals are more equal than others.
— George Orwell

All bridge hands are equally likely, but some are more equally likely than others.
— Alan Truscott

All Cretans are liars.
— Emoedocles the Cretan

All generalizations are false.

All great deeds and all great thoughts have a ridiculous beginning. Great works are often born on a street comer or in a restaurant's revolving door.
— Albert Camus

All greatness is achieved while performing outside your comfort zone.
— Greg Arnold

All human actions have one or more of these seven causes: chance, nature, compulsions, habit, reason, passion, desire.
— Aristotle

All I ask for is the opportunity to prove that money doesn't buy happiness.

All mankind is divided into three classes: those who are immovable, those who are movable; and those who move.
— Beniamin Franklin

All men can fly, but sadly, only in one direction, down.

All men need a faith that will not shrink when washed in the waters of affliction and adversity.

All modern American literature comes from one book by Mark Twain called Huckleberry Finn.
— Ernest Hemingway

All mothers are working mothers.

All my life, I always wanted to be somebody. Now I see that I should have been more specific.
— Jane Wagner

All of us are mad. If it weren't for the fact every one of us is slightly abnormal, there wouldn't be any point in giving each person a separate name.
— Ugo Betti

Proverbs

All parts should go together without forcing. You must remember that the parts you are reassembling were disassembled by you. Therefore, if you can't get them together again, there must be a reason. By all means, do not use a hammer.

All power corrupts, but we need the electricity.

All right everyone, line up alphabetically according to your height.
— *Casey Stengel*

All rumors should be fitted with girdles to keep them from spreading.

All that glitters is not gold.
— *Morocco*

All that I have to say to the world and to mankind is contained in the notion, reverence for life.
— *Albert Schweitzer*

All that is gold does not glitter; not all those that wander are lost.
— *J.R.R. Tolkien*

All that is necessary for the forces of evil to win in this world is for enough good men to do nothing.

All that we see or seem, is but a dream within a dream.
— *Edgar Allen Poe*

All that you are, all that I owe to you, justifies my love, and nothing, not even you, would keep me from adoring you.
— *Marquis de Lafayette*

All the other candidates were mere mortals.
— *Gray Davis*, on the reason he tost to Arnold Schwarzenegger

All the parts falling off this car are of the very finest British manufacture

All the passions make us commit faults; love makes us commit the most ridiculous ones.
— *Duc de La Rochefoucauld*

All the things one has forgotten scream for help in dreams.
— *Elias Canetti*

All truth goes through three steps: First, it is ridiculed; second, it is violently opposed; third it is accepted as self-evident.
— *Arthur Schopenhauer*

All we are guaranteed is the pursuit of happiness. You have to catch up with it yourself.

Alliance: In international politics, the union of two thieves who have their hands so deeply inserted in each other's pocket that they cannot separately plunder a third.

Almost always the creative, dedicated minority has made the world better.
— Martin Luther King Jr.

Although they have tried to cover up the fact that mad cow disease exists, the government has finally given up to public pressure demanding they reveal the truth, however they are still insisting that this fatal infection is no worse than a broken leg. No worse than a broken leg? I once had a broken leg and it hurt like hell!

Always and never are two words you should always remember never to use.
— Wendell Johnson

Always go to other peoples funerals, otherwise they won't come to yours.
— Yogi Berra

Always have some project under way...an ongoing project that goes over from day to day and thus makes each day a smaller unit of time.
— Lillian Troll

Always keep your words soft and sweet, just in case you have to eat them.

Always listen to experts. They'll tell you what can't be done, and why. Then do it.
— Robert A. Heinlein

Always look out for the sunlight the Lord sends into your days.

Always put yourself in other's shoes. If you feel that it hurts you, it probably does hurt the person too.

Always remember that it is better to give than to receive. Besides, you don't have to write thank-you notes.

Always remember: Life is for enjoying.

Always take the time to say what's in your heart.

Alymony is having an ex-husband you can bank on.

Alymony: Funds which allow a woman who lived unhappily married to live happily unmarried.

Am I not destroying my enemies when I make friends of them?
— Abraham Lincoln

Proverbs

America is a country where you buy a lifetime supply of aspirin for one dollar and use it up in two weeks.

America is a country which produces citizens who will cross the ocean to fight for democracy but won't cross the street to vote.

America is the only country in the world where the poor have a parking problem.

America is the only country that went from barbarism to decadence without civilization in between.
— *Oscar Wilde*

Among my most prized possessions are words that I have never spoken.
— *Orson Rega Card*

Among the innumerable monuments of architecture constructed by the Romans, how many have escaped the notice of history, how few have resisted the ravages of time and barbarism!
— *Edward Gibbon*

An acquaintance is someone we know well enough to borrow from, but not well enough to lend to.
— *Ambrose Bierce*

An action always subcomes to a reactions.

An adolescent is a person who acts like a baby when they aren't treated like an adult.

An angry man opens his mouth and shuts his eyes.
— *Cato*

An educational system isn't worth a great deal if it teaches young people how to make a living but doesn't teach them how to make a life.

An elephant is a mouse built to government specifications.

An emotion as much tells you nothing about reality, beyond the fact that something makes you feel something.
— *Ayn Rand*

An empty man is full of himself.

An empty stomach is not a good political advisor.
— *Albert Einstein*

An enthusiast is a fellow who feels perfectly sure of the things he is mistaken about.

An enthusiast is one who believes about four times as much as he can prove, and can prove about eight times as much as anyone will ever believe.

An error is not a mistake until you refuse to correct it

An expert is someone who knows some of the worst mistakes that can be made in his subject, and how to avoid them.
— *Werner Heisenberg*

An honest politician is one who, when he is bought, will stay bought.
— *Simon Cameron*

An inch of time is an inch of gold, but you can't buy that inch of time with an inch of gold.

An insincere and evil friend is more to be feared than a wild beast a wild beast may wound your body, but an evil friend will wound your mind.
— *Buddha*

An intellectual snob is someone who can listen to the William Tell Overture and not think of The Lone Ranger.
— *Dan Rather*

An interior is the natural projection of the soul.

An Oklahoma businessman reports that if his business gets any worse he won't have to lie on his next income-tax return.

An unusual child is one who asks questions that his parents can answer.

And in the end it's not the years in your life that count. It's the life in your years.
— *Abraham Lincoln*

And then, the Earth being small, mankind will migrate into space, and will cross the airless Saharas which separate planet from planet and sun from sun. The Earth will become a Holy Land which will be visited by pilgrims from all the quarters of the Universe. Finally, men will master the forces of Nature; they will become themselves architects of systems, manufacturers of worlds.
— *Winwood Reade*

And when the future hinges on the next words that are said, Don't let logic interfere, believe your heart instead.
— *Philip Robison*

Anger blows out the lamp of the mind. In the examination of a great and important question, everyone should be serene, slow-pulsed and calm.
— *Robert G. Ingersoll*

Anger is a state that starts with madness and ends with regret.

Anger is like the fire extinguisher in a building — it is to be used only in case of emergency.

Proverbs

Animals are such agreeable friends; they ask no questions, they make no criticisms.

Antidotes are what you take to prevent dotes.

Any fool can condemn others and most fools do.

Any girl can tell you that the only thing harder than a diamond is getting one.

Any intelligent fool can make things bigger, more complex, and more violent. It takes a touch of genius — and a lot of courage — to move in the opposite direction.
— *Albert Einstein*

Any man can be a father, but it takes a special man to be a dad.

Any man who laughs at women's clothes has never paid the bill for them.

Any man who tells you he understands women is either lying or isn't telling the truth.

Any philosophy that can fit into a nutshell belongs there.

Any religion or philosophy which is not based on a respect for life is not a true religion or philosophy.
— *Albert Schweitzer*

Any road followed to its end leads precisely nowhere. Climb the mountain just a little to test if's a mountain. From the top of the mountain, you cannot see the mountain.
— *Bene Gesserit*

Any stone in your boot always migrates against the pressure gradient to exactly the point of most pressure.
— *Milt Barber*

Any sufficient advanced technology is indistinguishable from magic.

Any sufficiently advanced bug is indistinguishable from a feature.
— *Kulawi*

Anyalyzing humour is like dissecting a frog: Nobody enjoys it, and the frog usually dies as a result.

Anybody who thinks talk is cheap never argued with a traffic cop.

Anyone can escape into sleep, we are all geniuses when we dream, the butcher's the poet's equal there.
— *E.M. Cioran*

Anyone can make a mistake; a fool insists on repeating it.

Anyone who attempts to generate random numbers by deterministic means is, of course, living in a state of sin.
— *John von Neumann*

Anyone who cannot cope with mathematics is not fully human. At best he is a tolerable subhuman who has learned to wear shoes, bathe and not make messes in the house.
— *Robert Heintein*

Anyone who has never made a mistake has never tried anything new.
— *Albert Einstein*

Anyone who has time to look for a four leaf clover needs to find one.

Anyone who is capable of getting themselves made President should on no account be allowed to do the job.

Anyone who is not a socialist at 16 has no heart, but anyone who still is at 32 has no mind.
— *Woodrow Wilson*

Anyone who makes a significant contribution to any field of endeavor, and stays in that field long enough, becomes an obstruction to its progress — in direct proportion to the importance of their original contribution

Anyone who proposes to do good must not expect people *to* roll stones out of his way, but must accept his lot calmly if they even roll a few more upon it.
— *Albert Schweitzer*

Anyone who says sunshine brings happiness has never danced in the rain.

Anything free is worth what you pay for it.

Anything in life worth having is worth working for.
— *Andrew Carnegie*

Anything less than mad, passionate, extraordinary love is a waste of time. There are too many mediocre things in life to deal with and love should not be one of them.

Anything more than the truth would be too much.
— *Robert Frost*

Anything on the ground is a cat toy. Anything not there yet, will be.

Anything that begins well, ends badly. Anything that begins badly, ends worse.

Anything that can be changed will be changed until there is no time left to change anything.

Proverbs

Anything you lose automatically doubles in value.
— *Mignon McLaughin*

Anywhere is walking distance, if you've got the time.
— *Steven Wright*

Applying computer technology is simply finding the right wrench to pound in the correct screw.

Archeologist: A man whose career lies in ruins.

Arithmetic is being able to count up to twenty without taking off your shoes.
— *Mickey Mouse*

Art does not tolerate reason.
— *Albert Camus*

Art is a collaboration between God and the artist, and the less the artist does the better.
— *Andre Gide*

Art is making something out of nothing and selling it.
— *Frank Zappa*

As a computer, I find your faith in technology amusing.

As a man begins to live more seriously within; he begins to live more simply without.

As a person learns more, the person becomes aware of the depths even more. Thus, there's more that one does not know, consciously speaking.

As a rule, the freedom of any people can be judged by the volume of their laughter.

As every cat owner knows, nobody owns a cat.
— *Ellen Perry Berkeley*

As far as the laws of mathematics refer to reality, they are not certain; and as far as they are certain, they do not refer to reality.
— *Albert Einstein*

As I grow older, I pay less attention to what men say. I just watch what they do.
— *Andrew Carnegie*

As I said before, I never repeat myself.

As long as a secret is secure in your heart, your are its master, and you can ride on it. As soon as you disclose it, it becomes your master and rides on you.

As long as mankind shall continue to bestow more liberal applause on their destroyers than on their benefactors, the

thirst of military glory will ever be the vice of the most exalted characters.
— *Edward Gibbon*

As memory may be a paradise from which we cannot be driven, it may also be a hell from which we cannot escape.
— *John Lancaster Spalding*

As soon as you delete a worthless file, you'll need it.

As we gain knowledge, we do not become more certain, we become certain of more.
— *Ayn Rand*

As your attorney, it is my duty to inform you that it is not important that you understand what I'm doing or why you're paying me so much money. What's important is that you continue to do so.

Asking the boss for a rise may not be patriotic but will help the government with extra tax if it comes off.

Associate yourself with men of good quality, if you esteem your own reputation; for it is better to be alone than in bad company.
— *George Washington Carver*

Assume a virtue if you have it not.

Assuming that the left wing or the right wing gained control of the country, it would probably fly around in circles.
— *Pat Paulsen*

At any street corner the feeling of absurdity can strike any man in the face.
— *Albert Camus*

At least dogs do what you tell them to do. Cats take a message and get back to you.

At the beginning and at the end of love, the two lovers are embarrassed to find themselves alone.
— *La Bruvere*

At the heart of all beauty lies something inhuman, and these hills, the softness of the sky, the outline of these trees at this very minute lose the illusory meaning with which we had clothed them, henceforth more remote than a lost paradise...that denseness and that strangeness of the world is absurd.
— *Albert Camus*

At the point in flattery where a woman would know you were lying, a man will think you've only begun to appreciate him.
— *Jessie Johnstone*

Proverbs

At the source of every error blamed on the computer, you will find at least two errors, including the error of blaming it on the computer.

Atheism is a non-prophet organization.

Avarice, envy, pride, three fatal sparks, have set the hearts of all on fire.

— *Dante Alighieri*

— x —

B

Bacteria: The only culture some people have.

Badness can be caught in great abundance, easily; the road to her is level, and she lives near by. But good is harder, for the gods have placed in front of her much sweat; the road is steep and long and rocky at first, but when you reach the top, she is not hard to find.
— Hesiod

Based on what you know about him in history books, what do you think Abraham Lincoln would be doing if he were alive today? (1) Writing his memoirs of the Civil War. (2) Advising the President. (3) Desperately clawing at the inside of his coffin.
— David Letterman

Batman costume warning label: Caution! Cape does not enable user to fly.

Be a good listener. Your ears will never get you in trouble.
— Frank Tyger

Be as kind as you can today, tomorrow you may not be there.

Be bold in what you stand for; and careful what you fall for.

Be careful of your thoughts, they may become words at any moment.

Be cautious in choosing friends, and be even more cautious in changing them.

Be courteous to all, but intimate with few, and let those few be well tried before you give them your confidence. True friendship is a plant of slow grow, and must undergo and withstand the shocks of adversity before it is entitled to the appellation.
— George Washington Carver

Be curious, not judgemental.
— Watt Whitman

Be good or be good at it!

Be kind, for everyone you meet is fighting a harder battle.
— Plato

Be modest! It is the kind of pride least likely to offend.
— Jules Renard

Proverbs

Be more concerned about your character than about your reputation, because your character is what you really are, while your reputation is merely what others think of you.

Be nice to everyone on your way to the top because you pass them all on the way down.
— *Fred A. Hufnagel Sr.*

Be not angry that you cannot make others as you wish them to be, since you cannot make yourself as you wish to be.
— *Thomas A' Kempis*

Be not indifferent to contempt, even from very ordinary people, but rather look well to the cause of it.
— *Charles Simmon*

Be slow in choosing a friend, slower in changing.
— *Benjamin Franklin*

Be strong and of good courage; be not afraid, neither be thou dismayed: for the Lord thy God is with thee whithersoever thou goest.

Be such is the irresistable nature of truth, that all it asks, and all it wants, is the liberty of appearing.
— *Thomas Paine*

Be thankful for problems. If they were less difficult, someone with less ability might have your job.

Be wary of strong drink. It can make you shoot at tax collectors, and miss.

Be who you are and say what you feel, because those who mind don't matter, and those who matter don't mind.
— *Dr. Suess*

Be yourself; who else is better qualified?
— *Frank J. Giblin II*

Beat me with the truth, don't torture me with lies.

Beauty is a form of genius - is higher, indeed, than genius, as it needs no explanation. It is of the great facts in the world like sunlight, or springtime, or the reflection in dark water of that silver shell we call the moon.
— *Oscar Wilde*

Beauty is eternity gazing at itself in a mirror.
— *Kahlil Gibran*

Beauty is in the eye of the beholder and I'm not one to judge.

Beauty is only skin deep, but ugly goes all the way to the bone!

Beauty is truth, truth beauty, a thing of beauty is a joy for ever.
— *John Keats*

Beauty is unbearable, drives us to despair, offering us for a minute the glimpse of an eternity that we should like to stretch out over the whole time.
— *Albert Camus*

Beauty that is unaware of itself is the most beautiful.

Because I have confidence in the power of Truth and of the spirit, I believe in the future of mankind.
— *Albert Schweitzer*

Been there, done that, and have the T-shirt to prove it.

Before a person sets out to test his faith by trying to move a mountain, he should begin with a molehill and work up.

Before holding another in any other way, you should first hold them in your heart. Love and affection start there, and everything else that is really important comes from that point.
— *Steve Ulrich*

Before marriage, he lies awake thinking about what you said. After marriage, he dozes off while you're saying it.

Before one can know what love really is one must have a fall and then pick oneself up.
— *Leo Tolstoy*

Before you can break out of prison, you must realize that you are locked up. Before you point your fingers be sure your hands are clean.

Beginning to think is beginning to be undermined.
— *Albert Camus*

Behavior is a mirror in which everyone shows his image.
— *Johann Wolfgang Goethe*

Behaviourism is the art of pulling habits out of rats.

Behind every advance of the human race is a germ of creation growing in the mind of some lone individual, an individual whose dreams waken him in the night while other contentedly sleeps.

Behind every great fortune there is a crime.
— *Honore de Balzac*

Behind every successful man is a surprised woman.
— *Maryon Pearson*

Being cool, is not trying to be cool.

Being politically correct means always having to say you're sorry.

Being right half the time beats being half-right all the time.

Proverbs 29

Being right is highly overrated. Even a stopped dock is right twice a day.

Being strong and silent only gets you so far... it's the things you don't say you regret the most.
— *Ericsson*

Being unknown does not mean being inferior.

Being with you is like walking on a very clear morning - definitely the sensation of belonging there.
— *E.B. White*

Belief in God will help you most if you also believe in yourself.

Believe all the good you can of everyone. Do not measure others by yourself. If they have advantages which you have not, let your liberality keep pace with their good fortune. Envy no one, and you need envy no one.
— *William Hazlitt*

Believe in miracles, but don't depend on them.

Believe nothing merely because you have been told it. Do not believe what your teacher tells you merely out of respect for the teacher. But whatsoever, after due examination and analysis, you find to be kind, conducive to the good, the benefit, the welfare of all beings - that doctrine believe and cling and take it as your guide.

Believe nothing! Belief is a confession of ignorance! Therefore do not even believe what even tell you! All I can do is to teach you to enlighten yourselves. Your first duty is to abolish your ignorance, and only you yourselves can do this.
— *Buddha*

Believe your beliefs and doubt your doubts.
— *F.F. Bosworth*

Beshere's formula for failure: There are two kinds of people who fail - those who listen to nobody and those who listen to everybody.

Better death than dishonor.

Better never to have met you in my dream than to wake and reach for hands that are not there.
— *Otomono Yakamochi*

Better to know the answer, than to live with the question.
— *Jason Q.*

Better to light a candle than to curse the darkness.

Better to remain silent and be thought a fool, than to speak and remove all doubt.
— Abraham Lincoln

Better to understand little than to misunderstand a lot.

Better to wear out than to rust out.

Better to write for yourself and have no public, than to write for the public and have no self.
— Cyril Connolly

Better untaught than ill-taught.

Between my mother and justice I choose my mother.
— Albert Camus

Between the legs of the women walking by, the dadaists imagined a monkey wrench and the surrealists a crystal cup. That's lost.
— Ivan Chtcheglov

Beware how you take away hope from another human being.
— Oliver Wendall Holmes

Beware of all enterprises that require new clothes.
— Henry David Tnoreau

Beware of bugs in the above code; I have only proved it correct, not tried it.
— Donald Knuth

Beware of fate - it loves to take advantage of anyone who believes in it.

Beware of the fury of the patient man.
— John Dryden

Beware of the man of one book.

Big doesn't necessarily mean better. Sunflowers aren't better than violets.

Big egos are big shields for lots of empty space.
— Diana Black

Big ideas are so hard to recognize, so fragile, so easy to kill. Don't forget that, all of you who don't have them.
— John Elliot Jr.

Big mouths and small brains don't mix!
— Ehren Metcalf

Bigamy is having one wife too many. Monogamy is the same.
— Oscar Wilde

Billions and billions of years ago, life as we know it arose from this primordial chocolate ooze.

Proverbs

Blessed are our enemies, for they tell us the truth when our friends flatter us.

Blessed are the flexible for they shall not break.

Blessed are those who can give without remembering and take without forgetting.

Blessed be those who initiate lively discussions with the hopelessly mute, for they shall be know as dentists.

Blessed is he who doesn't show hatefulness over what is lost, but instead, shows gratefulness over what is left.

Blessed is he who expects nothing, for he shall never be disappointed.
— *Jonathan Swift*

Blessed is he who, having nothing to say, refrained from giving wordy evidence of the fact.

Blessed is the home where each puts the other's happiness first.

Blessed is the man who can laugh at himself, for he will never cease to be amused. Blowing out another man's flame doesn't make yours shine any brighter, but less.

Blushing is the color of virtue.
— *Diogenes*

Bones; there are 206 in the human body. No need for dismay, however two bones of the middle ear have never been broken in a skiing accident.

Books say, "She did this because." Life says, "She did this." Books are where things are explained to you; life is where things aren't. I'm not surprised that some people prefer books. Books make sense. The only problem is that the lives they make sense of are other people's lives, never your own.
— *Julian Barnes*

Boredom sets into boring minds.

Born twice, die once. Born once, die twice

Both poverty and riches are the offspring of thought
— *Napoleon Hill*

Break the bones and the body will heal, break the spirit and the body will die.

Bureaucracy is a giant mechanism operated by pygmies.
— *Honore de Balzac*

Buses stop at bus stations, trains at train stations; my desk has a workstation.

But friendship is precious, not only in the shade, but in the sunshine of life. And thanks to a benevolent arrangement of things, the greater part of life is sunshine.
— *Thomas Jefferson*

But now everything will be different. It is nonsense to believe that life will not allow it, that the past will not allow it. I must struggle to live a better life, a far better life.
— *Leo Tolstoy*

But the fact that some geniuses were laughed at does not imply that all who are laughed at are geniuses. They laughed at Columbus, they laughed at Fulton, they laughed at the Wright brothers. But they also laughed at Bozo the Clown.
— *Carl Sagan*

But words are things, and a small drop of ink, falling like dew, upon a thought, produces that which makes thousands, perhaps millions, think.
— *Lord Byron*

Butcher's window. Let me meat your needs.

Buy a dog a toy and it will play with it for ever. Buy a cat a present and it will play with the wrapper for 10 minutes.

Buy more, and be happy.

By the time a man realizes his father was right, he has a son who thinks he's wrong.

By the time you can make ends meet, they move the ends.

By the time you decide to look for greener pastures, you're too old to climb the fence.

By the time you learn the rules of life, you're too old to play the game.

By three methods we may learn wisdom: First, by reflection, which is noblest; second, by imitation, which is easiest; and third by experience, which is the bitterest.
— *Confucius*

By trying we can easily endure adversity. Another man's, I mean.
— *Mark Twain*

— x —

C

C is often described, with a mixture of fondness and disdain varying according to the speaker, as "a language that combines all the elegance and power of assembly language with all the readability and maintainability of assembly language."

C makes it easy to shoot yourself in the foot. C++ makes it harder, but when you do, it blows away your whole leg.
— *Bjarne Stroustrup*

Calamities are of two kinds: misfortune to ourselves, and good fortune to others.
— *Ambrose Bierce*

Calvin: People think it must be fun to be a super genius, but they don't realize how hard it is to put up with all the idiots in the world. Hobbes: Isn't your pants' zipper supposed to be in the front?
— *Calvin and Hobbes*

Can't never could do anything until Could came along and whipped Can't butt; now Can't can do a lot. Can't never did anything but fail.
— *Mr. Eaton*

Canaries have to demonstrate their ability to sing before they can be imported. What a pity that this doesn't also apply to imported opera singers!

Cancer is so limited, It cannot corrode faith, It cannot shatter hope, It cannot kill friendships, It cannot cripple love, It cannot destroy peace, It cannot silence courage, It cannot suppress memories, It cannot conquer the spirit.

Capital punishment is our societies recognition of the sanctity of human life.
— *Orrin Hatch*

Casual drug users should be taken out and shot.
— *Darvl Gates*

Cat's motto: No matter what you've done wrong, always try to make it look like the dog did it.

Cats are rather delicate creatures and they are subject to a good many ailments, but I never heard of one who suffered from insomnia.
— *Joseph Wood Krutch*

Cats are smarter than dogs. You can't get eight cats to pull a sled through snow.
— *Jeff Valdez*

Cats don't hunt seals. They would if they knew what they were and where to find them. But they don't, so that's all right.
— *Terry Pratchett*

Cats instinctively know the exact moment their owners will wake up. Then they wake them 10 minutes sooner.

Cats know what we feel. They don't care, but they know.

Cats seem to go on the principle that it never does any harm to ask for what you want.
— *Joseph Wood Krutch*

Cauliflower is nothing but cabbage with a college education.
— *Mark Twain*

Certain flaws are necessary for the whole. It would seem strange if old friends lacked certain quirks.
— *Johann Wolfgang Goethe*

Certain scientists are working on a new scheme to abolish sleep. The new baby has beaten them to it.

Challenges can be stepping stones or stumbling blocks. Change is inevitable, except from a vending machine.

Change your thoughts and you change your world.
— *Norman Vincent Peale*

Changing one thing for the better is worth more than proving a thousand things wrong.

Character is what a person is in the dark.

Charity should begin at home, but most people don't stay at home long enough to begin it.

Charm is getting the answer yes without asking a dear question.
— *Albert Camus*

Cheerfulness is contagious, but don't wait to catch ft from others. Be a "carrier."

Cheerio, see you soon.

Cherish your visions; cherish your ideals; cherish the music that stirs in your heart, the beauty that forms in your mind, the loveliness that drapes your purest thoughts, for out of them will grow delightful conditions, all heavenly environment; of these if you but remain true to them, your world will at last be built.
— *James Alien*

Proverbs

Chess is a foolish expedient for making idle people believe they are doing something very clever when they are only wasting their time.
— *Georoe Bernard Shaw*

Chickens: The only animals you eat before they are born and after they are dead.

Childhood is that wonderful time of life when all you need do to lose weight is to take a bath.

Children are natural mimics. They act like their parents in spite of every attempt to teach them good manners.

Children begin by loving their parents. After a time they judge them. Rarely, if ever, do they forgive them.
— *Oscar Wilde*

Children do, indeed, help hold a marriage together, keeping their parents so busy they don't have time to quarrel.

Children in a family are like flowers in a bouquet - there's always one that will face the opposite direction.

Children in the back seats of cars cause accidents, but accidents in the back seats of cars cause children.

Children need love, especially when they do not deserve it.
— *Harold S. Hubert*

Children seldom misquote you. In fact, they usually repeat word for word what you shouldn't have said.

Children will still die unjustly even in a perfect society. Even by his greatest effort, man can only propose to diminish, arithmetically, the sufferings of the world.
— *Albert Camus*

Choice, not chance, determines destiny.

Choose a job you like and you will never have to work a day of your life.
— *Confucius*

Choose well. Your choice is brief, and yet endless.
— *Johann Wolfgang Goethe*

Choose your friends carefully. A negative attitude is very contagious and can rub off on you little by little without your knowledge.

Christian: One who believes that the New Testament is a divinely inspired book that is admirably suited to the spiritual needs of his neighbour.

Christianity claims over and over that the church is founded on Christ and is not dependent on any worldly reality, but in

actual fact it depends on women's bodies to give it its saints and sinners. It was the Word/God that divided the sexes, and established the war of desperate need between them. It is, time and time again, God's Word that women are not allowed to represent.
— *Rebecca S. Chopp*

Christianity has been studied and practiced for ages, but it has been studied far more than it has been practiced.

Christopher Robin Hood: He steals from the rich and gives to the Pooh.

Church members are either pillars or caterpillars. The pillars hold up the church, and the caterpillars just crawl in and out.

Classical music threatens to develop a tune with every other bar and then disappoints you.

Cleaning your house while your kids are still growing is like shoveling the walk before it has stopped snowing.

Clothes make the man. Naked people have little or no influence on society.
— *Mark Twain*

Clouds come floating into my life, no longer to cany rain or usher storm but to add color to my sunset sky.
— *Rabindranath Tagore*

Cole's Law: Thinly sliced cabbage.

College is that bright interlude of freedom a young man has between subjection to his mother and submission to his wife.

Come, work for the Lord. The work is hard, the hours long, and the pay is low. But the retirement benefits are out of this world.

Coming together is a beginning, staying together is progress, working together is success.
— *Henry Ford*

Committee: A body that keeps minutes and wastes hours.

Common sense is in spite of, not the result of, education.
— *Victor Hugo*

Common sense is the collection of prejudices acquired by age eighteen.
— *Albert Einstein*

Common sense is what tells you that the world is flat.

Communication by empathy is a talent that few possess.

Proverbs

Compromise does not satisfy, but dissatisfies everybody; it does not lead to any general fulfillment, but to general frustration; those who try to become everything to all people end up by not being anything to anyone.
— *Ayn Rand*

Compromise: Such an adjustment of conflicting interests as gives each adversary the satisfaction of thinking he has got what he ought not to have, and is deprived of nothing except what was justly his due.
— *Ambrose Bierce*

Compromise: The art of dividing a cake so that everybody believes he or she got the biggest piece.

Computers are composed of nothing more than logic gates stretched out to the horizon in a vast numerical irrigation system.
— *Stan Augarten*

Computers are like Old Testament gods; lots of rules and no mercy.
— *Joseph Campbell*

Computers are not intelligent. They only think they are.

Confidence is the feeling you have before you understand the situation.

Confront the dark parts of yourself, and work to banish them with illumination and forgiveness. Your willingness to wrestle with your demons will cause your angels to sing. Use the pain as fuel, as a reminder of your strength.
— *August Wilson*

Conquering any difficulty always gives one a secret joy, for it means pushing back a boundary-line and adding to one's liberty.
— *Henri Frederic Amiel*

Conscience is like a baby. It has to go to sleep before you can.

Consciousness: That annoying time between naps.

Conserve toilet paper, use both sides.

Consider how hard it is to change yourself; and you will understand what little chance you have trying to change others.

Consider how much more you often suffer from your anger and grief, than from those very things for which you are angry and grieved.
— *Marcus Antonius*

Constant use will wear out anything, especially friends.

Consumers are statistics, customers are people.

Courage is not the absence of fear, but rather the judgment that something else is more important than fear.
— Ambrose Redmoon

Courage is required if love is to be given.

Courage is what it takes to stand up and speak. Courage is also what it takes to sit down and listen.
— Winston Churchill

Courtesy is as much a mark of a gentleman as courage.
— Theodore Roosevelt

CPU: Central Propulsion Unit. The CPU is the computer's engine. It consists of a hard drive, an interface card and a tiny spinning wheel that's powered by a running rodent - a gerbil if the machine is a 286 model, a ferret if it's a 386, and a ferret on speed if it's a 486.

Creation of woman from the rib of man: She was not made from his head to top him; nor out of his feet to be trampled upon by him; but out of his side to be equal with him, under his arm to be protected, and near his heart to be loved.

Creditor One of a tribe of savages dwelling beyond the Financial Straits and dreaded for their desolating incursions.
— Ambrose Bierce

Crime does not pay.. .as well as politics.
— Alfred E. Neuman

Crows everywhere are equally black.

Cultivate friends who pray for you, not prey upon you.

Cupid's arrows rarely strike two people with the same definition of cleanliness.
— Margo Kaugman

Curiosity is the very basis of education and if you tell me that curiosity killed the cat, I say only the cat died nobly.
— Arnold Edinborouah

— x —

Proverbs

D

Darkness cannot drive out darkness. Only life can do that Hate cannot drive out hate. Only love can do that.
— *Martin Luther King Jr.*

Dear Jesus, please help Mommy and Daddy. Take care of Brother and Me. And please God, take care of yourself cause if anything happens to you we are in big trouble. Amen.

Death and the grave make no distinction of persons.

Death cannot kill what never dies.

Death during adolescence feels unfair. We're young. We're invincible. Death is supposed to come with old age. When death breaks into our lives and steals our innocence, its finality leaves us unnaturally older. There are too many elderly young people.
— *Sara Shandler*

Death for us all, but his own death to each.
— *Albert Camus*

Death is a black camel which kneels at every man's gate.

Death is a challenge. It tells us not to waste time... It tells us to tell each other right now that we love each other.
— *Leo Buscaglia*

Death is but death, and all in time shall die.

Death is deaf and will hear no denial.

Death is God's way of telling you not to be such a wise guy.

Death is life's way of telling you you're fired.

Death is not a period but a comma in the story of life.

Death is not the greatest loss in life. The greatest loss is what dies inside us while we live.
— *Norman Cousins*

Death is when eternity becomes a single dreamless nights sleep.
— *Plato*

Death rides with the drinking driver.

Dedication is not what others expect of you; it is what you can give to others.

Deeds cannot dream what dreams can do.
— E.E. Cummings

Defeat isn't bitter if you don't swallow it.

Definition of Stress: The confusion created when one's mind overrides the body's desire to beat or choke the living shit out of some asshole who desperately needs it.

Deja moo: The feeling that you've heard this bull before!

Democracy is a device that insures we shall be governed no better than we deserve.
— George Bernard Shaw

Democracy is a process by which people are free to choose the man who will get the blame.
— Laurence J. Peter

Democracy is three wolves and one sheep voting on what to have for supper.

Democracy, like love, can survive almost any attack - except neglect and indifference.

Dentist: A Prestidigitator who, putting metal in one's mouth, pulls coins out of one's pockets.
— Ambrose Bierce

Dentists have more faith in people than anybody. It's a miracle that more of them don't get their fingers bitten off.

Depression may be an exaggerated form of a response to loss that in less extreme form is adaptive. A depressed mood slows us down, makes us think realistically rather than optimistically, makes us turn away from goals that we can no longer hope to achieve, and signals to others that this is a time in life when we need some help.
— Peter Gray

Despite the high cost of living, it remains very popular.

Destiny is not a matter of chance, it is a matter of choice; it is not a thing to be waited for, it is a thing to be achieved.
— William Jennings Bryan

Did you ever notice when you blow in a dog's face he gets mad at you? But put him in a car and the first thing he does is stick his head out the window.

Did you ever walk into a room and forget why you walked in? I think that's how dogs spend their lives.
— Sue Murphy

Did you hear about the teenage boy who let his hair down - and smothered?

Proverbs

Did you know that dolphins are so intelligent that within only a few weeks of captivity, they can train Americans to stand at the very edge of the pod and throw them fish?

Die when I may, I want it said by those who knew me best that I always plucked a thistle and planted a flower where I thought a flower would grow.

— *Abraham Lincoln*

Dieting is wishful shrinking.

Diplomacy is convincing a man he's a liar without actually saying so.

Diplomacy is the art of saying nice doggy until you can find a rock.

Diplomacy: The art of letting someone have your own way.

Discipline without freedom is tyranny. Freedom without discipline is chaos.

— *Cullen Hightower*

Discovering the inner beauties of a person will also enhance your perceptions of the person's physical beauties.

Discovery consists of looking at the same thing as everyone else and thinking something different.

— *Albert Szent-Gyoroyi*

Discretion is being able to raise your eyebrow instead of your voice.

Diving into yourself is sometimes like diving into an icy river. You don't know the true depths of yourself until you close your eyes and let the water of your soul envelop you completely.

Do all things with love.

— *Og Mandino*

Do bad and remember, do good and forget.

Do for others with no desire of returned favor. We all should plant some trees we'll never sit under.

Do not admire a man for how strong he is, but rather how wisely he uses his strength.

Do not allow yourselves to be disheartened by any failure as long as you have done your best

— *Mother Teresa*

Do not believe in a thing because you have read about it in a book. Do not believe in a thing because another man has said it was true. Do not believe in words because they are hallowed by tradition. Find out the truth for yourself. Reason it out. That is realization.

— Swami Vivekananda

Do not go where the path may lead, go instead where there is no path and leave a trail.

— Ralph Waldo Emerson

Do not meddle in the affairs of cats, for they are subtle and will piss on your computer.

— Brian Gollum

Do not meddle in the affairs of dragons for you are crunchy and taste good with ketchup.

Do not meddle in the affairs of Unix, for it is subtle and quick to core dump

Do not repeat anything you will not sign your name to.

Do not speak of secret matters in a field that is full of little hills.

Do not spoil what you have by desiring what you have not Remember that what you have now was once among the things you only hoped for.

Do not the most moving moments of our lives find us without words?

— Marcel Marceau

Do not try to live forever. You will not succeed.

— George Bernard Shaw

Do not wait for leaders; do it alone - person to person.

— Mother Teresa

Do not wait for the last judgment. It comes every day.

— Albert Camus

Do not waste your time on social questions. What is the matter with poor is poverty; what is the matter with the rich is uselessness.

— George Bernard Shaw

Do not worry about your difficulties in Mathematics. I can assure you mine are still greater.

— Albert Einstein

Do nothing in great haste, except catching fleas and running from a mad dog.

Do one thing at time, with supreme excellence.

— NASA

Do something. Either lead, follow, or get out of the way!

Proverbs

Do what you can with what you have where you are.
— *Theodore Roosevelt*

Do you believe in love at first sight or should I drive by again?

Do you know how painful it is to tell someone you love him and not hear him say it back?
— *Monica*

Do you not hear me anymore? I know it's not your thing to care, I know it's cool to be so bored, but it sucks me in when you're aloof, it sucks me in, it sucks, it works, I guess it's cool to be alone.
— *Ben Folds Five*

Do you realize how many mistakes you'd make if you didn't sleep a third of your day?

Doctrines have proven expendable; yet the legacy of faith persists.
— *Bernard Meland*

Documentation is like sex: when it is good, it is very, very good; and when it is bad, it is better than nothing.
— *Dick Brandon*

Dog's have owners. Cat's have staff.

Dogs feel very strongly that they should always go with you in the car, in case the need should arise for them to bark violently at nothing right in your ear.
— *Dave Barry*

Doing a thing well is often a waste of time.
— *Robert Byrne*

Doing a thing wrong for a long period of time gives it the superficial appearance of being right.

Don't accept your dog's admiration as conclusive evidence that you are wonderful.
— *Ann Landers*

Don't ask what your community can do for you. Ask what you can do for your community.
— *Steve Andres*

Don't be afraid of death so much as an inadequate life.
— *Bertolt Brecht*

Don't be afraid of opposition; remember a kite rises against, not with the wind.

Don't be afraid of the space between your dreams and reality. If you can dream it, you can make it so.

Don't be afraid of tomorrow, for God has already been there.

Don't be irreplaceable - if you can't be replaced, you won't be promoted.

Don't be so Heavenly minded that you do no earthly good.

Don't be too timid and squeamish about your actions. All life is an experiment The more experiments you make, the better.
— *Ralph Waldo Emerson*

Don't believe your friends when they ask you to be honest with them. All they really want is to be maintained in the good opinion they have of themselves.
— *Albert Camus*

Don't bother just to be better than your contemporaries or predecessors. Try to be better than yourself.
— *William Faulkner*

Don't change horses while crossing a stream.

Don't control, be in control.
— *Kwai Chana Caine*

Don't count the days, make the days count.
— *Mohammed Ali*

Don't cry because it's over, smile because it happened.

Don't do that Son, you'll go blind! Dad, I'm over here...

Don't ever follow any leader until you know whom he is following.

Don't ever slam a door - you may want to go back.

Don't frown. You never know when someone is falling in love with your smile.

Don't get good at doing something if you don't like doing it.

Don't go for looks - it can deceive; don't go for wealth - even that fades away. Go for someone who makes you smile because only a smile makes a dark day seem bright. Hope you find that person.

Don't kill the dream - execute it!

Don't knock masturbation - it's sex with someone I love.
— *Woody Allen*

Don't laugh at the fallen; there may be slippery places in your path.

Don't let time take control of your destiny. Let your destiny take control of your time.
— *Ulrick Ricardo Milord*

Proverbs

Don't let your hearts grow numb. Stay alert. It is your soul which matters.
— *Albert Schweitzer*

Don't let your life slip through your fingers by living in the past or for the future.

Don't limit your challenges, challenge your limits.

Don't listen to what I say; listen to what I mean.

Don't marry for money; you can borrow it cheaper.

Don't measure your life by how many breaths you take, measure it by how many times you get your breath taken away.

Don't measure yourself by what you have accomplished, but what you should have accomplished with your ability.

Don't play stupid with me.. .I'm better at it!

Don't shut love out of your life by saying it's impossible to find. The quickest way to receive love is to give; the fastest way to lose love is to hold it too tightly; and the best way to keep love is to give it wings.

Don't sweat the petty things, and don't pet the sweaty things.

Don't take for granted the things closest to your heart.

Don't take life too seriously, you'll never get out of it alive.
— *Elbert Hubbard*

Don't take people for what they are! Most people do not deserve this. Take them rather for what they should be. Don't take me for what I should be. Take me for what I want to be. Yours friendly and faithfully!
— *Maraarethe Strnad*

Don't tell God how big your problems are; tell your problems how big your God is.

Don't tell. It's a big secret I used to do drugs.
— *Courtney Love,*
when she pleaded not guilty to felony drug charges

Don't think of it as being outnumbered, think of it as a wide target selection.

Don't think there are no crocodiles because the water is calm.

Don't think you're on the right road just because it's a well-beaten path.

Don't try to learn the tricks of the trade until you've learned the trade. Don't wait for your ship to come in. Row out to meet it.

Don't walk in front of me, I may not follow; don't walk behind me, I may not lead; walk beside me, and just be my friend.
— Albert Camus

Don't waste your youth growing up.

Don't wish to be anything but what you are, and try to be that perfectly.
— St. Francis De Sales

Don't work for recognition, but do work worthy of recognition.

Doubt makes the mountain which faith can move.

Doubt whom you will, but never yourself.

Dough is the wrong term for money. Dough sticks to your hands.

Down it came, the blessed deluge. The music of rain splashing on tents and tin sheds drove men to an ecstasy of rejoicing. They turned out to cheer lifted up their faces and opened their mouths to drink the bright drops; danced round, hallooing and shouting, getting drenched in the downpour.
— Katherine Susannah Prichard

Dream as if you'll live forever. Live as if you'll die today.
— James Dean

Dream different dreams while on the same bed.

Dream in light years, challenge miles, walk step by step.

Dream is not a revelation. If a dream affords the dreamer some light on himself, it is not the person with closed eyes who makes the discovery but the person with open eyes lucid enough to fit thoughts together. Dream - a scintillating mirage surrounded by shadows - is essentially poetry.
— Michel Leiris

Dream what you want to dream; go where you want to go; be what you want to be because you have only one life and one chance to do all the things you want in life.

Dreamers are those who have achieved in love and life, because it is a dream that got them there.
— Cindy Sherman

Dreams and visions are infused into men for their advantage and instruction...
— Artemidoros

Dreams are extremely important. You cant do it unless you imagine it.
— George Lucas

Dreams are renewable. No matter what our age or condition, there are still untapped possibilities within us and new beauty waiting to be born.
— *Dale Turner*

Dreams are the touchstones of our character.
— *Henry David Thoreau*

Dreams are what I am made of. Reality is what I am.
— *Clint Echols*

Dreams aren't in your head. Dreams are memories of another universe.
— *Everworld*

Dreams come true; without that possibility, nature would not incite us to have them.
— *John Uplike*

Drink wet cement and get really stoned.

Drive carefully! Remember, it's not only a car that can be recalled by it's maker.

Drive carefully, we need every taxpayer we can get.

Drive-in banks were established so most of the cars today could see their real owners.
— *E. Joseph Cossman*

Dyslexics of the world, untie!

— *x* —

Each generation has its few great mathematicians, and mathematics would not even notice the absence of the others. They are useful as teachers, and their research harms no one, but it is of no importance at all. A mathematician is great or he is nothing.
— *Alfred Adler*

Each minute should count, so be accountable for each minute.

Each of us wages a private battle each day between the grand fantasies we have for ourselves and what actually happens.
— *Cathy Guisewite*

Earlier people used to switch on TVs after getting bored with their routine work. Now they switch on to routine work after getting bored with TV.

Early to rise, early to bed, makes a man healthy but socially dead.
— *Anamaniacs*

Earth does not belong to Man. Man belongs to the Earth.

East or west, home is best.
— *Bon*

Eat one live toad the first thing in the morning and nothing worse will happen to you the rest of the day.

Eat right. Exercise. Die Anyway.

Education and intelligence aren't the same thing!

Education is a wonderful thing; if you couldn't sign your name, you'd have to pay cash.

Education is not received. It is achieved.

Education is that which discloses to the wise and disguises from the foolish their lack of understanding.
— *Ambrose Bierce*

Education is the best provision for old age.
— *Aristotle*

Education is what you have left when you have lost all your notes.

Egotist: A person of low taste, more interested in himself than me.

Proverbs

Engineer : A person who knows a great deal about very little and who goes along knowing more and more about less and less, until finally he knows practically everything about nothing.

Enthusiasm for hard work is most sincerely expressed by the person who is paying for it.

Enthusiasm is a good engine, but it needs intelligence for a driver.

Enthusiasm is apt to breed more action than accuracy.

Enthusiasm is contagious - and so is the lack of it.

Enthusiasm is contagious, so keep it to yourself.

Enthusiasm is that driving force that overcomes all obstacles.

Enthusiasm is the propelling force necessary for climbing the ladder of success.

Enthusiasm, like measles, mumps and the common cold, is highly contagious.

— *Emory Ward*

Envy is destroyed by true friendship.

Envy is what inclines us to speak evil of the virtuous rather than of the wicked.

Envy never dwells in noble souls.

Envy never has a holiday.

Eternity has no gray hairs.

Ethics is the activity of man directed to secure the inner perfection of his own personality.

— *Albert Schweitzer*

Even a happy life cannot be without a measure of darkness, and the word happy would lose its meaning if it were not balanced by sadness. It is far better to take things as they come along with patience and equanimity.

— *Carl Jung*

Even a hare will bite when it is cornered.

Even a short pencil is more reliable then the longest memory.

Even if I'm not asleep, that doesn't mean I'm awake.

Even if laughter and smiling were nothing more than sheer silliness and fun, it would still be a precious boon. But we now know that it is far more than that, that it is, in fact, an essential element in emotional health.

— *Steve Allen*

Dictionary of Proverbs

Even if rock 'n' roll music died tomorrow, it would take several weeks for the sound to fade away.

Even if you are on the right track, you'll get run over if you just sit there!
— *Will Rogers*

Even in a pile of manure, a flower will grow.

Even in its extreme form modem jazz will never replace the old-fashioned earache.

Even in the presence of others he was completely alone.
— *Robert M. Pirsia*

Even the boldest zebra fears the hungry lion. Even the smallest candle bums brighter in the dark.

Even though a marriage is made in heaven, the maintenance work has to be done here on earth!

Events are less important than our response to them.

Eventually, all things merge into one, and a river runs through it. The river was cut by the world's great flood and runs over rocks from the basement of time. On some of the rocks are timeless raindrops. Under the rocks are the words, and some of the words are theirs. I am haunted by waters.
— *Norman Maclean*

Ever notice that the person who never boasts is always bragging about that fact.

Ever tried. Ever failed. No matter. Try Again. Fail again. Fail better.
— *Samuel Beckett*

Every accomplishment great or small, starts with the right decision, "I'll try."

Every act of kindness done makes life nicer for someone.

Every act of rebellion expresses a nostalgia for innocence and an appeal to the essence of being.
— *Albert Camus*

Every adversity carries with it the seeds of a greater benefit!
— *Napoleon Hill*

Every closed eye is not sleeping; and every open eye is not seeing.

Every day cannot be a feast of lanterns.

Every error, of whatever type, is a result of the degeneration of instinct and vitiation of the will: One has thereby nearly defined the bad. Everything good is instinct.
— *Friedrich Nietzsche*

Proverbs

Every gain must have a loss.

Every girl should use what mother nature gives her before father time takes it away.

Every good friend once was a stranger.

Every institution I've ever been associated with has tried to screw me.
— *Stephen Wolfram*

Every job is a self-portrait of the person who did it.

Every man dies. Not every man truely lives.
— *William Wallace*

Every man has a right to his opinion - if ft parallels ours!

Every man is the architect of his own fortune.
— *Appius Claudius*

Every man knows when his life began... If I did not exist in the past, why should I, or could I, exist in the future? The purpose of man is like the purpose of the pollywog-to wiggle along as far as he can without dying, or, to hang onto life until death takes him.
— *Clarence Darrow*

Every man reaps what he sows, except the amateur gardener.

Every new beginning comes from some other beginnings end.
— *Semi-Sonic*

Every obstacle is a stepping stone to your success.

Every revolutionary ends up by becoming either an oppressor or a heretic.
— *Albert Camus*

Every successful man I have heard of has done the best he could with conditions as he found them, and not waited until the next year for better.
— *Edgar Watson Howe*

Every time a friend succeeds, I die a little.
— *Gore Vidal*

Every time you graduate from the school of experience, someone thinks up a new course.

Everybody has a photographic memory. Some don't have film.

Everybody is ignorant, only on different subjects.

Everybody loves a fat man, but not when he has the other half of the seat on the bus.

Everybody thinks thrift is a wonderful virtue, especially in our ancestors.

Everybody wants to go to heaven, but nobody wants to die.

Everyone I meet knows more about something than I do.

Everyone is a hero, if you catch them at the right time.
— *Alex Caswell*

Everyone should carefully observe which way his heart draws him, and then choose that way with all his strength.

Everyone should fear death until he has something that will live on after his death.

Everything is controlled by a small evil group to which, unfortunately, no one we know belongs.

Everything is possible, just not too probable.

Everything leaves, but love remains.

Everything should be made as simple as possible, but no simpler.
— *Albert Einstein*

Everything that can be counted doesn't necessarily count; everything that counts can't necessarily be counted.
— *Albert Einstein*

Everything that can be invented has been invented.
— *Charles H. Duell*

Everything that makes man work and get excited utilizes hope. The sole thought that is not mendacious is therefore a sterile thought
— *Albert Camus*

Everything's been thought of before, the problem is to think of it again.
— *Johann Wolfgang Goethe*

Everywhere children are schooled to become masters at answering questions and to remain novices at asking them.
— *Bob Dillon*

Examine what is said, not who speaks.

Excess weight is like sugar in iced coffee - after a while it settles to the bottom.

Excuses are the easiest things to manufacture, and the hardest things to sell.

Expect people to do better than they are; it helps them to become better. But don't be disappointed when they are not; it helps them to keep trying.

Proverbs

Expecting the world to treat you fairly because you are good is like expecting the bull not to charge because you are a vegetarian.
— *Dennis Wholey*

Experience is a great advantage. The problem is that when you get the experience, you're too damned old to do anything about it
— *Jimmy Connors*

Experience is a hard teacher. She gives the test first and the lessons afterwards.

Experience is a teacher who never tells us in advance what our next lesson will be.

Experience is not what happens to a man, it is what a man does with what happens to him.
— *Aldous Huxley*

Experience is one thing you can't get for nothing.
— *Oscar Wilde*

Experience is something you don't get until just after you need it.

Experience is that marvelous thing that enables you recognize a mistake when you make it again.
— *Franklin P. Jones*

Experience is the name everyone gives to their mistakes.
— *Oscar Wilde*

Experience is what you get when you don't get what you want.

Experience: that most brutal of teachers. But you learn, my God do you learn.
— *C.S. Lewis*

Experience: The wisdom that enables us to recognize in an undesirable old acquaintance the folly that we have already embraced.
— *Ambrose Bierce*

Explore daily the will of God.

— x —

Facts are stupid things.
— Ronald Reagan

Facts don't disappear just because they're ignored.

Fairness is required if progress is to endure.

Fairy tale: A horror story to prepare children for the newspapers.

Faith builds a bridge from this world to the next

Faith is not believing that God can, but that God will!

Faith is not faith until it's all you're holding onto.

Faith is the quality that enables you to eat blackberry jam on a picnic without looking to see whether the seeds move.

Faith is to the soul what a mainspring is to a watch.

Faith keeps the man who keeps his faith.

Faith makes all things possible. Love makes all things easy. Hope makes all things work.

Fall sick and you will know who is your friend and who is not.

Fame is chiefly a matter of dying at the right time.

Familiar acts are beautiful through love.

Families is where our nation finds hope, where wings take dream.
— George W. Bush

Fanaticism consists of redoubling your efforts when you have forgotten your aim.
— Santayana

Fans are interesting things. Rush fans just can't comprehend why the rest of the world doesn't like Rush. REM fans consider the rest of the world beneath their social level to notice. Kate Bush fans love the rest of the world, and the world loves them, but spend long nights plotting to knife one another.
— Richard Darwin

Fantasy is hardly an escape from reality. It's a way of understanding it.
— Lloyd Alexander

Proverbs

Far away there in the sunshine are my highest aspirations. I may not reach them, but I can look up and see their beauty, believe in them and try to follow where they may lead.
— *Louisa May Alcott*

Far better is it to dare mighty things, to win glorious triumphs, even though checkered by failure.. .than to rank with those poor spirits who neither enjoy much nor suffer much, because they live in a gray twilight that knows not victory nor defeat.
— *Theodore Roosevelt*

Far too many people spend their lives reading the menu instead of enjoying the banquet.

Fashion is a form of ugliness so intolerable that we have to alter it every six months.
— *Oscar Wilde*

Fast fat computers breed slow, lazy programmers.
— *Robert Hummel*

Fat people are harder to kidnap.

Fat people are usually good—natured because it takes them so long to get mad dear through.

Fat people have the kind of inflation that even the government cant keep down.

Faults are thick where love is thin.
— *Howell*

Fear doesn't overwhelm you; you let fear overwhelm you.

Fear knocked at the door. Faith answered and no one was there.

Fear of criticism is the kiss of death in the courtship of achievement

Feed the mind and the burden becomes lighter.

Feed your faith and doubt will starve to death.

Female passion is to masculine as an epic is to an epigram.
— *Karl Kraus*

Ferreting into our souls, we often ferret out something that might have lain there unnoticed.
— *Leo Tolstoy*

Few are the friends of your own self; most are the friends of your success.

Fifty is the old age of youth and the youth of old age.

Fill what's empty, empty what's full, and scratch where it itches.

Finagle's first law: If an experiment works, something has gone wrong.

Finagle's fourth law: Once a job is fouled up, anything done to improve it only makes it worse.

Finagte's second law: No matter what the anticipated result, there will always be someone eager to (a) misinterpret it, (b) fake it, or (c) believe it happened according to his own pet theory.

Finagle's third law: In any collection of data, the figure most obviously correct, beyond all need of checking, is the mistake

First law of procrastination: Procrastination shortens the job and places the responsibility for its termination on someone else (i.e., the authority who imposed the deadline).

First law of window cleaning: It's on the other side.

First love is a little foolishness and a lot of curiosity.

Flight by machines heavier than air is unpractical and insignificant, if not utterly impossible.
— Simon Newcomb

Flirtation: Attention without intention.

Flowers are the sweetest things God ever made and forgot to put a soul into.

Folks who are friends usually have the same virtues, the same enemies, or the same faults.

Follow love and it will flee; flee love and it will follow you.

Fool me once, shame on you; fool me twice, shame on me.

Fools rush in where angels fear to tread.
— Alexander Pope

For a good friend, the journey is never too long.

For a relationship to work, both side must be able to detect even the slightest uncomfort felt by the other person, even if it is not expressed directly.
— Bernard Yen

For Christ our Lord, all can give some, but some will give all.

For every complex problem, there is a solution that is simple, neat and wrong.
— H.L. Mencken

For every minute you are angry you lose sixty seconds of happiness.
— Ralph Waldo Emerson

Proverbs

For God is not against us because of our sin. He is with us, against our sin.

For good or ill, your conversation is your advertisement. Every time you open your mouth you let the people look into your mind.
— *Bruce Barton*

For it was not into my ear you whispered, but into my heart. It was not my lips you kissed, but my soul.
— *Judy Garland*

For my birthday I got a humidifier and a de-humidifier... I put them in the same room and let them fight it out.
— *Steven Wright*

For NASA, space is still a high priority.
— *Dan Quayle*

For one human being to love another that is perhaps the most difficult of our tasks; the ultimate, the last test and proof, the work for which all other work is but preparation.
— *Rainer Maria Rilke*

For people who like peace and quiet - a phoneless cord.

For small creatures such as we the vastness is bearable only through love.
— *Carl Sagan*

For the Angel of Death spread his wings on the blast, and breathed in the face of the foe as he pass'd; and the eyes of the sleepers wax'd deadly and chill, and their hearts but once heaved, and for ever grew still!
— *Lord Byron*

For those who understand you, no explanation is necessary; for those who don't, none is possible.
— *Kurt Cobain*

For you see, each day I love you more. Today more than yesterday and less than tomorrow.
— *Rosemonde Gerard*

Forever turned out to be too long.
— *Julia Ormond*

Forgetfulness: A gift of God bestowed upon debtors in compensation for their destitution of conscience.
— *Ambrose Bierce*

Forgetfulness: A gift of God bestowed upon debtors in compensation for their destitution of conscience.

Forgive, O Lord, any litttle jokes on Thee, and I'll forgive Thy great big one on me.

— *Robert Frost*

Forgiveness is like the fragrance a flower gives after it's been stepped on.

Forgiveness is the fragrance of the violet that clings fast to the heel that crushed it!

— *George Roemisch*

Forgiveness is the most tender part of love.

Formula for youth: keep your enthusiasm and forget your birthdays.

Fortune helps them that is willing to help themselves.

Fortune is like glass: ft breaks when it is brightest

Fortune makes friends; misfortune tries them.

Fortune never comes with both hands full.

Fortune smiles upon the man who can laugh at himself.

Fortune sometimes favors those she afterwards destroys.

Four things come not back: the spoken word, the spent arrow, the past and the neglected opportunity.

— *Omar Idn Al—Halif*

Four—word story of failure: Hired, tired, mired, fired.

Free love? As if love is anything but free. Man has bought brains, but all the millions in the world have foiled to buy love.

— *Emma Goldman*

Free your mind, and your clothes will follow.

Freedom is not the right to do as you please, but the liberty to do as you ought.

Friend is an overused word.

Friends are angels who lift us to our feet when our wings have trouble remembering how to fly.

Friends are chocolate chips in the cookie of life!

Friends are like a priceless treasure; he who has none is a social pauper.

Friends are those rare people who ask how you are and then wait to hear the answer

Friends are treasures.

— *Horace Bruns*

Friends last longer the less they are used.

Proverbs

Friends slowly won are long held.

Friends. They're the people you can share your secrets with, cry with, laugh with, and just have fun with. They don't judge you or make you change. They accept you exactly as you are. They look at you and they see a great person, one they love spending time with.
— *Kate Tierney*

Friends: People who borrow my books and set wet glasses on them.

Friendship is a golden chain, the links are friends so dear, and like a rare and precious jewel, it's treasured more each year.

Friendship is the hardest thing in the world to explain. It's not something you learn in school. But if you haven't learned the meaning of friendship, you really haven't learned anything.
— *Muhammad Ali*

Friendship often ends in love; but love in friendship — never.
— *Charles Caleb Cotton*

Friendship: A building contract you sign with laughter and break with tears.

Friendships are different from all other relationships. Unlike acquaintanceship, friendship is based on love. Unlike lovers and married couples, it is free of jealousy. Unlike children and parents, it knows neither criticism nor resentment. Friendship has no status in law. Business partnerships are based on a contract So is marriage. Parents are bound by law. But friendships are freely entered into, freely given, and freely exercised.
— *Stephen Ambrose*

Frisbeetarianism: The belief that when you die, your soul goes up the on roof and gets stuck.

From the moment absurdity is recognized, it becomes a passion, the most harrowing of all. But whether or not one can live with one's passions, whether or not one can accept their law, which is to bum the heart they simultaneously exalt — that is the whole question.
— *Albert Camus*

From what we get, we can make a living; what we give, however, makes a life.
— *Arthur Ashe*

Fruit is silver in the morning, gold at noon, and lead at night.

Funny how a dollar can look so big when you take it to church, and so small when you take it to the store.

— x —

G

Gambling: The sure way of getting nothing for something.

Generally by the time you are real, most of your hair has been loved off, and your eyes drop off, and you get loose in the joints and very shabby, but these things don't matter at all because once you are real, you can't be ugly, except to people who don't understand.
— *Margery Williams*

Generation X is not tost, those who should be nuturing them, cant find them.

Genetics explains why you took like your father, and if you don't, why you should.

Genius is nothing more than inflamed enthusiasm.

Genius is one per cent inspiration and ninety-nine per cent perspiration.
— *Thomas Edison*

Genocide is like a dessert It is made of the flesh and bones of woman and children, it is sweetened with the Wood of the innocent, and it is baked in the ovens of Auschwitz.

Genuine faith is assuring, insuring, and enduring.

Get a good idea and stay with it Dog it, and work at it until it's done right.
— *Walt Disney*

Get busy living, or get busy dying.
— *Shawshank Redemption*

Give a man a fish and he wont starve for a day. Teach a man how to fish and he wont starve for his entire life.

Give a man a fish, and you feed him for a day. Teach a man to fish, and he'll invite himself over for dinner.
— *Calvin Keegan*

Give according to your income, lest God will make your income like your giving.

Give me a lever long enough, and I shall move the world.
— *Archimedes*

Give plenty of what is given to you, and listen to pity's call; don't think the little you give is great and the much you get is small.
— *Phoebe Cary*

Proverbs

Give to a pig when it grunts and a child when it cries, and you will have a fine pig and a bad child.

Give until it hurts

— *Mother Teresa*

Give us dear vision that we may know where to stand and what to stand for, because unless we stand for something, we shall fall for anything.

— *Peter Marshall*

Giving money and power to government is like giving whiskey and car keys to teenage boys.

— *P. J. O'Rourke*

Giving someone all your love is never an assurance that they'll love you back! Don't expect love in return, just wait for it to grow in their hearts but if it doesn't, be content it grew in yours.

Glittering prizes and endless compromises shatter the illusion of integrity.

— *Neil Peart*

Goals are dreams with deadlines.

God alone is the judge of true greatness because He knows men's hearts.

— *Mahatma Gandhi*

God can mend a broken heart but he must have all the pieces.

God creates a worm for every bird, but He does not throw it in the nest.

God does not care about our mathematical difficulties. He integrates empirically.

— *Albert Einstein*

God does not think; he creates. He does not exist; he is eternal.

— *S. Kierkegaard*

God doesn't call people who are qualified. He calls people who are willing, and then He qualifies them.

— *Richard Parker*

God doesn't discriminate, only religions do.

God gave people a mouth that closes and ears that don't, which should tell us something.

God gave us memories, that we might have June roses in the December of our lives.

— *James M. Barrie*

God gave us time so that everything wouldn't happen all at once.

God gives us faces; we create our own expressions. God gives, but man must open his hand.

God heals, and the doctor takes the fee.
— *Benjamin Franklin*

God is a comic playing to an audience that's afraid to laugh.

God is more interested in your future and your relationships than you are.
— *Billy Graham*

God is not moved or impressed with our worship until our hearts are moved and impressed by Him.
— *Kelly Sparks*

God is real, unless declared integer.

God is too kind to do anything cruel; too wise to make a mistake; too deep to explain Himself.

God loves us the way we are, but too much to leave us that way.

God loves you right where you are but he doesn't want to leave you there.
— *Max Lucado*

God never gives us more than we can handle, just enough to let us see who we really are.

God never said it would be easy. He just said He would go with me.
— *J.G. Holland*

God not only plays dice, he also sometimes throws the dice where they cannot be seen.
— *Stephen Hawking*

God puts some in places of leadership to shoulder responsibility, not to enjoy privileges.

God uses broken things. It takes broken soil to produce a crop, broken clouds to give rain, broken grain to give bread, broken bread to give strength. It is the broken alabaster box that gives forth perfume. It is Peter, weeping bitterly, who returns to greater power than ever.
— *Vance Havner*

God will supply all your real needs.

God's will will not lead you where His grace cannot keep you.

God, grant me the serenity to accept the things I cannot change, the courage to change the things I can, and the wisdom to know the difference.
— *Reinhold Niebuhr*

Good advice is something a man gives when he is too old to set a bad example.
— *La Rouchefoucauld*

Good communications is as stimulating as black coffee and just as hard to sleep after.
— *Anne Morrow Lindbergh*

Good friends, good books and a sleepy conscience: this is the ideal life.
— *Mark Twain*

Good humor is one of the best articles of dress one can wear in public.

Good judgment comes from bad experience, and a lot of that comes from bad judgment

Good leaders are like baseball umpires; they go practically unnoticed when doing their jobs right.
—*Byrd Baggett*

Good manners are a way of making things easier for another person.
— *Jeanne Thevaites*

Good manners is what enables a person to wait at the counter patiently and quietly for service — while the blabber mouth gets all the service.

Goodness is the only investment that never fails.
— *Henry David Thoreau*

Grabel's Law: 2 is not equal to 3 — not even for large values of 2.

Grace is the divine ability to cope with every circumstance.

Grandchildren are God's way of compensdating us for growing old.

Grandparents: The people who think your children are wonderful even though they're sure you're not raising them right.

Grasshopper always wrong in argument with chicken.

Gratitude is not only the greatest of virtues, but the parent of all the others.

Gratitude is the rarest of all virtues, and yet we invariably expect it.

Gravitation cannot be held responsible for people falling in love.
— Albert Einstein

Gray hair and wrinkles never conceal dimples.

Great men may die, but their ideas won't.
— Kelly Nelson

Great minds discuss ideas. Average minds discuss events. Small minds discuss people.

Great music is that which penetrates the ear with facility and leaves the memory with difficulty. Magical music never leaves the memory.
— Thomas Beecham

Great spirits have always found violent opposition from mediocrities. The latter cannot understand it when a man does not thoughtlessly submit to hereditary prejudices but honestly and courageously uses his intelligence.
— Albert Einstein

Greater love has no one than this, that he lay down his life for his friends.

Grow old along with me, the best is yet to be.
— Robert Browning

Growing old is mandatory. Growing up is optional.

— x —

Proverbs

Habit never goes because if you remove H, Abit remains. If you remove A, Bit remains. If you remove B, It still remains.

Had the price of looking been blindness, I would have looked.
— *Ralph Ellison*

Half of the American people have never read a newspaper. Half never voted for President. One hopes it is the same half.
— *Gore Vidal*

Half of the people in the world are below average.

Half our troubles come in wanting our way; the other half comes in getting it.

Handicapped is not helpless.

Hanging is too good for a man who makes puns; he should be drawn and quoted.
—*Fred Allen*

Happiness can only be obtained when one is happy.

Happiness in intelligent people is the rarest thing I know.
— *Ernest Hemingway*

Happiness is a by—product of achievement.

Happiness is a path, not a destination.

Happiness is not something you have in your hands; it is something you carry in you heart.

Happiness is the conviction that we are loved in spite of ourselves.

Happiness isn't getting what you want; it's wanting what you get.
— *Garth Brooks*

Happiness isnt something you experience; it's something you remember.
— *Oscar Levant*

Happiness lies for those who cry, those who hurt, those who have searched and those who have tried. For only they can appreciate the importance of people who have touched their lives.

Happiness lies, first of all, in health.
— *G.W. Curtis*

Happiness makes up in height for what it lacks in length.
— Robert Frost

Happiness sneaks in through a door you didn't know you left open.

Happiness will never come to those who fail to appreciate what they already have.

Happiness, that grand mistress of the ceremonies in the dance of life, impels us through all its mazes and meanderings, but leads none of us by the same route.
— Charles Caleb Cotton

Happy laughter and family voices in the home will keep more kids off the streets at night than the strictest curfew.

Hard work brings more of it, smart work brings less of it.

Hard work doesn't harm anyone, but I do not want to take chances.

Hard work has future payoff. Laziness pays off now.

Hard work spotlights the character of people; some turn up their sleeves, some turn up their noses, and some don't turn up at all!

Hardware: the parts of a computer system that can be kicked.
— Jeff Pesis

Harvard Law: Under the most rigorously controlled conditions of pressure, temperature, volume, humidity, and other variables, the organism will do as it damn well pleases.

Hating people is like burning down your own house to get rid of a rat.

Have a mouth as sharp as a dagger, but a heart as soft as tofu.

Have patience with everything that remains unsolved in your heart. Try to love the questions themselves, like locked rooms and like books written in a foreign language. Do not now look for the answers. They cannot now be given to you because you could not live them. It is a question of experiencing everything. At present you need to live the question. Perhaps you will gradually, without even noticing it, find yourself experiencing the answer, some distant day.
— Rainer Maria Rilke

Have you ever wondered why, wondered why the night sky, Is always so dark and sinister? With a few clouds here and a few clouds there, And the moon, with the light it administers. May be it's the darkness in our souls that fills all hollows and

Proverbs

holes, darker than the darkest empty space. Or may be it's just there to see, not to be pondered about by you and me, so let it simply Rest in Peace.
— *Charles Edward Jaggard*

Have you found a penny in the street lately? It was probably a dime when someone dropped it.

Having no secrets means you have lived in isolation.

Having some place to go to is home. Having someone to love is family. Having both is a blessing.

Having teenagers is often what undermines a parent's belief in heredity.

Having the right to do it, doesn't mean it is right to do it.

He does not believe that does not live according to his belief.
— *Thomas Fuller*

He felt that his whole life was some kind of dream and he sometimes wondered whose it was and whether they were enjoying it

He has Van Gogh's ear for music.

He is a tool who cannot get angry, but he is a wise man who will not.

He is not afraid of work, you can tell by the way he fights it.

He is one of those people who would be enormously improved by death.

He only earns his freedom and his life, who takes them every day by storm.
— *Johann Wolfgang Goethe*

He painted a tiger, but it turned out a dog.

He seemed to indulge in all the usual pleasures without being a slave to any of them.
— *Albert Camus*

He that lets the small things bind him, leaves the great undone behind him.

He that will not reason is a bigot, he that cannot reason is a fool, he that dares not reason is a slave.
— *William Drummond*

He took his defeat like a man; he blamed it on his wife.

He was so narrow minded he could see through a keynote with both eyes.

He who asks is a fool for five minutes, but he who does not ask remains a fool forever.

He who believes that time will wear away the pain from love has not truly loved before.
— Bernard Yen

He who breaks a thing to find out what it is, has left the path of wisdom.
— J.R.R. Tolkien

He who can no longer pause to wonder and stand rapt in awe is as good as dead; his eyes are closed.
— Albert Einstein

He who can take no interest in what is small, will take false interest in what is great.

He who dies with the most toys, is, nonetheless, still dead.

He who fails to prepare, prepares to fail.

He who fights with monsters should look to it that he himself does not become a monster.. when you gaze long into the abyss, the abyss also gazes into you.
— Friedrich Nietzsche

He who forces love where none is found remains a fool the whole year around.

He who governs by his moral excellence may be compared to the Pole star which abides in its place while all other stars bow towards it.

He who has a thing to sell and goes and whispers in a well is not as apt to get the dollars as he who climbs a tree and hollers.

He who has a why to live can bear almost any how.
— Friedrich Nietzsche

He who has a why to live for can bear almost any how.
— Friedrich Nietzsche

He who has no fire in himself cannot warm others.

He who has the courage to laugh is almost as much a master of the world as he who is ready to die.
— Giacomo Leopardi

He who hesitates is not only lost, but miles from the next exit.

He who is not grateful for the good things he has would not be happy with what he wished he had.

He who kneels the most stands best.
— D.L. Moody

He who knows most, talks least

Proverbs

He who knows not and knows not that he knows not is a fool. Shun him. He who knows not and knows that he knows not is a child. Teach him. He who knows and knows not that he knows is asleep. Wake him. He who knows and knows that he knows is a wise man. Follow him.

He who laughs last didn't get the joke.

He who laughs last thinks slowest!

He who parades his virtues seldom leads the parade.

He who receives a good turn should never forget it; he who does one should never remember it.

He who runs against time is against an adversary not subject to defeat.

He who sleeps late has short days.

He who slings mud looses ground.

Heal the past; live the present; dream the future.

Health is merely the slowest possible rate at which one can die.

Heaven can wait, but I cannot. I cannot take for granted that time is on my side.

— *Bonny Hicks*

Heaven doesn't want me and hell is scared I am going to take over.

— *Eve Toth*

Heaven is where the police are British, the cooks are French, the mechanics German, the lovers Italian and it's all organised by the Swiss. Hell is where the chefs are British, the mechanics French, the lover's Swiss, the police German and it's all organised by the Italians.

— *Eliane Kirchner*

Heavens above! The reason why I'm so jealous of you is obvious enough! If you weren't so damned attractive physically, do you think my heart would beat almost to suffocation whenever I see you speak to someone? If you don't realize how attractive you are in that way, let me tell you, other people do, and have told me so.

— *Violet Trefussis*

Heavier-than-air flying machines are impossible.

— *Lord Kelvin*

Heavy drinkers have what is known as saloon arthritis — every night they get stiff in a different joint.

Hell is when there is no reason to live and no courage to die.
— *William Markiewicz*

Help Wanted: Telepath. You know where to apply.

Herblock's Law. If it is good, they will stop making it.

Here at last we shall be free; the Almighty hath not built here for his envy, will not drive us hence: here we may reign secure, and in my choice to reign is worth ambition though in Hell: better to reign in Hell, than serve in Heaven.
— *John Milton*

Here is a good joke to do during an earthquake: Straddle a big crack in the ground, and if it opens wider, go "Whoa! Whoa!" and flail your arms around, like you're going to fall in.

Here is a test to find whether your mission on earth is finished: If you're alive, it isn't.
— *Richard Bach*

Here's to you and here's to me and may we never disagree, but if we do I'll still love you.

Highway billboards must go — we need the room for roadsigns, garbage dumps, and junkyards.

Highway sign near San Antonio: Thirty days hath September, April, June, and November — and anyone exceeding trie speed limit"

Hiroshima '45, Tchemobyl '86, Windows '95.

His [Johann Sebastian Bach] skill is no longer simply a technique, but an interpretation of the world, an image of Being; and his music is a phenomenon of the reality of the inconceivable as the cosmos itself.
— *Albert Schweitzer*

History books which contain no falsehoods are extremely dull.

History does repeat itself, but not as often as old movies.

History is a selective interpretation of events designed to justify those currently in power. Memory is the same thing on an individual scale.

History is now costing us more than the stuff is worth.

History is simply a record of man's intelligence — or lack of it.

History is something that never happened told by someone who wasn't there.
— *Gomez de la Serna*

History records only one indispensable man
— *Adam.*

Proverbs

History repeats itself, and that's one of the things wrong with history

History repeats itself, but each time the price goes up.

History will be kind to me for I intend to write it.
— *Winston Churchill*

History, which undertakes to record the transactions of the past, for the instruction of future ages, would ill deserve that honourable office if she condescended to plead the cause of tyrants, or to justify the maxims of persecution.
— *Edward Gibbon*

History.. .is, indeed, little more than the register of the crimes, follies, and misfortune of mankind.
— *Edward Gibbon*

Hitch your wagon to a star.
— *Ralph Waldo Emerson*

Hold fast to dreams, for if dreams die, life is a broken bird that cannot fly.
— *Langston Hughes*

Hold your head up because you have every right to.

Holding on to anger is like grasping a hot coal with the intent of throwing it at someone else; you are the one getting burned.
— *Buddha*

Holding your baby in your arms is one of life's great moments. All problems disappear as your gaze into the eyes of your offspring.

Home is a place where teenagers go to refuel.

Home is an invention on which no one has yet improved.
—*Ann Douglas*

Honest criticism is hard to take, particularly from a relative, a friend, an acquaintance, or a stranger.
— *Franklin P. Jones*

Honor cannot be found in the false. Honor makes a perfect gift to yourself.

Hope begins in the dark, the stubborn hope that if you just show up and try to do the right thing, the dawn will come. You wait and watch and work: you don't give up.
—*Anne Lamott*

Hope cannot be killed.

Hope is a good thing - may be the best thing, and no good thing ever dies.
— *Stephen King*

Hope is a waking dream.
— Aristotle

Hope is not the conviction that something will turn out well but the certainty that something makes sense, regardless of how it turns out
— Vaclay Havel

Hope is putting faith to work when doubting would be easier.

Hope sees the invisible, feels the intangible, and achieves the impossible.

Hospital is a place where they wake you up to give you a sleeping pill.

Hot heads and cold hearts never solved anything.

Housework is something you do that nobody notices until you don't do it.

How come we don't always know when love begins, but we always know when it ends?

How do you start your days? Good morning Lord or Good Lord, morning.

How far a fisherman stretches the truth depends on the length of his arms.

How happy the lot of the mathematician. He is judged solely by his peers, and the standard is so high that no colleague or rival can ever win a reputation he does not deserve.
— W.H. Auden

How I wish that somewhere there existed an island for those who are wise and of goodwill.
— Albert Einstein

How long a minute is depends on what side of the bathroom door you're on.

How many legs does a dog have if you call the tail a leg? Four. Calling a tail a leg doesn't make it a leg.
— Abraham Lincoln

How many of you believe in telekinesis? Raise MY hand!

How would you like to spend eternity, smoking or non-smoking?

However great the ills a man may have to bear, he but adds to them when he allows himself to give away to despair.
— Confucius

Hug an ogre - enrich the emotionally needy.

Hugs are not measured by quantity, they are measured by quality.

Proverbs

Human beings have will power while a mule has won't power.

Human beings, who are almost unique in having the ability to learn from the experience of others, are also remarkable for their apparent disinclination to do so.
— *Douglas Adams*

Human diseases are the same as they were five thousand years ago, but doctors have selected more expensive names for them.

Human experience is the starting point and ending point of the hermeneutical circle. Codified tradition both reaches back to roots in experience and is constantly renewed or discarded through the test of experience. "Experience" includes experience of the divine, experience of oneself, and experience of the community and the world, in an interacting dialectic.
— *Rosemary Radford Ruether*

Human relationships always help us to carry on because they always presuppose further developments, a future - and also because we live as if our only task was precisely to have relationships with other people.
— *Albert Camus*

Human things must be known to be loved, but Divine things must be loved to be known.

Humanity today is not safe in the presence of humanity. The old cannibalism has given way to anonymous action in which the killer and the killed do not know each other, and in which, indeed, the very fact of mass death has the effect of making mass killing less reprehensible than the death of a single individual.
— *Norman Cousins*

Humans are like tea bags. They never realize their strength until they are put in hot water.

Hurewitz's Memory Principle: The chance of forgetting something is directly proportional to.. .uh...

Hurt leads to bitterness, bitterness to anger, travel too far that road and the way is lost.
— *Terry Brooks*

— x —

I

I always get what I want because I always want what I get.
— Tim Bischoff

I always knew that looking back at my tears would make me laugh, but I never thought that looking back at my laughter would make me cry.
— Cat Stevens

I always thought looking back on the times I cried would make me laugh; but I never knew looking back on the times I laughed would make me cry.

I always try to go the extra mile at work, but my boss always finds me and brings me back.

I am a little man and this is a little town but there must be a spark in a little man that can burst into flame.
— John Steinbeck

I am always going to be true to myself.
— Princess of Wales Diana

I am an insomniac, agnostic, egotist: I lie awake nights wondering whether I believe that I am as great as I think I am.

I am convinced that He (God) does not play dice.
— Albert Einstein

I am convinced that life is 10% what happens to me and 96% how I react to it.

I am never less alone than when alone.
— Scipio Africanus

I am not a vegetarian because I love animals; I am a vegetarian because I hate plants.
— A. Whitney Brown

I am not afraid of storms for I am learning how to sail my ship.
— Louisa May Alcott

I am not as think as you stoned I am.

I am not part of the problem. I am a Republican.
— Dan Quayle

I am not religious, I just love the Lord.

I am not young enough to know everything.
— Oscar Wilde

Proverbs

I am on a thirty day diet. So far, I have lost 15 days.

I am Pentium of Borg. Division is futile. You will be approximated.

I am reading a very interesting book about anti-gravity. I just cant put it down.

I am serious; it was a joke.

I am so glad God sees the whole video tape of my life, and not just a snapshot of where I am now.

I am sorry I offended you - I should have lied.

I am the world's greatest authority on my own opinion.

I asked for everything so I could enjoy life. Instead, He gave me life so I could enjoy everything.

I asked Mom if I was a gifted child. She said they certainly wouldn't have paid for me.

I believe I found the missing link between animal and civilized man. It is us.

— *Konrad Lorenz*

I believe in the Big Bang theory. God spoke and BANG! It was.

I believe in the brotherhood of man, all men, but I don't believe in brotherhood with anybody who doesn't want brotherhood with me. I believe in treating people right, but I'm not going to waste my time trying to treat somebody right who doesn't know how to return the treatment.

— *Malcolm X*

I believe that every human has a finite number of heartbeats. I don't intend to waste any of mine running around doing exercises.

— *Neil Armstrong*

I believe the true road to preeminent success in any line is to make yourself master in that line.

— *Andrew Carnegie*

I believe we are on an irreversible trend toward more freedom and democracy, but that could change.

— *Dan Quayle*

I belong to no organized party. I am a Democrat.

— *Will Rogers*

I bend, but I do not break.

I bought some batteries but they weren't included, so I had to buy them again.

— *Steven Wright*

I can get more out of God by believing Him for one minute than by snouting at Him all night.
— Smith Wiggtesworth

I can lead you to the water but I can't let you drink.

I can't dial 911. There's no 11 on my phone.

I cannot walk through the suburbs in the solitude of the night without thinking that the night pleases us because it suppresses idle details, just as our memory does.
— Jorge Luis Bonnes

I close my eyes in order to see.

I contend that we are both atheists. I just believe in one fewer god than you do. When you understand why you dismiss all the other possible gods, you will understand why I dismiss yours.
— Stephen F. Roberts

I could never convince the financiers that Disneyland was feasible because dreams offer too little collateral.
— Walt Disney

I couldn't repair your brakes, so I made your horn louder.

I deserve respect for the things I did not do.
— Dan Quayle

I did what any normal person would do at that age. You call home. You call home to mother and father and say, "I'd like to get into the National Guard."
— Dan Quayle

I didn't have time to write a short letter, so I wrote a long one instead.
— Mark Twain

I disapprove of what you say, but I will defend to the death your right to say it.
— Voltaire

I dislike arguments of any kind. They are always vulgar, and often convincing.
— Oscar Wilde

I do love nothing in the world so well as you: is not that strange?
— William Shakespeare

I do not know what I may appear to the world; but to myself I seem to have been only like a boy playing on the sea—shore, and diverting myself in now and then finding a smoother pebble or a prettier shell than ordinary, whilst the great ocean of truth lay all undiscovered before me.
— Isaac Newton

Proverbs

I DO want your money, because God wants your money!

I don't blame Congress. If I had $600 billion, I'd be irresponsible too.

I don't care who you are, what you drive, or where you'd rather be.

I don't even know what street Canada is on.
—Al Capone

I don't feel obliged to believe that the same God who has endowed us with sense, reason, and intellect has intended us to forgo their use.
— Galileo Galilei

I don't have a solution but I admire the problem.

I don't have an attitude problem. You have a perception problem.

I don't know what tomorrow holds, but I know who holds tomorrow.

I don't know what's worse, finding the love of your life and losing them — or never knowing if you will.
— Carerea

I don't like to stand out. It consumes too much of your life to be in the limelight.

I don't necessarily agree with everything I say.

I don't need your attitude; I have one of my own.

I don't remember how we happened to meet each other. I don't remember who got along with whom first. All I can remember is all of us together...always.

I don't think of all the misery, but of all the beauty that still remains.
— Anne Frank

I don't think so, therefore I'm probably not.
— Alan Smithee

I don't use drugs, my dreams are frightening enough.
— M.C. Escher

I don't want any yes - men around me. I want everybody to tell me the truth even if it costs them their jobs.
— Samuel Goldwyn

I don't want to achieve immortality through my work. I want to achieve it through not dying.
— Woody Alien

I don't want to be a genius - I have enough problems just trying to be a man.
— Albert Camus

I dread success. To have succeeded is to have finished one's business on earth, like the male spider, who is killed by the female the moment he has succeeded in his courtship. I like a state of continual becoming, with a goal in front and not behind.
— *George Bernard Shaw*

I dreamed a thousand new paths... I woke and walked my old one.

I drink to make other people interesting.
— *George Jean Nathan*

I either want less corruption, or more chance to participate in it.
— *Ashley Brilliant*

I emerged from the woods that day into a different world, an adult world, where memories of first love linger, but summers always end.
— *Tim Madigan*

I enjoyed my own nature to the fullest, and we all know that there lies happiness, although, to soothe one another mutually, we occasionally pretend to condemn such joys as selfishness.
— *Albert Camus*

I feel more fellowship with the defeated than with saints.
— *Albert Camus*

I finally managed to teach my dog to beg. Last night he came home with $15.00.

I got a fortune cookie that said, "To remember is to understand." I have never forgotten it. A good judge remembers what it was like to be a lawyer. A good editor remembers being a writer. A good parent remembers what it was like to be a child.
— *Anna Quindlen*

I had a lovely evening. Unfortunately, this wasn't it
— *Groucho Marx*

I had dreams and I've had nightmares. I overcame the nightmares because of my dreams.

I had the ambition to not only go farther than man had gone before, but to go as far as it was possible to go.
— *Captain Cook*

I had to get rid of my wife. The cat was allergic.

I had to go on two diets at the same time because one diet wasn't giving me enough food.
— *Barry Matter*

I hate quotations, let me know what you know.
— *Ralph Waldo Emerson*

I hate television. I hate it as much as peanuts. But I can't stop eating peanuts.
— Orson Welles

I have a microwave fireplace. I can have a relaxing evening in front of the fire in 8 minutes.
— Steven Wright

I have a most peaceable disposition. My desires are for a modest hut, a thatched roof, but a good bed, good food, very fresh milk and butter, flowers in front of my window and a few pretty trees by my door. And should the good Lord wish to make me really happy, he will allow me the pleasure of seeing about six or seven of my enemies hanged upon those trees.
— Heinrich Heine

I have a perfect cure for a sore throat. Cut it
— Alfred Hitchcock

I have all the answers, it's just that most of them aren't right.

I have all the money I'll ever need if I die by 4 today.
— Henny Youngman

I have always thought the actions of men the best interpreters of their thoughts.
— John Locke

I have an everyday religion that works for me. Love yourself first and everything else falls into line. You really have to love yourself to get anything done in this world.
— Lucille Ball

I have approximate answers and possible beliefs and different degrees of certainty about different things, but I'm not absolutely sure of anything, and many things I don't know anything about, such as whether it means anything to ask why we're here, and what the question might mean. I might think about it a little bit, but if I can't figure it out then I go on to something else. But I don't have to know an answer. I don't have to.. .I don't feel frightened by not knowing things, by being lost in the mysterious universe without having any purpose, which is the way it really is, as far as I can tell, possibly. It doesn't frighten me.
— Richard Feynman

I have called this principle, by which each slight variation, if useful, is preserved, by the term Natural Selection.
— Charles Darwin

I have changed my mind a dozen times. It seems to work better now.

I have every sympathy with the American who was so horrified by what he has read of the effects of smoking that he gave up reading.
— *Henry G. Strauss*

I have great faith in fools — self confidence my friends call it.
— *Edgar Allen Poe*

I have learned this at least by my experiment: If one advances confidently in the direction of his dreams, and endeavors to live the life he has imagined, he will meet with a success unexpected in common hours.
— *Henry David Thoreau*

I have memories — but only a fool stores his past in the future.
— *David Gerrold*

I have never let my schooling intererfere with my education.
— *Mark Twain*

I have never met a person whose greatest need was anything other than real, unconditional love. You can find it in a simple act of kindness toward someone who needs help. There is no mistaking love. You feel it in your heart. It is the common fiber of life, the flame that heals our soul, energizes our spirit and supplies passion to our lives. It is our connection to God and to each other.
— *Elisabeth Kibler—Ross*

I have not failed. I've just found 10,000 ways that won't work.
— *Thomas Edison*

I have not yet begun to procrastinate!

I have opinions of my own - strong opinions - but I don't always agree with them.
— *George Bush*

I have studied many philosophers and many cats. The wisdom of cats is infinitely superior.
— *Hippolyte Taine*

I have to remind myself that some birds weren't meant to be caged. Their feathers are just too bright. And when they fly away, the part of you that knew it was a sin to lock them up does rejoice. But your world is just that much colder and emptier that they're gone. I don't know... may be I just miss my friend.
— *Stephen King*

I hear and I forget, I see and I remember, I do and I understand.

I hope this match never ends. When the match ends, the memories begin.
— *Ryan Giggs*

Proverbs

I hope to be the kind of person my dog thinks I am.

I just got lost in thought. It was unfamiliar territory.

I just want to turn on the light and have it work. I don't want to know where the electricity comes from.

I keep my good health by having a very bad temper, kept under good control.
— *Theodore Roosevelt*

I know God will not give me anything I can't handle. I just wish that He didn't trust me so much.
— *Mother Teresa*

I know Karate and several other Japanese words.

I know no method to secure the repeal of bad or obnoxious laws so effectual as their strict construction.
— *Ulysses S. Grant*

I know not with what weapons World War III will be fought, but World War IV will be fought with sticks and stones.
— *Albert Einstein*

I know that if I had had a chance to take possession of your soul, I would have made it smile.
— *Jimmy*

I know they say love is blind, but does it also have to be deaf, dumb, and stupid?

I know UNIX, PASCAL, C, FORTRAN, COBOL, and nineteen other high-tech word.

I learned that it is the weak who are cruel, and that gentleness is to be expected only from the strong.
— *Leo Rosten*

I like libraries. It makes me feel comfortable and secure to have walls of words, beautiful and wise, all around me. I always feel better when I can see that there is something to hold back the shadows.
— *Roger Zelazny*

I like pigs. Dogs look up to us. Cats look down on us. Pigs treat us as equals.
— *Winston Churchill*

I loathe people who keep dogs. They are cowards who haven't got the guts to bite people themselves.
— *August Strindberg*

I love California. I practically grew up in Phoenix.
— *Dan Quayle*

I love thee to the level of everyday's most quiet need, by the sun and candle light... I love thee with the breath, smiles, tears of all my life.
— E.B. Browning

I love this world as a dead world. And always there comes an hour when one is weary of prisons, and all one craves for is a warm face, the warmth and wonder of the living heart.
— Albert Camus

I love to think of nature as an unlimited broadcasting system through which God speaks to us every hour, if we will only tune in.
— George Washington Carver

I love you so passionately, that I hide a great part of my love, so as not to oppress you with it.
— Marie De Rabutin—Chantal

I may not be totally perfect, but parts of me are excellent
— Ashtey Brilliant

I must admit I personally measure success in terms of the contributions an individual makes to her or his fellow human beings.
— Margaret Mead

I must study politics and war that my sons may have liberty to study mathematics and philosophy - My sons ought to study mathematics and philosophy, geography, natural history, naval architecture, navigation, commerce and agriculture in order to give their children a right to study painting, poetry, music, architecture, statuary, tapestry, and porcelain.
— John Adams

I never found the companion that was so companionable as solitude. We are for the most part more lonely when we go abroad among men than when we stay in our chambers. A man thinking or working is always alone, let him be where he will.
— Henry David Thorsau

I never think of the future. It comes soon enough.
— Albert Einstein

I no longer worry about being a brilliant conversationalist. I simply try to be a good listener. I notice that people who do that are usually welcome wherever they go.
— Frank Bettger

I once saw this sign on a diner wall: "I have an agreement with the bank: They don't fry hamburgers, and I don't cash checks."

Proverbs

I only hope that we never lose sight of one thing — that it was all started by a mouse.
— *Walt Disney*

I preached as never sure to preach again, and as a dying man to dying men.
— *Richard Baxter*

I put instant coffee into a microwave oven and almost went back in time.
— *Steven Wright*

I refuse to engage in an intellectual battle with an unarmed man.

I regret not the things I have done, only those I have yet to do.
— *George Lucas*

I regret to say that we of the F.B.I. are powerless to act in cases of oral-genital intimacy, unless it has in some way obstructed interstate commerce.
— *J. Edgar Hoover*

I remember little things that break my heart. We were coming out of Michael's house one day, and he noticed my shoelaces were undone. He bent down and tied them. I almost cried. To me, it was such a gesture of love.
— *Kirk Douglas*

I saw some piglets suckling their dead mother. After a short while they shuddered and went away. They had sensed that she could no longer see them and that she wasn't like them any more. What they loved in their mother wasn't her body, but whatever it was that made her body live.
— *Confucius*

I shall be telling this with a sigh. Somewhere ages and ages hence: two roads diverged in a wood, and I.

I signed up for an exercise class and was told to wear loose fitting clothing. If I "had" any loose fitting clothing, I wouldn't have signed up in the first place!

I spilled spot remover on my dog. He's gone now.

I stand by all the misstatements that I've made.
— *Dan Quayle*

I tell my students that artificial intelligence is a property that a machine has if it astounds you.
— *Herbert Freeman*

I think all right thinking people in this country are sick and tired of being told that ordinary, decent people are fed up in

this country with being sick and tired. Well, I'm certainly not, and I'm sick and tired of being told that I am.
— Monty Python

I think animal testing is a terrible idea; they get all nervous and give the wrong answers.

I think I've found the trouble with our economy. There are far more ways to get into debt, than there are to get out of it.

I think my favorite sport in the Olympics is the one in which you make your way through the snow, you stop, you shoot a gun, and then you continue on. In most of the world, it is known as the biathlon, except in New York City, where it is known as winter.
— Michael Ventre

I think that i shall never see a billboard as lovely as a tree. Perhaps, unless the billboards fall I'll never see a tree at all.
— Ogden Nash

I think that the undecideds could go one way or the other.
— Georoe Bush

I think there's a world market for about 5 computers.
— Thomas J. Watson

I took a speed-reading course and read War and Peace in twenty minutes. It involves Russia.
— Woody Allon

I took the one less traveled by, and that has made all the difference.
— Robert Frost

I treasure every moment spent with you, every smile from you, and every thought about you!

I used to be indecisive, but now I'm not so sure.

I used to be Snow White, but I drifted.
— Mae West

I used to have a photographic memory, but it was never developed.

I used to have an open mind but my brains kept falling out.

I walk alone, assaulted it seems, by tears from heaven.
— Patti Smith

I want to die in my sleep like my grandfather, not screaming and yelling like the passengers in his car.

I want to know God's thoughts; the rest are details.
— Albert Einstein

Proverbs

I was about half in love with her by the time we sat down. That's the thing about girls. Every time they do something pretty, even if they're not much to look at, or even if they're sort of stupid, you fall half in love with them, and then you never know where the hell you are.
— J.D. Salinger

I was angered, for I had no shoes. Then I met a man who had no feet.

I was angry with my friend I told my wrath my wrath did end; i was angry with my foe I told it not my wrath did grow.
— William Stake

I was born not knowing and have had little time to change that here and there.
— Richard Feynman

I was born when you kissed me, and I died when you left me, but I lived for the two weeks you loved me.

I was not lying. I said things that later on seemed to be untrue.
— Richard Nixon

I was recently on a tour of Latin America, and the only regret I have is that I didn't study my Latin harder in school so I could converse with those people.
— Dan Quayle

I was regretting the past and fearing the future. Suddenly God was speaking: "My name is I am." I waited and God continued: "When you live in the past, with its mistakes and regrets, it is hard. I am not there. My name is not I was. When you live in the future, with its problems and fears, it is hard. I am not there. My name is not I will be. When you live in this moment, it is not hard. I am here. My name is I am."
— Helen Mellincost

I was thrown out of college for cheating on the metaphysics exam. I looked into the soul of the boy next to me.
— Woody Allen

I was under medication when I made the decision to burn the tapes.
— Richard Nixon

I was walking home one night and a guy hammering on a roof called me a paranoid little weirdo.. .in morse code...

I wear my wife's eyeglasses because she wants me to see things her way.
— Jayson Feinburg

I went to a general store. They wouldn't let me buy anything specifically.
— Steven Wright

I went to a place to eat. The menu said breakfast served any time. I ordered French toast during the Renaissance.
— Steven Wright

I will be correspondent to command, and do my spiriting gentry.
— William Shakespeare

I will set you free, to roam in lands far away, and hope you return. If and when you do come back, I shall hold you, and kiss you to make my world right. And then I will set you free once more.
— Anne Forehand

I wonder if other dogs think poodles are members of a weird religious cult.
— Rita Rudner

I wonder why you can always read a doctor's bill and never his prescription.
— Fintey Peter Dunne

I would fain die a dry death.
— William Shakespeare

I would like to learn, or remember, how to live.
— Annie Dillard

I would rather have a moment of wonderful than a lifetime of nothing special.
— Steel Magnolias

I wrote a song, but I can't read music. Every time I hear a new song on the radio, I think "Hey, may be I wrote that."

I'd give my right arm to be ambidextrous.
— Brian W. Kernighan

I'd like to help you out, which way did you come in?

I'd love to make up my mind, but I can't remember where I left it.

I'd probably be famous now if I wasn't such a good waitress.
— Jane Siberry

I'd rather do something and fail than do nothing and succeed!

I'd rather have a bottle in front of me than a frontal tobotomy.

I'm a Leo. Leos don't believe in this astrology stuff.
— Tom Neff

I'm moving to Mars next week, so if you have any boxes...
— Steven Wright

Proverbs

I'm not confused, I'm well mixed.

— Robert Frost

I'm old enough to know better but I'm still to young to care.

I'm sorry, you seem to have mistaken me for someone who cares.

I'm the one who's got to die when it's time for me to die, so let me live my life the way I want to.

— Jimi Hendrix

I'm writing an unauthorized autobiography.

— Steven Wright

I've always believed that you shouldn't want to mend a broken heart, because that's someone you don't want to forget Scars can be good.

— Joseph Fiennes

I've been to all parts of this grand world and have seen no great tragedy than the heart that loves and sees it not returned. The tragedy, of course, is for both parties.

— Ryan Vooris

I've discovered the whole problem with the National Debt Most of us work 5 days a week, and the government spends.

I've gotten to the age where I need my false teeth and hearing aid before I can ask where I left my glasses.

I've learned that if someone says something unkind about me, I must live so that no one will believe it.

I've noticed your hostility towards him... I ought to have guessed you were friends.

I've read about foreign policy and studied; I know the number of continents.

— George Wallace

I've to say NO to the good so I can say YES to the best

I've tried all season to put my thumb on it but perhaps the problem is bigger than my thumb.

— Reyna Thompson

I, thus neglecting worldly ends, all dedicated to closeness and the bettering of my mind.

— William Shakespeare

I've been to all parts of this grand world and have seen no great tragedy than the heart that loves and sees it not returned. The tragedy, of course,' is for both I parties.

— Ryan Vooris

I've discovered the whole problem with the National Debt Most of us work 5 days a week, and the government spends.

I've gotten to the age where I need my false teeth and hearing aid before I can ask where I left my glasses.

I've learned that if someone says something unkind about me, I must live so that no one will believe it.

I've noticed your hostility towards him... I ought to have guessed you were friends.

I've read about foreign policy and studied; I know the number of continents.

— *George Wallace*

I've to say NO to the good so I can say YES to the best

I've tried all season to put my thumb on it, but perhaps the problem is bigger than my thumb.

— *Reyna Thompson*

I, thus neglecting worldly ends, all dedicated to closeness and the bettering of my mind.

— *William Shakespeare*

Identity would seem to be the garment with which one covers the nakedness of the self, in which case, it is best that the garment be loose, a little like the robes of the desert, through which one's nakedness can always be felt, and, sometimes, discerned. This trust in one's nakedness is all that gives one the power to change one's robes.

— *James Baldwin*

Idiot box: The part of the envelope that tells a person where to place the stamp when they cant quite figure it out for themselves

— *Rich Hall*

If A = B and B = C, then A = C. except where void or prohibited by law.

— *Roy Santoro*

If a home doesn't make sense, nothing does.

If A is a success in life, then A equals X plus Y plus Z. Work is X; Y is play; and Z is keeping your mouth shut

— *Albert Einstein*

If a June night could talk, it would probably boast that it invented romance.

— *Bern Williams*

If a kid asks where rain comes from, I think a cute thing to tell him is "God is crying." And if he asks why God is crying, another cute thing to tell him is "probably because of something you did."

If a man does not keep pace with his companions, perhaps it is because he hears a different drummer. Let him step to the music which he hears, however measured or far away.

— *Henry David Thoreau*

If a small thing has the power to make you angry, does that not indicate something about your size?

— *Sidney J. Harris*

If a word in the dictionary were mispelled, how would we know?

— *Steven Wright*

If absence makes the heart grow fonder, some people must really love church.

If I am given a formula, and I am ignorant of its meaning, it cannot teach me anything, but if I already know it what does the formula teach me?

— *St. Augustine*

If I could reach up and hold a star for every time you've made me smile, the entire evening sky would be in the palm of my hand.

If I could reach up and hold a star for every time you've made me smile, the entire evening sky would be in the palm of my hand.

If I could reach up and hold a star for every time you've made me smile, the entire evening sky would be in the palm of my hand.

— *Carina*

If I ever needed a brain transplant, I'd choose a sportswriter's because I'd want a brain that had never been used.

— *Norm Van Brocklin*

If I had my life to live over I would have burned the pink candle sculpted like a rose before it melted in storage.

— *Erma Bombeck*

If I had my life to live over I would have cried and laughed less while watching television, and more while watching life.

— *Erma Bombeck*

If I had my life to live over I would have eaten the popcorn in the 'good' living room and worried much less about the dirt when someone wanted to light a fire in the fireplace.

—*Erma Bombeck*

If I had my life to live over I would have gone to bed when I was sick instead of pretending the earth would go into a holding pattern if I weren't there for the day.
—Erma Bombeck

If I had my life to live over I would have invited friends over to dinner even if the carpet was stained and the sofa faded.
—Erma Bombeck

If I had my life to live over I would have sat on the lawn with my children and not worried aboutgrass stains.
—Erma Bombeck

If I had my life to live over I would have taken the time to listen to my grandfather ramble about his youth.
—Erma Bombeck

If I had my life to live over I would have talked less and listened more.
—Erma Bombeck

If I had my life to live over I would never have insisted the car windows be rolled up on a summer day because my hair had just been teased and sprayed.

If I had only known, I would have been a locksmith.
— Albert Einstein

If I have seen farther than others, it is because I was standing on the shoulders of giants.
—Isaac Newton

If I knew that, I'd fall in love over and over again. Hearts aren't supposed to be mended. If you fall in love and it doesn't work out, you get a broken heart. What comes out of that will make you a better lover and partner next time.
— Griffin Dunne

If I love you, what business is it of yours?
— Johann Wolfgang Goethe

If I want your opinion, I'll ask you to fill out the necessary forms.

If I was led by God to love God, step by step, as it seemed, if I accept that the beauty and rapture were real and true, then the rest of it was God's will too and that is the cause for bitterness. But if I'm simply a deluded ape who took a lot of old folktales far too seriously, then I brought all this on myself and my companions. The problem with atheism is that I have no—one to despise but myself. If, however, I choose to believe that God is vicious, then at least I have the solace of hating God.
— Mary Doria Russell

Proverbs

If innocence can leave, guilt can come.

If instead of a gem, or even a flower, we should cast a lovely thought on a friend, that would be giving as the angels give.
— *Georoge MacDonald*

If it jams, force it. If it breaks, it needed to be replaced anyway.

If it takes a lot of words to say what you have in mind, give it more thought.
— *Dennis Roch*

If it were as easy to arouse enthusiasm as it is suspicion, just think what could be accomplished!

If it's worth doing, it's worth overdoing!
— *Stacey Brown*

If Jesus was Jewish, how come he's got a Mexican name?
— *Tom Waits*

If life is a waste of time, and time is a waste of life, lets all get wasted together and have the time of our lives!
— *Sahir Sait*

If life were a novel, then dead would mark the end of the first chapter.
— *Kelly Nelson*

If life were fair, Dan Quayle would be making a living asking, "Do you want fries with that?"
— *John Cleese*

If loving you is wrong, I don't want to be right.

If money could talk, it would say goodbye.

If my film makes one more person miserable, I've done my job.
— *Woody Allen*

If Noah had been truly wise, he would have swatted those two flies.
— *Helen Castle*

If nobody knows the troubles you've seen, then you don't live in a small town.

If one dream should fall and break into a thousand pieces, never be afraid to pick one of those pieces up and begin again.
— *Flavia Weedn*

If one is lucky, a solitary fantasy can totally transform one million realities.
— *Maya Angelou*

If only God would give me some dear sign! Like making a large deposit in my name at a Swiss Bank.
— *Woody Allen*

If people are injured from the use of liquor, the injury arises not from the use of a bad thing, but from the abuse of a good thing.
— Abraham Lincoln

If people behaved like governments, you'd call the cops.
— Kelvin Throop

If people bring so much courage to this world the world has to kill them, so of course it kills them. The world breaks everyone and afterward many are strong at the broken places. But those that will not break it kills, it kills the very good and the very gentle and the very brave...
— Ernest Hemingway

If quitters never win, and winners never quit, then who is the fool that first said "Quit while you are ahead?"

If somebody has a bad heart, they can plug this jack in at night as they go to bed and it will monitor their heart throughout the night And the next morning, when they wake up dead, there'll be a record.
— Mark S. Fowler

If someone had told me I would be Pope one day, I would have studied harder.
— Pope John Paull

If someone is too tired to give you a smile, leave one of your own, because no one needs a smile as much as those who have none to give.

If someone says something unkind about me, I must live so that no one will believe it.

If success attend me, grant me humility; if failure, resignation to Thy will.
— David Livingstone

If suffering brings wisdom, I would wish to be less wise.
— William Butler Yeats

If the automobile had followed the same development cycle as the computer, a Rolls—Royce would today cost $100, get a million miles per gallon, and explode once a year, killing everyone inside.
— Robert X. Cringely

If the Devil can get into the church, nine times out of ten he'll come in through the choir.
— Thomas Brantley Winstead

If the human brain was simple enough for us to understand, we'd be so simple we couldn't understand.

Proverbs

If the human brain were so simple that we could understand it we would be so simple that we couldn't.

If the lawmaker is above the law, then, by definition, there is no law.

If the new software you want requires new hardware to run, you don't need the new software.

If the road you travel has no obstacles, it leads nowhere.

If the world didn't have evil, two faced, backstabbing, lying, theiving, assholes void of any moral obligation to humanity in general.. .who'd run for president?

if the world laughs at you, laugh right back - its as funny as you are.

If there is a sin against life, it consists perhaps not so much in despairing of life as in hoping for another life and in eluding the implacable grandeur of this life.

— *Albert Camus*

If there is anything we wish to change in the child, we should first examine it and see whether it is not something that could better be changed in ourselves.

— *Carl Jung*

If they squeeze olives to make olive oil, how do they make baby oil?

If things get any worse, I'll have to ask you to stop helping me.

If things get better with age, I'm approaching magnificent!

If this is a crush, then I don't know if I could take if the real thing ever happened.

— *Holden*

If this is tea, please bring me some coffee.. .but if this is coffee, please bring me some tea.

— *Abraham Lincoln*

If thou art able, stranger, to find out all these things and gather them together in your mind, giving all the relations, thou shaft depart crowned with glory and knowing that thou hast been adjudged perfect in this species of wisdom.

If time heals all wounds, how come the belly button stays the same?

If toast always lands butter-side down, and cats always land on their feet, what happen if you strap toast on the back of a cat and drop it?

— *Steven Wright*

If we are walking in joy, we are trusting God.

If we deny love that is given to us, if we refuse to give love because we fear pain or loss, then our lives will be empty, our loss greater.

If we don't know our own history, we are doomed to live it.
— *Hannah Arendt*

If we don't succeed, we run the risk of failure.
— *Dan Quayle*

If we get involved in a nuclear war, would the electromagnetic pulses from exploding bombs damage my videotapes?

If we only wanted to be happy it would be easy; but we want to be happier than other people, which is almost always difficult, since we think them happier than they are.
— *Charles de Montesquieu*

If we think of love as in itself the answer to all the problems human beings face, we will constantly be disappointed by it. If we search for perfection in a mate and refuse to be satisfied by anything less than that, we will never really experience sexual or marital love. If we are unwilling to undergo the interpersonal negotiations... we will never be able to give our love to anyone. Since love does not simply happen, as I have been suggesting, it must emerge as the saving remnant of our endless yearning for happy and meaningful lives.
— *Irving Singer*

If we'd confess our sins to one another we'd all laugh at the lack of originality.

If Yoda so strong in Force is, why words in right order he cannot put?

if you always do what you always did, you'll always get what you always got.

If you always watch the demons behind you, then you will never see the angels ahead.

If you are killed, you've lost a very important part of your life.
— *Brooke Shields*

If you are never scared, embarrassed, or hurt, it means you never take chances.

If you are patient in one moment of anger, you will escape a hundred days of sorrow.

If you are too careful, you are so occupied in being careful that you are sure to stumble over something.
— *Gertrude Stien*

Proverbs

If you begin to live life looking for the God that is all around you, every moment becomes a prayer.

— *Frank Bianco*

If you begin to understand what you are without trying to change it, then what you are undergoes a transformation.

— *Jiddu Krishnamurti*

If you build your life on dreams it's prudent to recall; a man with moonlight in his hands has nothing there at all.

— *Don Quixote*

If you can keep your head while all about are losing theirs and blaming it on you, perhaps you have underestimated the seriousness of the situation.

If you can laugh at it you can live with it.

If you can laugh when things go wrong, you have someone in mind to blame.

If you can not get rid of the family skeleton, you may as well make it dance.

— *George Bernard Shaw*

If you can read this, I've lost my trailer.

If you can't be a good example, then you'll just have to be a horrible warning.

— *Catherine Aird*

If you can't be content with what you have received, be thankful for what you have escaped.

If you can't control the wind, adjust your sail.

If you can't feed a hundred people, then feed just one.

— *Mother Teresa*

If you can't say something nice, become a reporter.

If you can't sleep, don't count sheep. Talk to the shepherd.

If you can't sleep, then get up and do something instead of lying there worrying. It's the worry that gets you, not the lack of sleep.

— *Date Carnegie*

If you could kick the person responsible for most of your troubles in the backside, you wouldn't be able to sit down for two weeks.

If you count sheep two at a time you'll fall asleep twice as fast.

If you cry because the sun has gone out of your life, your tears will prevent you from seeing the stars.

If you decide not to choose then you've already made the wrong choice!

If you depend on others to make you happy, you will be endlessly disappointed.

If you disregard the very simplest cases, there is in all of mathematics not a single infinite series whose sum has been rigorously determined. In other words, the most important parts of mathematics stand without a foundation.
— Niels H. Abet

If you do not know the way, seek where His footprints are.

If you don't care where you are, then you aren't lost.

If you don't do it, you'll never know what would have happened if you had done it
— Ashley Brilliant

If you don't have time to do it right you must have time to do it over.

If you don't know where you're going, how do you expect to get there.

If you don't like the way the world is, you change it You have an obligation to change it. You just do it one step at a time.
— Marian Wright Edelman

If you don't love, you cant live; if you don't live, you cant love.
— Jason Benson

If you don't stand for something, you'll fall for anything.

If you ever need a helping hand, there is one at the end of your arm.

If you expect nothing, you're apt to be surprised. You'll get it.
— Malcolm S. Forbes

If you fear death, you're already dead.

if you fear nothing, you love nothing. If you love nothing, what joy can there be in life?
—Sean Connery

If you gave me something I need more than you do, you've given me a gift; if you've given me something you need more than I do, you've gifted me with love.

If you get to thinking you're a person of some influence, try ordering somebody else's dog around.

If you give 100%, God will make up the difference!

If you give a smile right now, I'll give you the whole damn world.
— Leo Roth

Proverbs

If you give me six lines written by the most honest man, I will find something in them to hang him.

— *Cardinal de Richelieu*

If you go out looking for friends, you're going to find they are very scarce. If you go out to be a friend, you'll find them everywhere.

— *Zig Zigler*

If you have built castles in the air, your work need not be lost that is where they should be. Now put foundations under them.

— *Henry David Thoreau*

If you have much, give of your wealth; if you have little, give of your heart.

If you have the desire, you are halfway there.

— *E. Crique*

If you have virtue, acquire also the graces and beauties of virtue.

If you haven't all the things that you want, be thankful for all the things that you don't have that you didn't want

If you haven't much education you must use your brain.

If you hit two keys on the keyboard, the one you don't want will appear on the screen.

If you judge people, you have no time to love them.

—*Mother Teresa*

If you keep your mind sufficiently open, people will throw a lot of rubbish into it.

— *William A. Orton*

If you laugh a lot, when you get older your wrinkles will be in the right places.

— *Andrew Mason*

If you lend someone $20, and never see that person again, it was probably worth it.

If you let your children grow without trimming their buds, don't expect many blossoms.

If you love life, people call you an optimist If you hate life, people call you a pessimist. But if you think nothing at all of life, they think nothing of you.

If you love somebody, let them go, for if they return, they were always yours. And if they don't, they never were.

— *Kahlil Gibran*

If you love someone, you say it, you say it right then, out loud... or the moment just passes you by.

If you make friends with yourself, you will never be alone.

If you make people think they're thinking, they'll love you, but if you really make them think they'll hate you.

If you meet the Buddha in the lane, feed him the ball.
— Phil Jackson

If you must hold yourself up to your children as an object lesson, hold yourself up as a warning and not as an example.
— George Bernard Shaw

If you only have the Word, you will dry up. If you only have the Spirit, you will blow up. But if you have the Word and the Spirit, you will go up and grow up.

If you pick up a starving dog and make him prosperous, he will not bite you; that is the principal difference between a dog and a man.
— Mark Twain

If you set the example, you won't need to set many rules.
— Zig Zigler

If you still have the courage after losing all, you can be rest assured that you have not lost everything.

If you suck on a tit the movie gets an R rating. If you hack the tit off with an axe it will be PG.
— Jack Nicholson

If you tame me, then we shall need each other. To me, you will be unique in all the world. To you, I shall be unique in all the world.
— Antoine De Saint—Exupery

If you tell a joke in the forest and nobody laughs, was it a joke?

If you tell the truth you don't have to remember anything.
— Mark Twain

If you think dogs can't count, try putting three dog biscuits in your pocket then giving Fido only two of them.
— Phil Pastoret

If you think I am weird, you should meet my invisible friends!

If you think it's expensive to hire a professional to do the job, wait until you hire an amateur.
— Red Adair

If you think nobody cares if you're alive, try missing a couple of car payments.

Proverbs

If you think someone as a friend, you can approach him or her more easily.

— Howie

If you think that something small cannot make a difference, try going to sleep with a mosquito in the room.

If you think you can, or you think you cant, your right!

— Henry Ford

If you think you're getting too much government these days, just be happy that you're not getting all you are paying for.

If you treat a man as he is, he will remain as he is; if you treat him as he ought to be and could be, he will become as he ought to be and could be.

— Johann Wolfgang Goethe

If you treat every situation like a life or death matter, be prepared to die a lot of times.

If you understand something today, it must be obsolete.

If you wait to have kids until you can afford them, you probably never will. If you want a baby, have a new one. Don't baby the old one.

— Jessamyn West

If you want a definition of poverty, ask parents with three or four teenagers in the family.

If you want a place in the sun, you will have to expect some blisters.

If you want a thing well done, do it yourself.

— Charles Haddon Sourgeon

If you want something said, ask a man. If you want something done, ask a woman.

— Margaret Thatcher

If you want to bake an apple pie from scratch, you must first create the Universe.

— Carl Sagan

If you want to be well liked never lie about yourself, and be careful when telling the truth about others.

If you want to feel rich, just count all the things you have that money cant buy.

If you want to know yourself, observe the behavior of others. If you want to understand others, look in your own heart.

— Johann Wolfgang Goethe

If you want to make your dreams come true, the first thing you have to do is wake up.

If you want your dreams to come true, don't oversleep.

If you want your spouse to listen and pay strict attention to every word you say, talk in your sleep.

If you weep because the sun has set, your own tears will never let you see the stars.

If you will regret it in the morning, steep till noon.

If you wish your merit to be known, acknowledge that of other people.

If you're not part of the solution, you're part of the precipitate.
— *Steven Wright*

If you're too busy to laugh, you're entirely too busy.

If your faith cannot move mountains, it ought to at least dimb them.

If your morals make you dreary, depend upon it, they are wrong. I do not say give them up, for they may be all you have, but conceal them like a vice lest they should spoil the lives of better and simpler people.
— *Rober Loius Stevenson*

If your parents didn't have any children, there is a good chance you wont have any.
— *Clarence Dav*

If your vision doesn't scare you, then both your vision and your God are too small.
— *Brother Andrew*

If, after all, men cannot always make history have meaning, they can always act so that their own lives have one.
— *Albert Camus*

Ignorance and prejudice are the ballast of our ship of state — however, ships without ballast are not seaworthy and cannot sail in the tempests, nor reach a safe harbor.

Imagination is more important than knowledge. Knowledge is limited. Imagination encircles the world.
— *Albert Einstein*

Imagination is the one weapon in the war against reality.
— *Jules de Gaultier*

Imagination was given to man to compensate him for what he isn't, and a sense of humor to console him for what he is.

Imagine If every Thursday your shoes exploded if you tied them the usual way. This happens to us all the time with computers, and nobody thinks of complaining.
— *Jeff Raskin*

Proverbs

Imbesi's Law of the Conservation of Filth: "In order for something to become dean, something else must become dirty." Freeman's Extension: "but you can get everything dirty without getting anything dean."

Immature love says: "I love you because I need you." Mature love says "I need you because I love you."
— *Erich Fromm*

Immense power is acquired by assuring yourself in your secret reveries that you were born to control affairs.
— *Andrew Carnegie*

Important letters that contain no errors will develop errors on the way to the printer.

In a cat's eye, all things belong to cats.

In a universe suddenly divested of illusion and lights, man feels an alien, a stranger. His exile is without remedy since he is deprived of the memory of a lost home or the hope of a promised land.
— *Albert Camus*

In a world where death is, we should have no time to hate.

In all love affairs there conies a moment when desire demands possession.

In all relationships to life, faith is worthless unless it leads to action.

In an atomic war there would be neither conqueror or vanquished. During such a bombardment both sides would suffer the same fate. A continuous destruction would take place and no armistice nor peace proposals would bring it to an end.
— *Albert Schweitzer*

In communism, man oppresses man. In capitalism, it's the other way around.

In computer science, we stand on each other's feet.
— *Brian K. Reid*

In default of inexhaustible happiness, eternal suffering would at least give us a destiny. But we do not even have that consolation, and our worst agonies come to an end one day.
— *Albert Camus*

In describing my experience I am recording not what happened or what exists, but how I perceive it. In doing so I define myself. As I create my diary, I create myself.
— *Tristine Rainer*

In dog years, I'm dead.

In essentials, unity; in nonessentials, liberty; in all things, charity.
— *Melanchthon*

In every real man a child is hidden that wants to play.
— *Friedrich Nietzsche*

In everyone's life, at some time, our inner fire goes out. It is then burst into flame by an encounter with another human being. We should all be thankful for those people who rekindle the inner spirit.
— *Albert Schweitzer*

In Hollywood husbands are as hard to keep as secrets.

In India, "cold weather" is merely a conventional phrase and has come into use through the necessity of having some way to distinguish between weather which will melt a brass door - knob and weather which will only make it mushy.
— *Mark Twain*

In life, there are three things you can count on: death, taxes, and the accidental wiping of your most important files.
— *Download Dispatch*

In life, we are all in the gutter. Some of us just tend to look up at the stars.
— *Oscar Wilde*

In love the paradox occurs that two beings become one and yet remain two.
— *Erich Fromm*

In many circumstances, the most important thing about a proposition is not that it be true, but that it be interesting.
— *Whitehead*

In matters of style, swim with the current; in matters of principle, stand like a rock.
— *Thomas Jefferson*

In Old English, "woma" means sound, noise; thus we have the word woman. "Man" in Old English means evil deed, wickedness in order to form an immaculate member of a flock of sheep one must, above all, be a sheep.
— *Albert Einstein*

in order to keep a true perspective of one's importance, everyone should have a dog that will worship him and a cat that will ignore him.
— *Dereke Bruce*

Proverbs

In prayer it is better to have a heart without words than words without a heart.

— *John Bunyan*

In science it often happens that scientists say, "You know that's a really good argument; my position is mistaken," and then they would actually change their minds and you never hear that old view from them again. They really do it it doesn't happen as often as it should, because scientists are human and change is sometimes painful. But it happens every day. I cannot recall the last time something like that happened in politics or religion.

— *Carl Sagan*

In science one tries to tell people, in such a way as to be understood by everyone, something that no one ever knew before. But in poetry, it's the exact opposite.

— *Paul Dirac*

In short, the habits we form from childhood make no small difference, but rather they make all the difference.

— *Aristotle*

In terms of the game theory, we might say the universe is so constituted as to maximize play. The best games are not those in which all goes smoothly and steadily toward a certain conclusion, but those in which the outcome is always in doubt Similarly, the geometry of life is designed to keep us at the point of maximum tension between certainty and uncertainty, order and chaos. Every important call is a close one. We survive and evolve by the skin of our teeth. We really wouldn't want it any other way.

— *George Leonard*

In the 60's people took acid to make the world weird. Now the world is weird, people take prozac to make it normal.

In the beginning the Universe was created. This made a lot of people angry and was widely regarded as a bad move.

— *Douglas Adams*

In the company of friends, writers can discuss their books, economists the state of the economy, lawyers their latest cases, and businessmen their latest acquisitions, but mathematicians cannot discuss their mathematics at all. And the more profound their work, the less understandable it is.

— *Alfred Adler*

In the constant confrontation between the rock and the water, the water wins finally, not by strength, but by perseverance.

In the country the darkness of night is friendly and familiar, but in a city, with its blaze of lights, it is unnatural, hostile and menacing. It is like a monstrous vulture that hovers, biding its time
— Somerset Maugham

In the dark of the moon, we have our dreams to light the path.

In the end, we will remember not the words of our enemies, but the silence of our friends.
— Martin Luther King Jr.

In the final analysis it is not what you do for your children but what you have taught them to do for themselves that will make them successful human being.
— Ann Landaus

In the hope of reaching the moon men fail to see the flowers that blossom at their feet.
— Albert Schweitzer

In the long run men hit only what they aim at.
— Henry David Thoreau

In the old days charity was a virtue instead of an industry.

In the purer ages of the commonwealth, the use of arms was reserved for those ranks of citizens who had a country to love, a properly to defend, and some share in enacting those laws, which it was their interest as well as duty, to maintain. But in proportion as the public freedom was lost in extent of conquest, war was gradually improved into an art, and degraded into a trade.
— Edward Gibbon

in the sciences, we are now uniquely privileged to sit side by side with the giants on whose shoulders we stand.
— Gerald Holton

In the topsy - turvy world of heavy rock, it's often useful to have a nice, solid piece of wood in your hands.
— Ian Faith

In theory there is no difference between theory and practice. In practice there is.
—Yogi Berra

In this modern age of inovation and invention, there are few moments to cherish. and those that should be neglected.
— Emil Wentezzel

in this world nothing can be said to be certain, except death and taxes.
— Benjamin Franklin

In three words I can sum up everything I've learned about life. It goes on.
— Robert Frost

In three words I can sum up everything I've learned about life: It goes on.

In weightlifting, I don't think sudden, uncontrolled urination should automatically disqualify you.

In words as fashions the same rule will hold, alike fantastic if too new or old: Be not the first by whom the new are tried, nor yet the last to lay the old aside.
— Alexander Pope

Inch by inch life's a cinch, yard by yard life is hard.

Incompatibility: In matrimony a similarity of tastes, particularly the taste for domination.
— Ambrose Bierce

Incontinence Hotline.. .can you hold please.

Indian build small fire stand real close. White man build BIG fire stand way back.

Indulge not thyself in the passion of anger; it is whetting a sword to wound thine own breast, or murder thy friend.
— Akhenaton

information is giving out. Communication is getting through.

Initiative is the ability to do the right thing. Efficiency is the ability to do the thing right. Effectiveness is doing the right tilings.

Insane people are always sure that they are fine, it is only the sane people who are willing to admit that they are crazy.
— Nora Ephron

Insanity is often the logic of an accurate mind overtaxed.
— Oliver Wendall Holmes

Instead of killing and dying in order to produce the being that we are not, we have to live and let live in order to create what we are.
— Albert Camus

Integrity is when what you say, what you do, what you think, and who you are all come from the same place.
— Madelyn Griffith—Haynie

Intelligence is like underwear, everyone has it but you don't have to show it off.

Interestingly, according to modern astronomers, space is finite. This is a very comforting thought - particularly for people who can never remember where they have left things.
—Woody Allen

International problems are becoming so complex that even taxi drivers and teenagers don't have the solutions.

Into the closed mouth the fly does not get
— Confucius

Is ignorance or apathy the biggest problem with the world today? I don't know and I don't care.

Is it a fact — or have I dreamt it — that, by means of electricity, the world of matter has become a great nerve, vibrating thousands of mites in a breathless point of time? Rather, the round globe is a vast head, a brain, instinct with intelligence!
— Nathaniel Hawthorne

Is it better to be bored, wishing you're not, or not to be bored, wishing that you were?

Is it possible to grow wiser without knowing it? One hopes so. We all hope so.

Is that love I see in your eyes, or merely a reflection of mine?

Is there any music as sweet as that of a car starting on a cold morning?

Isolation is aloneness that feels forced upon you, like a punishment. Solitude is aloneness you choose and embrace. I think great things can come out of solitude, out of going to a place where all is quiet except the beating of your heart.
— Jeanne Marie Laskas

It does not matter what temperature the room is; it's always room-temperature.

It does not pay a prophet to be too specific.
— L. Sorague de Camp

It has become appallingly obvious that our technology has exceeded our humanity.
— Albert Einstein

It has been observed that one's nose is never so happy as when it is thrust into the affairs of another, from which some physiologists have drawn the inference that the nose is devoid of the sense of smell.
— Ambrose Bierce

It has recently been discovered that research causes cancer in rats.

Proverbs

It hurts to love someone and not be loved in return, but what is the most painful is to love someone and never find the courage to let the person know how you feel.

It is a funny thing that when a woman hasn't got anything on earth to worry about, she goes off and gets married.

It is a good idea to be ambitious, to have goals, to want to be good at what you do, but it is a terrible mistake to let drive and ambition get in the way of treating people with kindness and decency. The point is not that they will then be nice to you. It is that you will feel better about yourself.

— *Robert Solow*

It is a good idea to obey all the rules when you are young just so you'll have the strength to break them when you are old.

— *Mark Twain*

It is a poor workman who blames his tools.

It is a rash man who reaches a conclusion, before he gets to it.

— *Jacob Levin*

It is all right to have an open mind if you know what to let in.

It is always a sad thing to understand those who were once obscured by the mystery and intangibility of the thoughtlessly loved.

— *Howard Spring*

It is always the best policy to tell the truth, unless, of course, you are an exceptionally good liar.

— *Jerome K. Jerome*

It is always the ones who talk loudest who do the least.

It is amazing how complete is the delusion that beauty is goodness.

— *Leo Tolstoy*

It is amazing how nice people are to you when they know you're going away.

— *Michael Aden*

It is amusing that a virtue is made of the vice of chastity; and it's a pretty odd sort of chastity at that, which leads men straight into the sin of Onan, and girls to the waning of their color.

— *Voltaire*

It is as necessary for men to hear the Gospel, as it was for Christ to die.

It is best to love wisely, no doubt; but to love foolishly is better than not to be able to love at all.

— *William Makepeace Thackeray*

It is better to be 5 minutes late than dead for 5 minutes.
— John Leighton

It is better to deserve honors and not have them than to have them and not deserve them.
— Mark Twain

It is better to forget and smile, than to remember and be sad.

It is better to have bad breath than to have no breath at all.

It is better to have one friend of great value than to have many friends of little value.

It is better to live day by day for you might not be here tomorrow,

it is better to regret something you did, rather than to regret something you didn't do.

It is better to sleep on what you intend doing than to stay awake over what you've done.

It is better to train ten people, than to do the work of ten people. But it is harder.
— Moody

It is better, I submit, to believe in something passionately even if it is wrong, than to believe in nothing at all.
— Chua Mui Hoong

It is difficult to "go with the flow" when you are swimming upstream.

It is easier to change the specification to fit the program than vice versa.

It is easier to pull down than to build up. It is easy to be flexible when one is spineless!

It is easy to have a balanced personality. Just forget your troubles as easily as you do your blessings.

It is far more impressive when others discover your good qualities without your help.

It is funny how we can see this outside world using our eyes; and we can see someone's inside world looking into their eyes.

It is greatness to do little things well.

It is hard to read a cartoon aloud.

It is hard to stumble when you're on your knees.

It is hard to understand how a cemetery raised its burial charges and blamed it on the cost of living.

Proverbs

It is important that man dreams, but it is perhaps equally important that he can laugh at his own dreams.
— *Yutang Lin*

It is important to stay cool, but be sure to not get frostbite.

It is impossible for a man to team what he thinks he already knows.
— *Epictetus*

It is impossible to give a dear account of the world, but art can teach us to reproduce it — just as the world reproduces itself in the course of its eternal gyrations. The primordial sea indefatigably repeats the same words and casts up the same astonished beings on the same seashore.
— *Albert Camus*

It is impossible to travel faster than light and certainly not desirable, as one's hat keeps blowing off.
— *Woody Allen*

It is in changing that things find repose.
— *Heraclitus of Ephesus*

It is in men as in soils where sometimes there is a vien of gold which the owner knows not of.
— *Jonathan Swift*

It is in virtue that happiness consists, for virtue is the state of mind which tends to make the whole life harmonious.

It is infinitely more exciting to live a life of catastrophic failures than a life of could-haves, should-haves and would-haves.
— *Moh Hon Meng*

It is love, not reason, that is stronger than death.
— *Thomas Mann*

It is much easier to be critical than to be correct
— *Benjamin Disraeli*

It is my firm belief that people should not hold firm beliefs.
—*Malaclypse*

It is nice to be important, but it's more important to be nice.

It is no exaggeration to say that the undecided could go one way or another.
—*George Bush*

It is normal to give away a little of one's life in order not to lose it all.
— *Albert Camus*

It is not a war on drugs; it's a war on people.

It is not against the law to be stupid, but it is stupid to be against the law.

It is not always easy to apologize, begin over, take advice, be unselfish, keep trying, be considerate, think and then act, profit by mistakes, forgive and forget, but it usually pays.
— Richard Hamilton

It is not clear that intelligence has any long—term survival value.
— Stephen Hawking

It is not enough to have a good mind; the main thing is to use it well.
— Rene Descartes

It is not enough to succeed. Others must fail.
— Gore Vidal

It is not how busy you are, but why you are busy — the bee is praised, the mosquito is swatted.

It is not now much we do, but how much love we put into doing it. It is not how much we give, but how much love we put into giving.
— Mother Teresa

It is not necessary to light a candle to the sun.

It is not once nor twice but times without number that the same ideas make their appearance in the world.
— Aristotle

It is not only what you do, but also what you don't do, for which you are accountable.

It is not raining. The sky leaks.

It is not real work unless you would rather be doing something else.
— J.M. Barrie

It is not the critic who counts. Not the man who points out how the strong man stumbled or where the doer of deeds could have done better. The credit belongs to the man who is actually in the arena, whose face is marred by dust and sweat and blood; who strives valiantly; who errs and comes short again and again; who knows the great enthusiasms, the great devotions; who spends himself in a worthy cause. Who, at the best knows in the end the triumph of high achievement, and who at the worst, at least fails while daring greatly, so that his place shall never be with those timid souls who know neither victory nor defeat.
— Theodore Roosevelt

Proverbs

It is not the employer who pays wages; he only handles the money, it is the product that pays wages.

It is not the knowing that is difficult, but the doing.

It is not the relation which is important but the relationship that is important!

It is not what a teenager knows that worries his parents, it's how he found out

It is now quite lawful for a Catholic woman to avoid pregnancy by resorting to mathematics, though she is still forbidden to resort to physics or chemistry.
— H.L. Mencken

It is one of the blessings of old friends that you can afford to be stupid with them.
— Ralph Waldo Emerson

It is our responsibility, not ourselves that we should take seriously.

It is said that for money you can have everything, but you cannot. You can buy food, but not appetite; medicine, but not health; knowledge but not wisdom; glitter, but not beauty; fun, but not joy; acquaintances, but not friends; servants, but not faithfulness; leisure, but not peace. You can have the husk of everything for money, but not the kernel.
— Ame Garborg

It is said that the lonely eagle flies to the mountain peaks while the lowly ant crawls the ground, but cannot the soul of the ant soar as high as the eagle?

It is seldom indeed that one parts on good terms, because if one were on good terms one would not part
— Marcel Proust

It is sickly faith that is shaken because some frail human being goes wrong.

It is strange how an earthquake 4,000 miles away seems less of a catastrophe

than the first scratch on your new car.

It is the business of the future to be dangerous.
—Hawkwind

It is the mark of an educated mind to be able to entertain a thought without accepting it.
— Aristotle

It is the mind that makes the body rich. The richest heritage a young man can have is to be born into poverty.
— Andrew Carnegie

It is the stretched soul that makes music, and souls are stretched by the pull of opposites-opposite bents, tastes, yearnings, loyalties. Where there is no polarity-where energies flow smoothly in one direction-there will be much doing but no music.
— Eric Hoffer

It is the wounded oyster that mends its shell with the pearl.

It is time for the human race to enter the solar system.
— Dan Quayle

It is time to quit playing church and start being the church.
— Keith Green

It is true that we don't know what we've got until we lose it, but it's also true that we don't know what we've been missing until it arrives.

It is unbecoming for young men to utter maxims.
— Aristotle

It is very hard to be in love with someone who no longer loves you, but it is far worse to be loved by someone with whom you are no longer in love.
— Georges Courteline

It is when we forget ourselves that we do things that are most likely to be remembered.

It is wonderful to be here in the great state of Chicago...
— Dan Quayle

It is your attitude and not your aptitude that determines your altitude.
— Zia Zigler

It isn't pollution that's harming the environment it's the impurities in our air and water that are doing it.
— Pan Quayle

It isn't what you have, or who you are, or where you are, or what you are doing that makes you happy or unhappy. It is what you think about.
— Date Carnegie

It looks like the people of San Francisco are an endangered species. That's probably good news for the country. Did I just say that out loud?
— *Jeb Bush, while looking at a map showing the prevalence of wildlife in California*

It matters not whether you win or lose; what matters is whether I win or lose.
— Damn Weinberg

It may be called puppy love, but it's real to the puppy.

Proverbs

It may be that your sole purpose in life is simply to serve as a warning to others.

It never occurs to a boy of sixteen that someday he will be as dumb as his father is now.

It sometimes looks foolish for folks to be spending so much time loving their enemies when they should be treating their friends a little better.

It takes a minute to have a crush on someone, an hour to like someone, and a day to love someone - but it takes a lifetime to forget someone.

It takes more money to amuse todays children than it took to educate their parents.

It takes two flints to make a fire.

— *Louisa May Alcott*

It was Christianity which first painted the devil on the worlds walls. It was Christianity which first brought sin into the world. Belief in the cure which it offered has now been shaken to it's deepest roots; but belief in the sickness which it taught and propagated continues to exists.

— *Friedrich Nietzsche*

It was then that I began to took into the seams of your doctrine. I wanted only to pick at a single knot; but when I had got that undone, the whole thing raveled out. And then I understood that it was all machine - sewn.

— *Henrik Ibsen*

It was very good of God to let Carlyle and Mrs Carlyle marry one another and so make only two people miserable instead of four, besides being very amusing.

— *Samuel Butler*

It will be interesting to hear the teenagers of today tell their children what they had to do without when they were young.

It will ever remain incomprehensible that our generation, which has shown itself so great by its achievements in discovery and invention, could fail so low spiritually as to give up thinking.

— *Albert Schweitzer*

It would not be better if things happened to people just as they wish.

— *Heraclitus of Ephesus*

It's a damn poor mind that can only think of one way to spell a word.

— *Andrew Jackson*

It's a funny world but not an hilarious one, unless you have a sick sense of humor.

It's a grand person indeed who can laugh at himself with others and enjoy it as much as they do.

It's a journey, not a destination.
— Aerosmith

It's a small world, but I wouldn't want to paint it.
— Steven Wright

It's better to be aware of your sorrows so that you can appreciate what you have rather than dwell on what you never recieved.
— Caroline Yawn

It's difficult to decide whether growing pains are something teenagers have — or are!

It's difficult to inspire others to accomplish what you haven't been willing to try.

It's disconcerting to fail asleep in church and have a fly buzz into one's open mouth.

It's easier to float a rumor than to sink one.

It's inexcusable for scientists to torture animals; let them make their experiments on journalists and politicians.
— Henrik Ibsen

Its kind of fun to do the impossible.
— Walt Disney

It's not that I'm afraid to die, I just don't want to be there when it happens.
— Woody Allen

It's really a wonder that I haven't dropped all my ideals, because they seem so absurd and impossible to carry out Yet I keep them, because in spite of everything I still believe that people are really good at heart.
— Anne Frank

It's smart to pick your friends — but not to pieces.

it's strange how death mocks us, that only in death do we cherish the ones we love.
— Jamie Yeo

Its failings notwithstanding, there is much to be said in favor of journalism in that by giving us the opinion of the uneducated, it keeps us in touch with the ignorance of the community.
— Oscar Wilde

It's funny, isn't it, how you can be surrounded by people and by lonely, yet one person can bring infinite contentment
— Matthew Yearout

— x —

Proverbs

J

Jazz music is an appeal to the emotions by an attack on the nerves.

Jesus paid a debt he didn't owe because we had a debt we couldn't pay.

Jesus saves souls, and turns them in for fabulous cash prizes!

Joy is what happens to us when we allow ourselves to recognize how good things really are.
— *Marianne Williamson*

Joy shared is joy doubled; sorrow shared is sorrow halved.

Joy, sorrow, tears, lamentations, laughter — to all these music gives voice, but in such a way that we are transported from the world of unrest to the world of peace, and see reality in a new way, as if we were sitting by a mountain fake and contemplating hills and woods and clouds in the tranquil and fathomless water.
— *Albert Schweitzer*

Junk in, junk out.
— *Janis McDowell*

Jury: Twelve people who determine which client has the better lawyer.

Just because a person grows older, it doesn't mean he necessarily grows up.

Just because your doctor has a name for your condition doesn't mean he knows what it is.

Just trust yourself, then you will know how to live.

Just when I was getting used to yesterday along came today.

— *x* —

K

Karl Marx's Mother. If Karl, instead of writing a lot about capital, had made a lot of it, it would have been much better.

Keep away from people who try to be little your ambitions. Small people always do that but the really great make you feel that you too, can become great
— *Mark Twain*

Keep on going and the chances are you will stumble on something, perhaps when you are least expecting it I have never heard of anyone stumbling on something sitting down.
— *Charles F. Kettering*

Keep your eyes on the stars, and your feet on the ground.
— *Theodore Roosevelt*

Keep your head in the clouds; you're the first to know when it rains, and it's easier to see the silver lining.

Keep your ideals high enough to inspire you and low enough to encourage you.

Keep your knees bent head to the sky and always be true to yourself.
— *D'Monroe*

Kids need love the most when they're acting most unlovable.
— *Erma Bombeck*

Killing time murders opportunities.

Kind words can be short and easy to speak, but their echoes are truly endless.
— *Mother Teresa*

Kindness has converted more sinners, than zeal, eloquence or learning.
— *F.W. Faber*

Kindness is a language which the deaf ear can hear and the blind can see.
— *Mark Twain*

Kindness is the insignia of a loving heart.

Kissing is the most pleasant way of spreading germs yet devised.

Kissing is the practice that shortens life — single life!

Kleptomaniac: One who can't help himself from helping himself.

Proverbs 117

Knock on the sky and listen to the sound.

Know thyself? If I knew myself I'd run away.
— *Johann Wolfgang Goethe*

Knowing without doing is like plowing without sowing.

Knowledge is information acquired by some people for the sake of knowing it and by other people for the sake of telling it.

Knowledge is like dynamite dangerous unless handled wisely.

Knowledge is love and light and vision.
— *Helen Keller*

Knowledge is power only when it is turned on.

Knowledge is the train; wisdom is the engine that pulls it

Knowledge without wisdom is as dangerous as an automobile with neither steering wheel nor brakes.

Knowledge, like lumber, is best when well-seasoned.

— *x* —

L

Lady Astor: "Mr. Churchill, you're drunk!" Winston Churchill: "Yes, and you, Madam, are ugly. But tomorrow, I shall be sober."

Last night I dreamed I ate a ten-pound marshmallow, and when I woke up the pillow was gone.
— *Tommy Cooper*

Laugh and the world laughs with you; cry and the other guy has an even better sob story.

Laugh at yourself first, before anyone else can.
— *Elsa Maxwell*

Laugh with people — not at them.

Laughing at our mistakes can lengthen our own life. Laughing at someone else's can shorten it!

Laughter is a tranquilizer with no side effects.

Laughter is but a frown turned upside down.

Laughter is like changing a baby's diaper. It doesn't permanently solve any problems, but it makes thing more acceptable for awhile.

Laughter is the brush that sweeps away the cobwebs of the heart.

Laughter is the closest distance between two people.
— *Victor Borge*

Laughter is the shock absorber that eases the blows of life.

Laughter is the sweetest music that ever greeted the human ear.

Laughter: An interior convulsion, producing a distortion of the features and accompanied by inarticulate noises. It is infectious and, though intermittent, incurable.
— *Ambrose Bierce*

Laundry instructions on a shirt made by HEET: For best results: Wash in cold water separately, hang dry and iron with warm iron. For not so good results: Drag behind car through puddles, blow-dry on roofrack.

Lawyer (n): Larval stage of Politician.

Laziness is a luxury that few people can afford.

Learn from the past, live for today, look for tomorrow. Take a nap this afternoon.

Learn to listen, opportunity often knocks softly.

Learn to reverence night and to put away the vulgar fear of it, for with the banishment of night from the experience of man, there vanishes as well a religious emotion, a poetic mood, which gives depth to the adventure of humanity.
— Henry Beston

Lesser artists borrow, great artists steal.
— Igor Stravinsky

Let a joy keep you. Reach out your hands and take it when it runs by.

Let me give you one definition of ethics: It is good to maintain life and to further life; it is bad to damage and destroy Life. And this ethic, profound, universal, has the significance of a religion. It is religion.
— Albert Schweitzer

Let nature take its course and hope it passes.

Let no guilty man escape, if it can be avoided. No personal considerations should stand in the way of performing a duty.
— Ulysses S. Grant

Let no one ever come to you without leaving better and happier. Be the living expression of God's kindness: Kindness in your face, kindness in your eyes, kindness in your smile.
— Mother Teresa

Let no one who loves be unhappy...even love unreturned has its rainbow.

Let us more and more insist on raising funds of love, of kindness, of understanding, of peace. The rest will be given.
—Mother Teresa

Let us not look back in anger or forward in fear, but around in awareness.
— James Thurber

Let us realize that the privilege to work is a gift, the power to work is a blessing, the love of work is success!
— David O. McKay

Let your ambition be the train tracks to your destiny and your experiences be the locomotive that takes you there.
— Ulrick Ricardo Milord

Let your midday sleep be short or none at all.

Lets face it, the world would be a boring place without oppressive governments. If we were free to do or say whatever we wanted, it wouldn't be exciting to do or say anything.
— James Maverick Cook

Life can be magnificent and overwhelming — that is its whole tragedy. Without beauty, love, or danger, it would be almost easy to live.
— *Albert Camus*

Life can only be understood backwards, but it must be lived forwards.

Life does not cease to be funny when people die any more than it ceases to be serious when people laugh.
— *George Bernard Shaw*

Life has a practice of living you, if you don't live it.
— *Philip Larkin*

Life is a picture, so paint it well.

Life insurance is like a football game-our relatives sit around and wait for us to "kick off."

Life insurance is the last thing on earth a man wants, but its too late then.

Life is a comedy for those who think and a tragedy for those who feel.

Life is a dark walking game which you walk without torch but with your team members. We do not know when we will collapse ,we do not know where there is a pit It is similar to that we can not understand what will happen in the coming days. So, every step should be taken with a dear and careful mind. There are ups and downs for us in our journey. We should face those problems bravely, squarely and share our happiness with our team members, our friends. In our journey, we should offer help and love to our team members. At the same time, our members may do the same to us. On the way, we cannot abandon the chance for us to walk but instead with determination and perseverance we shall finish our walk-life.
— *Ice Tang*

Life is a great big canvas, and you should throw all the paint on it you can.
— *Danny Kaye*

Life is a grindstone. Whether it grinds you down or polishes you up, depends upon what you're made of.

Life is a journey. Perhaps we may be more or less pointed towards a general direction, but whether we pave that road with diamonds and gold or just plain dirt and cement is up to us.
— *Alex Tan*

Life is a moderately good play with a badly written third act.
— *Truman Capote*

Proverbs

Life is a song. Love is the music.

Life is a waste of time, time is a waste of life, so get wasted all the time and have the time of your life.

Life is both sad and solemn. We are let into a wonderful world, we meet one another here, greet each other — and wander together for a brief moment. Then we lose each other and disappear as suddenly and unreasonably as we arrived.

Life is full of surprises. Just say "never" and you'll see.

Life is good for only two things, discovering mathematics and teaching mathematics
— Simeon Poisson

Life is hard, no one makes it out alive.

Life is like a box of chocolates; you never know when you'll find a nut.

Life is like a game of cards. The hand that is dealt you represents determinism; the way you play it is free will.
— Jawaharlal Nehru

Life is like a ladder, the higher you climb, the more expansive your view is.
— Taimi Megivern

Life is like a mirror, if you frown at it it frowns back; if you smile, it returns the greeting.

Life is like a movie. How good you do depends on your critics.

Life is like an onion. You peel it off layer by layer and sometimes you cry.

Life is more than willing to treat you civilly. Are you willing to acknowledge it?

Life is no brief candle to me. It is a sort of splendid torch which I have got a hold of for the moment, and I want to make it burn as brightly as possible before handing it onto future generations.
— George Bernard Shaw

Life is not a cup to be drained, but a measure to be filled.

Life is not so much a matter of position as of disposition.
— Andrew Carnegie

Life is richer when one gives it to another.

Life is so much simpler when you tell the truth.

Life is something that happens when you cant get to sleep.
— Fran Lebowitz

Life is the art of drawing sufficient conclusions from insufficient premises.
— Samuel Butler

Life is the crossroads of Heaven and Hell.
— Leigh Hunter

Life is the first gift, love is the second, and understanding the third.

Life is to be lived, not controlled, and humanity is won by continuing to play in face of certain defeat.
— Ralph Ellison

Life is what happens between responsibilities and death.

Life is what happens to you while you're busy making other plans.
— John Lennon

Life isn't fair, but we do try to make it equally unfair for everyone.

Life itself cannot give you joy unless you really will it Life just gives you time and space. It's up to you to fill it.

Life itself is a grand show. To perform well, you'll need to take showers everyday.
— Kenny Huang

Life may have no meaning. Or even worse, it may have a meaning of which I disapprove.
— Ashley Brilliant

Life moves pretty fast. If you don't stop and look around once in a while, you might miss it.
— Ferris Bueller

Life should be treated as a picture. We should draw and paint it colorfully.
— Ice Tang

Life shrinks or expands in proportion to one's courage.
— Anais Nin

Life was not meant to be fair, but meant to be lived.

Life without love is like a tree without blossoms or fruit.
— Kahlil Gibran

Life's splendor forever lies in wait about each one of us in all its fullness, but veiled from view, deep down, invisible, far off. It is there, though, not hostile, not reluctant, not deaf. If you summon it by the right word, by its right name, it will come.
— Franz Kafka

Proverbs

Life's too short for chess.
— *H.J. Byron*

Like the crest of a peacock so is mathematics at the head of all knowledge.

Likely as not, the child you can do the least with will do the most to make you proud.
— *Mignon McLaughlin*

Liquor is a lubricant only if a man is going downhill.

Liquor kills everything that's alive and preserves everything that's dead.

Liquor may not be so bad after all; it makes men fight and shoot at each other-and miss!

Liquor will kill germs, but you cant get them to drink it.

Little minds are tamed and subdued by misfortune; but great minds rise above them.
— *Washington Irving*

Little wonder why computers are so popular. They represent perfection.

Live by what you trust, not by what you fear.

Live life because you want to, not because you have to.

Live your life so that you won't be afraid to have your phone tapped.

Living in a vacuum sucks.
— *Adrienne E. Gusoff*

Living without faith is like driving in a fog.

Logic merely enables one to be wrong with authority.
— *Doctor Who*

Long engagements give people the opportunity of finding out each other's character before marriage, which is never advisable.
— *Oscar Wilde*

Longevity of life is weighed by events, experiences and impressions, not time.

Looking back, I have this to regret that too often when I loved, I did not say so.
— *David Grayson*

Looking back, may I be filled with gratitude; looking forward, may I be filled with hope; looking upward, may I be aware of strength; looking inward, may I find peace.

Lord give me an answer, or give me the patience to wait for one, just do it now please!

Lord, be merciful, shut me up when my life speaks so much louder than my words.

Lord, give me chastity. But not yet.
— *St. Augustine*

Lord, grant me the serenity to accept the things I can not change, the courage to change the things I can, and the wisdom to hide the bodies of those I had to kill because they pissed me off.

Lord, grant that I may always desire more than I can accomplish.
— *Michelangelo*

Lord, may others treat me tomorrow as I have treated them today.

Lost in you, I found myself.
— *Sarah Balodis*

Lots of people want to ride with you in the limo, but what you want is someone who will take the bus with you when the limo breaks down.
— *Oprah Winfrey*

Love and hate are the two closest emotions.

Love asks faith, and faith asks firmness.
— *Herbert*

Love at first sight is cured by a second look.

Love at first sight usually ends with divorce at first slight.

Love begets love.
— *Hark*

Love begins with a smile, grows with a kiss and ends with a tear.

Love can be a blessing or a curse.

Love can neither be bought nor sold; its only price is love.

Love can sometimes be magic. But magic can sometimes...just be an illusion.
— *Javan*

Love can turn the cottage into a golden palace.

Love comes to those who still hope even though they've been disappointed, to those who still believe even though they've been betrayed, and to those who still love even though they've been hurt before.

Love comes without warning. No banners, flashy signs, or wakeup calls. It is always there, but take it for granted, and one day it will be gone.
— *Betsy Lawson*

Proverbs

Love comforts like sunshine after rain.

Love cures the very wound it makes.

Love does not begin and end the way we seem to think it does. Love is a battle, love is a war; love is a growing up.
— *James Baldwin*

Love does not consist in gazing at each other but in looking outward together in the same direction.
— *Antoine De Saint=Exupery*

Love doesn't hide. It stays and fights. It goes the distance. That's why God made love so strong. So it can carry you. All the way home.

Love doesn't make the world go 'round. Love is what makes the ride worthwhile.
— *Franklin P. Jones*

Love doesn't really make the world go round. It just makes people so dizzy it looks like it.

Love goes toward love as schoolboys from their books. But love from love, toward school with heavy looks.
— *William Shakespeare*

Love has been defined as something that makes a fellow feel funny and act foolish.

Love has no law but the law of love.

Love has nothing to do with what you are expecting to get its what you are expected to give — which is everything.

Love has reasons that reason knows nothing of.

Love in your heart wasn't put there to stay. Love isn't love till you give it away.

Love is a disease you can't "catch" without being properly exposed.

Love is a fire. But whether it is going to warm your hearth or burn down your house, you can never tell.
— *Joan Crawford*

Love is a force that connects us to every strand of the universe, an unconditional state that characterizes human nature, a form of knowledge that is always there tor us if only we can open ourselves to it.
— *Emily H. Sell*

Love is a fruit in season at all times, and within reach of every hand.
— *Mother Teresa*

Love is a little word; people make it big.

Love is a perky elf dancing a merry little jig and then suddenly he turns on you with a miniature machine gun.
— *Matt Groening*

Love is a sour delight, a sugur'd grief, a living death, an ever-dying life.
— *Thomas Watson*

Love is a sweet torment.
— *Draxe*

Love is a well from which we can drink only as much as we have put in, and the stars that shine from it are only our eyes looking in.
— *Stendhal*

Love is an attachment to another self. Humour is a form of self-detachment — a way of looking at one's existence, one's misfortune or one's discomfort If you really love, if you really know how to laugh, the result is the same: you forget yourself.
— *Claude Roy*

Love is an attempt to change a piece of a dream world into reality.
— *Theordor Reik*

Love is an unusual game. There are either two winners or none.

Love is blind, but friendship doses its eyes.

Love is blind. Marriage is the eye-opener.

Love is but the discovery of ourselves in others, and the delight in the recognition.
— *Alexander Smith*

Love is composed of a single soul inhabiting two bodies.

Love is friendship set on fire.
— *Jeremy Taylor*

Love is growing old together, contentedly. Sharing a sunset as you've shared your lives. Happy that your worlds are entwined.
— *Jan Brazill*

Love is like an hourglass, with the heart filling up as the brain empties.
— *Jules Renard*

Love is like Pi: natural, irrational, and very important.
— *Lisa Hoffman*

Love is like playing the piano. First you must learn to play by the rules, then you must forget the rules and play from your heart.

Love is like quicksilver in the hand. Leave the fingers open and it stays. Clutch it, and it darts away.

— *Dorothy Parker*

Love is like scarlet fever — one has to go through it and get it over.

— *Leo Tolstoy*

Love is never away; it is the only way.

Love is not blind, it sees more not less; But because it sees more it chooses to see less.

Love is not obedience, conformity, or submission. It is a counterfeit love that is contingent upon authority, punishment, or reward. True love is respect and admiration, compassion and kindness, freely given by a healthy, unafraid human being.

— *Dan Barker*

Love is not what makes the world go around, but it sure makes the ride worthwhile.

Love is only an illusion until it lasts forever.

— *Delilah*

Love is perhaps the only glimpse we are permitted of eternity.

— *Helen Hayes*

Love is so short, and forgetting so long.

— *Pablo Neruda*

Love is something different from delirium, but it's hard to tell the difference.

Love is something that you can leave behind you when you die. It's I that powerful.

Love is sunshine, hate is shadow, life is checkered shade and sunshine.

— *Longfellow*

Love is the answer, but while you are waiting for the answer sex raises some pretty good questions.

— *Woody Allen*

Love is the child of illusion and the parent of disillusion.

— *Miguel de Unamuno*

Love is the extremely difficult realization that something other than oneself is real.

— *Iris Murdoch*

Love is the immortal flow of energy that nourishes, extends and preserves. Its eternal goal is life.

— *Smiley Blanton*

Love is the master of all arts.

Love is the only fire against which there is no insurance.

Love is the only game in which two can play and both lose.

Love is the only service that power cannot command and money cannot buy.

Love is the pain you can't refuse.
— Rhodez

Love is the quest, marriage the conquest divorce the inquest.

Love is the triumph of imagination over intelligence.
— Henry Louis Mencken

Love is the unity of two hearts beating together as one.

Love is the wisdom of the fool and the folly of the wise.
— Samuel Johnson

Love is when two people who care for each other get confused.
— Bob Schneider

Love is when you take away the feeling, the passion, the romance and you find out you still care for that person.

Love lasts when the relationship comes first.

Love like paint can make things beautiful when you spread it but it simply dries up when you don't use it

Love looks through a telescope; envy, through a microscope.

Love makes the world go round.
— Charles Dickens

Love many, trust few, and always paddle your own canoe.

Love me, love my dog.
— St. Bernard

Love means never having to say you're sorry.
— Erich Segal

Love never dies a natural death. It dies because we don't know how to replenish its source. It dies of blindness and errors and betrayals. It dies of illness and wounds.
— Anais Nin

Love plays a stringed instrument, the heart.

Love sees no color.

Love sought is good, but given unsought is better.
— William Shakespeare

Love takes off masks that we fear we cannot live without and know we cannot live within.
— James Baldwin

Love will creep where it cannot go.

Love will make you forget time, and time will make you forget love.

Love won't be tampered with, love won't go away. Push it to one side and it creeps to the other.
— *Louise Erdrich*

Love your enemies just in case your friends turn out to be a bunch of bastards.
— *R.A. Dickson*

Lovers don't meet somewhere along the way; they are in each other all along.
— *Rumi*

Loving word may heal and bless.

Loving you contains not one of my emotions, it contains all of them.

LSD melts in your mind, not in your hand.

Luck is a loser's excuse for a winner's position!

Lust isn't all there is to sex. Sex isn't all there is to love. But love is almost all there is to life.
— *Eddie Cantor*

— x —

M

Make it idiot proof and someone will make a better idiot.

Make lots of money, enjoy the work, operate within the law. choose two.

Make this your motto: Don't die until you are dead.

Make your life a mission, not an intermission.
— Arnold Glasgow

Making mistakes isn't stupid; disregarding them is.

Man blames fate for other accidents, but feels personally responsible when he makes a hole-in-one!

Man cannot discover new oceans unless he has courage to lose sight of the shore.

Man ceased to be an ape, vanquished the ape, on the day the first book was written.
— Yevoeny Zamyatin

Man has lost the capacity to foresee and forestall. He will end by destroying the earth.
— Albert Schweitzer

Man invented language to satisfy his deep need to complain.
— Lily Tomlin

Man is a dog's idea of what God should be.
— Holbrook Jackson

Man is a peculiar creature. He spends a fortune making his home insect-proof and air-conditioned, and then eats in the yard.

Man is a rational animal who always loses his temper when he is called upon to act in accordance with the dictates of reason.
— Oscar Wilde

Man is the only creature who refuses to be what he is.
— Albert Camus

Man wants to live, but it is useless to hope that this desire will dictate all his actions.
— Albert Camus

Man's greatest vices are the misuses of his virtues.

Man's maximum achievement often falls short of God's minimum demands.

Man's real life is happy, chiefly because he is never expecting it to be so.

Proverbs 131

Many a man thinks he is buying pleasure, when he is really selling himself to it.
— *Benjamin Franklin*

Many Christians debate whether the devil is on earth or in hell. Can he dwell in Christians or only in the world? The fact is: the devil is in darkness. Wherever there is spiritual darkness, there the devil will be.

Many churches are now serving coffee after the sermon. Presumably this is to get the people thoroughly awake before they start to drive home.

Many people lose their tempers merely by seeing you keep yours.
— *Frank Moore Colby*

Many people quit looking for work when they find a job.

Many people spend their health for wealth, and then try to spend their wealth for health.
—*Mikey*

Many people would sooner die than think; in fact, they do so.
— *Bertrand Russell*

Marital problems? You don't need a new wife, you need a new life!

Mark all mathematical heads which be wholly and only bent on these sciences, how solitary they be themselves, how unfit to live with others, how unapt to serve the world.
— *Roger Ascham*

Marriage is an expensive way of getting your laundry done for free.

Marriage is the triumph of imagination over intelligence. Second marriage is the triumph of hope over experience.

Marriage. Don't be pressured into it. Is the fear of loneliness really greater than the fear of bondage?
— *Sumiko Tan*

Mars is essentially in the same orbit. Mars is somewhat the same distance from the Sun, which is very important. We have seen pictures where there are canals, we believe, and water. If there is water, that

Mathematicians are like Frenchmen: Whatever you say to them they translate into their own language and forthwith it is something entirely different.
— *Johann Wotfgang Goethe*

Mathematics is not a careful march down a well— cleared highway, but a journey into a strange wilderness, where the

explorers often get lost Rigour should be a signal to the historian that the maps have been made, and the real explorers have gone elsewhere.
—W.S. Anglin

Maturity is knowing when and where to be immature.

May the heart felt warmth of those who truly care make the sorrow in your heart less harder to bear.

May the roof above us never fall in, and may we friends gathered below never fall out.

May you have enough happiness to make you sweet, enough trials to make you strong, enough sorrow to keep you human, enough hope to make you happy and enough money to buy me gifts.

May you live all the days of your life.
— Jonathan Swift

May your life be long and useful like a roll of toilet paper.

May your trouble be like the old man's teeth, few and far between.

Maybe all one can do is hope to end up with the right regrets.
— Arthur Miller

May be God wants us to meet a few wrong people before meeting the right one so that when we finally meet the right person, we should know how to be grateful for that gift.

Maybe I am not very human — what I wanted to do was to paint sunlight on the side of a house.
— Edward Hopper

Maybe kids would eat better if you installed a drive-up window off the kitchen and handed them dinner in a bag.

Maybe this world is another planet's Hell.
— Aldous Huxley

Maybe we can never see angels or there just aren't any from heaven but that's all right. Whatever we're going through, be sure we have our spirit faith and love.

We are angels for someone of happiness. Maybe, for ourselves too.
— Deserts Chiao

Maybe we were better off when charity was a virtue instead of a deduction.

Measure your success by the challenges and lessons you team along the way.

Meeting a girl is about looking across a room and catching a smile.
— *A.J. McLean*

Memories are meant to fade, Lenny. They're designed that way for a reason.
— *Angela Basset*

Men always want to be a woman's first love. Women have a more subtle instinct; what they like to be is a man's last romance.

Men are never convinced of your reasons, of your sincerity, of the seriousness of your sufferings, except by your death. So long as you are alive, your case is doubtful; you have a right only to your skepticism.
— *Albert Camus*

Men are never realty willing to die except for the sake of freedom: therefore they do not believe in dying completely.
— *Albert Camus*

Men in general judge more from appearances than from reality. All men have eyes, but few have the gift of penetration.
— *Machiavelli*

Men marry because they are tired, women because they are curious; both are disappointed
— *Oscar Wilde*

Men mistake friendship, but not sex, for love; women mistake sex, but not friendship, for love.
— *Peter Wastnolm*

Men occasionally stumble over the truth, but most of them pick themselves up and hurry off as if nothing had happened.
— *Winston Churchill*

Men tell you the facts, but God will tell you the truth!

Men trip not on mountains! They trip on molehills.

Mercy to the guilty is cruelty to the innocent.

Merrily, merrily shall I live now, under the blossom that hangs on the bough.
— *William Shakespeare*

Middle age is when you go all out and end up all in.

Middle age starts when you have been warned to stow down, not by a motorcycle cop, but by your doctor.

Military intelligence is a contradiction in terms.
— *Groucho Marx*

Minds are like parachutes; they work best when open.
— *Lord Thomas Dewar*

Misery acquaints a man with strange bedfellows.
— William Shakespeare

Modern medicine still hasn't decided whether it's harder on a middle-aged man to mow the lawn himself or argue to get his teenage son to do it

Modern politics is mostly the province of people too lazy to work.

Money is an excellent servant but a horrible master.

Money may be the husk of many things, but not the kernel. It buys you food, but not appetite; medicine, but not health; acquaintances, but not friends; servants, but not loyalty; days of joy, but not peace or happiness.
— Henrik Ibsen

Moral rules are directions for running the human machine. Every moral rule is there to prevent a breakdown, or a strain, or a friction, in the running of that machine.
— C.S. Lewis

More and more, when faced with the world of men, the only reaction is one of individualism. Man atone is an end unto himself. Everything one tries to do for the common good ends in failure.
— Albert Camus

More doors are opened with "please" than with keys.

More people are flattered into virtue than bullied out of vice.

More than any time in history mankind faces a crossroads. One path leads to despair and utter hopelessness, the other to total extinction. Let us pray that we have the wisdom to choose correctly.
— Woody Allon

Mosquitoes are a great moral force; it forces mankind to wear more clothes for modesty.

Most accidents happen at home, maybe we oughta move.

Most books now say our sun is a star. But it still knows how to change back into a sun in the daytime.

Most folks are about as happy as they make up their minds to be.
— Abraham Lincoln

Most great men and women are not perfectly rounded in their personalities, but are instead people whose one driving enthusiasm is so great it makes their faults seem insignificant.
— Charles A. Cerami

Most of our suspicions of others are aroused by our knowledge of ourselves.

Most of the trouble in the world is caused by people wanting to be important.
— *T.S. Elliot*

Most of us can read the writing on the wall; we just assume it's addressed to someone else.
— *Ivorn Ball*

Most of us spend a lifetime going to sleep when we're not sleepy and getting up when we are.

Most paradigms are worth a nickle.
— *Jim Hadorn*

Most parents of teenagers seem to agree that one "hang-up" their kids don't have is when on the tetepehone.

Most people have a skeleton in their cupboard.
— *Leo Tolstoy*

Most people never run far enough on their first wind to find out they've got a second. Give your dreams all you've got and you'll be amazed at the energy that comes out of you.
— *William James*

Most people wish for riches, but few people provide the definite plan and burning desire which pave the road to wealth.
— *Napoleon Hill*

Mothers are fonder than fathers of their children because they are more certain they are their own.
— *Aristotle*

Motif 2.0 will ship well before the sun burns out, unless we decide to change the name first, and will contain a free plastic spaceman in every box
— *David Brooks*

Mozart has the classic purity of light and the blue ocean; Beethoven the romantic grandeur which belongs to the storms of air and sea, and while the soul of Mozart seems to dwell on the ethereal peaks of Olympus, that of Beethoven climbs shuddering the storm—beaten sides of a Sinai. Blessed be they both! Each represents a moment of the ideal life, each does us good. Our love is due to both.
— *Henri Frederic Amiel*

Much may be known of a man's character by what excites his laughter.

Murphy's Law isn't recursive. Washing your car to make it rain doesn't work.

Music has been called medicine, and some of it is hard to take.

Music has charm to soothe the savage beast.

Music is a higher revelation than all wisdom and philosophy.
— Ludwig van Beethoven

Music is an attempt to express emotions that are beyond speech.

Music is certainly not less clear than the defining word; music often speaks more subtly about states of mind than would be possible with words. There are shades that cannot be described by any single adjective.
— Felix—Bartholdy Mendelssohn

Music is love, love is music, music is my life and I love my life. Take care and goodnight!
— A. J. McLean

Music is the best cure for a sorrowing mind.

Music is the best means we have of digesting time.
— W.H. Auden

Music is the effort we make to explain to ourselves how our brains work. We listen to Bach transfixed because this is listening to a human mind.
— Lewis Thomas

Music is the most perfect art.
— Albert Camus

Music is the vernacular of the human soul.
— Geoffrey Latham

Music is well said to be the speech of angels; in fact, nothing among the utterances allowed to man is felt to be so divine. It brings us near to the Infinite.
— Thomas Carlyle

Music provokes love.

Music takes us out of the actual and whispers to us dim secrets that startle our wonder as to who we are, and for what, whence, and whereto.
— Ralph Waldo Emerson

My advice to you is not to inquire why or whither, but just enjoy your ice cream while it's on your plate-that's my philosophy.
— Thornton Wilder

My advice to you is to get married. If you find a good wife you'll be happy; if not you'll become a philosopher.
— Socrates

Proverbs

My aim is that when my hands will work no longer, that the works of my hands will still continue to keep on working.

My biggest problem is that I believe almost everything I tell myself.

My definition of an expert in any field is a person who knows enough about what's really going to be scared.
— P. J. Plauger

My dog is very obedient, he does what he is bid. A sign said "wet paint," and that's just what he did.

My dog is worried about the economy because Alpo is up to 99 cents a can. That's almost $7.00 in dog money.
— Joe Weinstein

My eyes are an ocean in which my dreams are reflected.
— Anna M. Uhlich

My father was a Creole, his father a Negro, and his father a monkey; my family, it seems, begins where yours left off.
— Alexander Dumas

My God, these folks don't know how to love — that's why they love so easily.
— D. H. Lawrence

My karma just ran over your dogma.

My library was dukedom large enough.
— William Shakespeare

My old dreams were good dreams that didn't come true but I am glad I had them.

My opinions may have changed, but not the fact that I am right.
— Ashley Brilliant

My own business bores me to death. I prefer other people's.
— Oscar Wilde

My play was a complete success. The audience was a failure.
— Ashley Brilliant

My religion consists of a humble admiration of the illimitable superior spirit who reveals himself in the slight details we are able to perceive with our frail and feeble mind.
— Albert Einstein

My sources are unreliable, but their information is fascinating.
— Ashley Brilliant

My worst day of vacation has always been better than my best day at work.

— x —

N

Names are not idetifiers, only labels for those we identify.

Nature has a funny way of breaking what does not bend.

Nature is a burning and frigid, transparent and limited universe in which nothing is possible but everything is given.

— *Albert Camus*

Nature uses only the longest threads to weave her patterns, so that each small piece of her fabric reveals the organization of the entire tapestry.

— *Richard Feynman*

Nearly all men can stand adversity, but if you want to test a man's character, give him power.

— *Abraham Lincoln*

Need some time to be alone, try washing the dishes!

Never be afraid to sit awhile and think.

— *Lorraine Hansberry*

Never before has the fate of so many been at the whim of so few.

Never confuse having a career with having a life.

Never doubt that a small group of thoughtful, committed citizens can change the world. Indeed, it's the only thing that ever has.

— *Margaret Mead*

Never drive faster than your guardian angel can fly.

Never exaggerate your faults — leave that for your friends.

Never explain — your friends do not need it and your enemies will not believe you anyway.

— *Elbert Hubbard*

Never express yourself more dearly than you are able to think.

— *Niels Bohr*

Never fear shadows. They simply mean that there's a light somewhere nearby.

— *Ruth E. Renkei*

Never give up on a dream just because of the time it will take to accomplish it. The time will pass anyway.

Never imagine yourself not to be otherwise than what it might appear to others that what you were or might have been was not otherwise than what you had been would have appeared to them to be otherwise.

Never interrupt your enemy when he is maiding a mistake.
— *Napoleon Bonaparte*

Never judge a book by its movie.
— *J.W. Eagan*

Never let a problem become an excuse!

Never let a problem to be solved become more important than the person to be loved.
— *Barbara Johnson*

Never put off until tomorrow what you can do today. There might be a law against it by that time.

Never say anything unless it is kind, necessary and true.

Never say goodbye when you still want to try; never give up when you still feel you can take it; never say you don't love that person anymore when you can't let go.

Never say there is nothing beautiful in the world anymore. There is always something to make you wonder in the shape of a tree, the trembling of a leaf.
— *Albert Schweitzer*

Never seek the wind in the field, ft is useless to try and find what is gone.

Never stand between a dog and a tree.

Never stop trying to succeed. It's always the last key that opens the lock.

Never think of the consequences of failing, you will always think of a negative results. Think only positive thoughts and your mind will gravitate towards those thoughts!
— *Michael Jordan*

Never underestimate the power of stupid people in large groups.

Never wrestle with a pig. You both get all dirty, and the pig likes it.

Next to being shot at and missed, nothing is really quite as satisfying as an income tax refund.
— *F.J. Raymond*

Next to debt, the hardest thing to get out of is a warm bed on a cold morning. Next year 3½ million kids will turn sixteen, and 7 million parents will turn pale.

Night brings our troubles to the light, rather than banishes them.
— *Seneca*

Night, the beloved. Night, when words fade and things come alive. When the destructive analysis of day is done, and all that is truly important becomes whole and sound again. When man reassembles his fragmentary self and grows with the calm of a tree.
— *Antoine De Saint—Exupery*

Ninety percent of politicians give the other ten percent a bad name.
— *Henry Kissinger*

No amount of ability is of the slightest avail without honor.
— *Andrew Carnegie*

No answer is also an answer.

No bird soars too high, if he soars with his own wings.
— *William Blake*

No cord or cable can draw so forcibly, or bind so fast, as love can do with a single thread.
— *Robert Burton*

No day is complete until you've heard the laughter of a child.

No distance of place or lapse of time can lessen the friendship of those who are thoroughly persuaded of each other's worth.
— *Robert Southey*

No drug, not even alcohol, causes the fundamental ills of society. If we're looking for the sources of our troubles, we shouldn't test people for drugs; we should test them for stupidity, ignorance, greed and love of power.
— *P. J. O'Rourke*

No great discovery was ever made without a bold guess.
— *Isaac Newton*

No happy time is really gone, if it leaves a special memory.

No horse goes as fast as the money you bet on him.

No individual raindrop ever considers itself responsible for the flood.

No Jesus, No Love. Know Jesus, Know Love.

No man is a failure who has friends.
— *Clarence*

No man is fully accomplished until he has acquired the ability to attend to his own business.

No man is rich enough to buy back his past.
— *Oscar Wilde*

No matter how much a woman loved a man, it would still give her a glow to see him commit suicide for her.
— *Henry Louis Mencken*

Proverbs

No matter if you win or lose, it's how much pride you retained in doing so.

No matter what kind of diet you're on, you can usually eat as much as you want of anything you don't like.

No matter what you want to do, there's always something else that has to be done first.

No moving parts, no batteries. No monthly payments and no fees. Inflation proof, non—taxable, in fact it's quite reliable. It can't be stolen, won't pollute, one size fits all, do not dilute. It uses little energy, but yields results enormously. Relieves your tension and your stress, invigorates your happiness. Combats depression, makes you beam and elevates your self esteem. Your circulation it corrects without complicated side effects. It is, I think, the perfect drug. May I prescribe, my friend — the hug!

No one appreciates the very special genius of your conversation as the dog does.
— *Christopher Morley*

No one can become a Christian on his own terms. No one can live in doubt when he has prayed in faith.

No one can make you feel inferior without your permission.
— *Eleanor Roosevelt*

No one can predict to what heights you can soar. Even you will not know until you spread your wings.

No one can whistle a symphony. It takes an orchestra to play it.

No one ever injured his eyesight by looking on the bright side of things.

No one feels another's grief, no one can understand another's joy. People imagine that they can reach one another. In reality, they only pass each other by.
— *Franz Schubert*

No one has ever come back from the other world. I can't console you, but one thing I can tell you, as long as my ideas are alive I will be alive.
— *Albert Schweitzer*

No one is dead as long as he is remembered by someone.

No one is listening until you make a mistake.

No one is responsible for all the things that happen to him, but he is responsible for the way he acts when they do happen.

No one knows what is in the secret heart of another.
— *Charles Dickens*

No one plans to fail but people can fail to plan.

No problem is so large it cant be fit in somewhere.

No sense being pessimistic. It wouldn't work anyway.

No wind, no waves.

No! Try not. Do. Or do not. There is no try.
— Yoda

No, this trick won't work... How on earth are you ever going to explain in terms of chemistry and physics so important a biological phenomenon as first love?
— Albert Einstein

Nobody can be exactly like me. Even I have trouble doing it.
— Tallulah Bankhead

Nobody can have too many friends, but one enemy may constitute a surplus.

Nobody ever went broke underestimating the tastes of the American people.
— H.L. Mencken

Nobody knows what will happen in the next second — we can only strive for our best in this moment In my mind, if friendship, family, and love are not there, there is no support or encouragement.
— Ice Tang

Nobody realizes that some people expend tremendous energy merely to be normal.
— Albert Camus

Nobody really cares if you're miserable, so you might as well be happy.
— Cynthia Nelms

Non-smoking area: If we see you smoking we will assume you are on fire and take appropriate action.

Nostalgia has really caught on in show business. Some Hollywood actors are remarrying their ex-wives.

Nostalgia isn't what it used to be.

Not being beautiful forced me to develop my inner resources. The pretty girl has a handicap to overcome.
— Golda Meir

Not being beautiful was the true blessing.

Not everything that counts can be counted, and not everything that can be counted counts.
— Albert Einstein

Proverbs 143

Not everything that is faced can be changed, but nothing can be changed until it is faced.
— *James Baldwin*

Note on a door Out to lunch; if not back by five, out for dinner also.

Nothing but blackness above and nothing that moves but the cars... God, if you wish for our love, fling us a handful of stars!
— *Louis Untermeyer*

Nothing endures but change.
— *Heraclitus*

Nothing fills me with a more ever increasing awe than the stars above me and the moral law within me.
— *Immanuel Kant*

Nothing is as soft as water, yet who can withstand the raging flood?
— *Lao Ma*

Nothing is ever accomplished by a reasonable man.
— *George Bernard Shaw*

Nothing is like it seems, but everything is exactly like it is.
— *Yogi Berra*

Nothing is more beautiful than a guitar, save perhaps two.
— *Frederic Chopin*

Nothing is more humiliating than to see idiots succeed in enterprises we have failed in.
— *Flaubert*

Nothing is more stressful than a trying to be a different person than who you are.

Nothing is really work unless you would rather be doing something else.

Nothing is wrong with California that a rise in the ocean level wouldn't cure.
— *Ross MacDonald*

Nothing makes us so lonely as our secrets.
— *Paul Tournier*

Nothing seems impossible for the man who doesn't have to do it himself.

Nothing seems to bring on an emergency as quickly as putting money aside in case of one.

Nothing splendid has ever been achieved except by those who dared believe that something inside of them was superior to circumstance.
— *Bruce Barton*

Nothing spoils the taste of peanut butter like unrequited love.
— *Charlie Brown*

Nothing would please the Kremlin more than to have the people of this country choose a second rate president.
— *Richard Nixon*

Notice: The only person getting his work done by Friday was Robinson Crusoe.

Now for a brief lesson in music: B—sharp, never B—flat, always B—natural.

Now he has departed from this strange world a little ahead of me. That means nothing. People like us, who believe in physics, know that the distinction between past, present, and future is only a stubbornly persistent illusion.
— *Albert Einstein*

Now I beg of you to tell me whether I must love a human being simply because he exists or resembles me and whether for those reasons alone I must suddenly prefer him to myself?
— *Marquis de Sade*

Now that I've given up hope I feel much better.

Now that practical skills have developed enough to provide adequately for material needs, one of these sciences which are not devoted to utilitarian ends has been able to arise in Egypt, the priestly caste there having the leisure necessary for disinterested research.
— *Aristotle*

Now that we know what we know, there is so much more we need to know.. .life is truely a journey and a blessing.
— *Paul Signorino*

Now would I give a thousand furlongs of sea for an acre of barren ground.
— *William Shakespeare*

Numbers written on restaurant bills within the confines of restaurants do not follow the same mathematical laws as numbers written on any other pieces of paper in any other parts of the Universe.
— *Douglas Adams*

Nurture your mind with great thoughts.
— *Benjamin Disraeli*

— x —

Proverbs

bjective evidence and certitude are doubtless very fine ideals to play with, but where on this moonlit and dream—visited planet are they found?
— *William James*

Obstacles are those frightful things you see when you take your eyes off the goal.
— *Hannah More*

Occupy my mind with motivational monologue. Set and implement realistic goals. Isolate negative thinking and influences. Take control and conquer my fears. Identify and eliminate stress. Visualize my success. Expect the best from each day.
— *Alexander Lockhart*

October is crisp days and cool nights, a time to curl up around the dancing flames and sink into a good book.
— *John Sinor*

Of all forms of caution, caution in love is the most fatal.

Of all sad words of tongue or pen, the saddest are these: "It might have been!"
— *John Greenleaf Whittier*

Of all the flowers in the Garden, there are a few that will and die. That's something we should both remember, when its time to say goodbye.
— *Audie Kirk Harrelson*

Of all the strategems, to know when to quit is the best.

Of all the things I miss from veterinary practice, puppy breath is one of the most fond memories!

Of all the things I've lost, I miss my mind the most.
— *Ozzy Osbom*

Of the various forms of government which have prevailed in the world, an hereditary monarchy seems to present the fairest scope for ridicule.
— *Edward Gibbon*

Oh Lord, help me to keep my big mouth shut until I know what I'm talking about.

Oh my ultra bestest, beautifulest, gloriest ICQ Goddess: Your grace is something I cannot conceal yet can never express.
— *Shergl Cheung*

Oh, the worst of all tragedies is not to die young, but to live until I am seventy—five and yet not ever truly to have lived.
— *Martin Luther King Jr.*

Oh, you who are born of the blood of the gods, Trojan son of Anchises, easy is the descent to Hell; the door of dark Dis stands open day and night. But to retrace your steps and come out to the air above, that is work, that is labor!
— *Virgil*

Old age is always 15 years older than you are.

Old age is the most unexpected of things that can happen to a man.
— *Trotsky*

On a front door: Everyone on the premises is a vegetarian except the dog. On a tombstone: "I told you I was sick."

On the whole, age comes more gently to those who have some doorway into an abstract world—art, or philosophy, or learning—regions where the years are scarcely noticed and the young and old can meet in a pale truthful light.
— *Freva Stark*

On your own is the way of life.

Once I dreamed I was a butterfly, and now I no longer know whether I am Chuang Tzu, who dreamed I was a butterfly, or whether I am a butterfly dreaming that I am Chuang Tzu.
— *Chuano Tzu*

Once on a tiger's back, it is hard to alight.

Once the realization is accepted that even between the closest human beings infinite distances continue to exist, a wonderful living side by side can grow up, if they succeed in loving the distance between them which makes it possible for each to see each other whole against the sky.
— *Rainer Maria Rilke*

Once upon a time, I had a good girl. Once upon a girl, I had a good time...

One can never consent to creep when one feels an impulse to soar.
— *Helen Keller*

One cannot be a part time nihilist.
— *Albert Camus*

One cannot know the quality of the iron until it has been in the fire.
— *Gabriel Knight*

Proverbs

One cat just leads to another.
— *Ernest Hemingway*

One does not find happiness in marriage, but takes happiness into marriage.

One good hearty laugh together could be the greatest insurance of lasting peace that men of all nations could contrive.

One good thing about being wrong is the joy it brings to others.

One good thing about forgetting is that you can no longer worry about whatever it was you forgot.

One hour's sleep before midnight is worth three after.

One lives in the hope of becoming a memory.
— *Antonio Porchia*

One man scorned and covered with scars still strive with his last ounce of courage to reach the unreachable stars; and the world will be better for this.

One Man's Sunset is another Man's Dawn.
— *Fievel Mouskawitz*

One may have a blazing hearth in one's soul and yet no one ever come to sit by it Passers-by see only a wisp of smoke from the chimney and continue on the way.
— *Vincent Van Gogh*

One may smile, and smile, and be a villain.
— *William Shakespeare*

One monk shoulders water by himself; two can still share the labor among them. When it comes to three, they have to go thirsty.

One must always maintain one's connection to the past and yet ceaselessly pull away from it.
— *Gaston Bachelard*

One must have the right to choose, even to choose wrong, if he is ever to learn to choose right.

One must never look for happiness; one meets it by the way.

One never loses by doing a good turn.

One of the advantages of being disorderly is that one is constantly making exciting discoveries.
— *A.A. Milne*

One of the indictments of civilization is that happiness and intelligence are so rarely found in the same person.
— *William Feather*

One of the lessons of history is that nothing is often a good thing to do and always a clever thing to say.

One of the major functions of skin is to keep people who look at you from throwing up.

One of the most adventurous things left us is to go to bed. For no one can lay a hand on our dreams.
— E.V. Lucas

One of the most common causes of failure is the habit of quitting when one is overtaken by temporary defeat Every person is guilty of this mistake at one time or another.
— Napoleon Hill

One of the most dangerous things you can ask for when it comes to love, is a warranty card.
— Jason Q.

One of the most important things a father can do for his children is to love their mother.

One of the most lasting pleasures you can experience is the feeling that comes over you when you genuinely forgive an enemy - whether he knows it or not.
— O.A. Battista

One of the sorriest spectacles imaginable is the anger of two people who have gotten into an argument over something that neither of them knows anything about.

One of the surest hindrances to the recovery of the sick is the centering of attention upon themselves.
— Ellen White

One of the wonders of life is just that — the wonder of life.

One of their children, Cain, once asked, "Am I my brother's son?"
— Student Bloopers

One often learns more from ten days of agony than from ten years of contentment.
— Merle Shain

One ought every day to listen to a little song, read a beautiful poem, see a worthwhile painting, and, if possible, say a flew sensible words.
— Johann Wolfgang Goethe

One reason why computers can do more work than people is that they never have to stop and answer the phone.

One should always play fairly when one has the winning cards.
— Oscar Wilde

One should always prefer the probable impossible to the improbable possible.

One thing I'll say for him, "Jesus is cool."
— Caiaphas

Proverbs

One thing is certain. If you can laugh at your troubles, you will always have something to laugh at.

One thing we know: Our God is the same; this earth is precious to Him. This we know: The earth does not belong to man; man belongs to the earth. This we know: All things are connected like the blood that unites one family; all things are connected; whatever befalls the earth, befalls the sons of the earth. Man did not weave the web of life - he is purely a strand in it. Whatever he does to the web he does to himself.
— *Chief Seattle*

One thing you can give and still keep, is your word.

One thorn of experience is worth a whole wilderness of warning.

One time a windshield wiper will work property is when it is holding a parking ticket.

One with God is a majority.
— *Billy Graham*

One word sums up probably the responsibility of any vice president and that one word is to be prepared.'
— *Dan Quayle*

One would like to stroke and caress human beings, but one dares not do so, because they bite.
— *Vladimir Lenin*

One youngster was explaining to another what "mixed emotions" meant. "It's like watching the school bum down when your new catcher's mitt is in your desk," he said.

One's past is what one is. It is the only way by which people should be judged.
— *Oscar Wilde*

Only a mediocre person is always at his best
— *W. Somerset Maugham*

Only a person who risks is free. The pessimist complains about the wind; the optimist expects it to change and the realist adjusts the sails.
— *William Arthur Ward*

Only boring people get bored.
— *Robin Beyer*

Only I can change my life. No one can do it for me.
— *Carol Burnett*

Only intolerance is intolerant.

Only presidents, editors and people with tapeworm have the right to use the editorial 'we'.
— *Mark Twain*

Only the winners decide what were war crimes.
— Gary Willis

Only thing to do is jump over the moon!
— Maureen

Only two things are infinite, the universe and human stupidity, and I'm not sure about the former.
— Albert Einstein

Only weird people wants others to think they are weird. Huh? Oh, no, I'm not weird at all. I only want you to think I am.
— Kenny Huang

Open up my head and let me out!

Opera is when a guy gets stabbed in the back and instead of bleeding, sings.
— Ed Gardner

Opportunities are like sunrises. If you wait too long, you miss them.
— William Arthur Ward

Opportunity is missed by most people because it is dressed in overalls and looks like work.
— Thomas Edison

Optimism is the faith that leads to achievement Nothing can be done without hope and confidence.

Optimism: The doctrine or belief that everything is beautiful, including what is ugly.
— Ambrose Bierce

Optometrist's office: If you don't see what you're looking for, you've come to the right place.

Ordinarily he was insane, but he had lucid moments when he was merely stupid.
— Heinrich Heine

Ordinary people believe only in the possible. Extraordinary people visualize not what is possible or probable, but rather what is impossible. And by visualizing the impossible, they begin to see it as possible.
— Cherie Carter-Scott

Ordinary riches can be stolen, real riches cannot. In your soul are infinitely precious things that cannot be taken from you.
— Oscar Wilde

Originality is the art of concealing your source.
— Franklin P. Jones

Other people's opinion of you does not have to become your reality.
— Les Brown

Proverbs 151

Our arms are the only ones God has to hug His children.

Our blend of youth and experience worked well. The exerienced players stood around watching the youngsters do all the work.
— *Graham Gooch*

Our chief want in life is somebody who will make us do what we can.
— *Ralph Waldo Emerson*

Our Congress is like the circus, but less talented.

Our degeneration, when it is traced back to its origin in our view of the world really consists in the fact that true optimism has vanished unperceived from our midst.
— *Albert Schweitzer*

Our eyes are placed in front because it is more important to look ahead than look back.

Our favorite attitude should be gratitude.

Our heritage and ideals, our codes and standards — the things we live by and teach our children — are preserved or diminished by how freely we exchange ideas and feelings.
— *Walt Disney*

Our mind is capable of passing beyond the dividing line we have drawn for it. Beyond the pairs of opposites of which the world consists, other, new insights begin.
—*Herman Hesse*

Out of difficulties grow miracles.
— *Jean De La Bruyere*

Out the 10Base—T, through the router, down the T1, over the leased line, off the bridge, past the firewall.. .nothing but Net
— *Tony Milter*

Outer agitation reveals inner instability.

Outside of a dog, a book is probably man's best friend. Inside of a dog, it's too dark to read.
— *Groucho Marx*

Outside of the killings, Washington has one of the lowest crime rates in the country.
— *Marion Barry*

Over the hill means the hardest climb is over and the view is terrific.

— *x* —

P

Pain is temporary, victory is forever.

Pain is the breaking of the shell that encloses your understanding.
— *Kahlil Gibran*

Paper cant wrap up a fire.

Paranoids are people, too; they have their own problems. It's easy to criticize, but if everybody hated you, you'd be paranoid too.
— *D.J. Hicks*

Passion: A feeling you feel when you feel a feeling you've never felt before.
— *Andrew Edgerton*

Passion: There are many things in life that will catch your eye, but only a few will catch your heart Pursue those.

Patience is the silken cord on which are strung the pearls of virtue.

Patience strengthens the spirit sweetens the temper, stifles anger, subdues pride, and bridles the tongue.

Pay attention to your enemies, for they are the first to discover your mistakes.
— *Antisthenes*

Peace cannot be kept by force. It can only be achieved by understanding.
— *Albert Einstein*

Pentiums melt in your PC, not in your hand.

People are always blaming their circumstances for what they are. I don't believe in circumstances. The people who get on in the world are the people who get up and look for the circumstances they want and if they cant find them, make them.
— *George Bernard Shaw*

People are like stained-glass windows. They sparkle and shine when the sun is out but when the darkness sets in, their true beauty is revealed only if there is a light from within.
— *Elisabeth Kibler-Ross*

People are lonely because they build walls instead of bridges.
— *J.F. Newton*

Proverbs

People are more likely to be killed by a champagne cork than by a poisonous snake.

People do not lack strength; they lack will.

— *Victor Hugo*

People don't care how much you know until they know how much you care.

People don't form relationships, they take hostages.

People don't grow old; they merely get old by not growing.

People don't run out of dreams — people just run out of time.

— *Glenn Frey*

People forget how fast you did a job, but they remember how well you did it.

People make enemies by complaining too much to their friends.

People may not always believe what you say, but they will believe what you do.

People may say I cant sing, but no one can ever say I didn't sing.

— *Florence Foster Jenkins*

People never say, "It's only a game" when they're winning.

People pick bad things from bad company very quickly but good company takes a good time to gift good things to them.

People say true friends must hold hands, but true friends don't need to hold hands because they know the other hand will always be there.

People see God every day, they just don't recognize Him.

People that are really very weird can get into sensitive positions and have a tremendous impact on history.

— *Dan Quayle*

People that hate cats will come back as mice in their next life.

— *Faith Resnick*

People travel to wonder at the height of mountains, at the huge waves of the sea, at the long courses of rivers, at the vast compass of the ocean, at the circular motion of the stars, and they pass by themselves without wondering.

— *St. Augustine*

People who are afraid of death are usually afraid of life.

People who are often in a hurry imagine they are energetic, when in most cases they are simply inefficient

— *Sydney J. Harris*

People who do not succeed have one distinguishing trait in common. They know all the reasons for failure and have what

they believe to be air-tight alibis to explain their own lack of achievement
— *Napoleon Hill*

People who do the world's real work don't usually wear neckties.

People who say they sleep like a baby haven't got one.

People who think they're out of this world always make you wish they were.

People who value their privileges above their principles, soon lose both.

People who want by the yard, but try by the inch, should be kicked by the foot!

People whose main concern is their own happiness seldom finds it.

People would enjoy life more if, once they got what they wanted, they could remember how much they wanted it.

People would worry less about what others think of them if they only realized how seldom they do.

Perfect love is rare indeed — for to be a lover will require that you continually have the subtlety of the very wise, the flexibility of the child, the sensitivity of the artist, the understanding of the philosopher, the acceptance of the saint the tolerance of the scholar and the fortitude of the certain.
— *Leo Buscaglia*

Perfection is reached, not when there is no longer anything to add, but when there is no longer anything to take away.
— *A. Saint-Exupery*

Perhaps I'm old and tired, but I always think that the chances of finding out what really is going on are so absurdly remote that the only thing to do is to say hang the sense of it and just keep yourself occupied.

Perhaps our eyes need to be washed by our tears once in a while, so that we can see Life with a clearer view again.
— *Alex Tan*

Perhaps the best thing about the future is that it only comes one day at a time.
— *Dean Acheson*

Perseverance is not a long race; it is many short races one after another.

Persistence is to the character of man what carbon is to steel.
— *Napoleon Hill*

Person Man, Person Man, hit on the head with a frying pan, lives his life in a garbage pan, Person Man. Is he depressed, or is he a mess? Does he feel totally worthless? Who came up with person man? Degraded Man, Person Man.

Philosophy alone can boast (and perhaps it is no more than the boast of philosophy), that her gentle hand is able to eradicate from the human mind the latent and deadly principle of fanaticism.

— *Edward Gibbon*

Philosophy: A route of many roads leading from nowhere to nothing.

— *Ambrose Bierce*

Physician: One upon whom we set our hopes when ill and our dogs when well.

— *Ambrose Bierce*

Piano teachers make liars out of all children.

Plan ahead: It wasn't raining when Noah built the ark!

Plans are nothing, planning is everything.

— *Dwight Eisenhower*

Plant a little gossip and you will reap a harvest of regret.

Please don't ask me what the score is, I'm not even sure what the game is.

— *Ashley Brilliant*

Please provide the date of your death.

Please understand there is no depression in this house and we are not interested in the possibilities of defeat. They do not exist.

— *Queen Victoria*

Poetry is an echo, asking a shadow to dance.

— *Carl Sandburg*

Poetry is an impish attempt to paint the color of the wind.

Poetry is simply the most beautiful, impressive and widely effective mode of saying things, and hence their importance.

— *George Arnold*

Poetry is the journal of the sea animal living on land, wanting to fly in the air. Poetry is a search for syllables to shoot at the barriers of the unknown and the unknowable. Poetry is a phantom script telling how rainbows are made and why they go away.

— *Carl Sandburg*

Politicians are interested in people. Not that this is always a virtue. Fleas are interested in dogs.

Politics and the shape of mankind are shaped by men without ideals and without greatness. Men who have greatness within them don't concern themselves with politics.
— Albert Camus

Politics: Poly (many) + ticks (bloodsucking parasites).

Popular music just has to come from the brain of the composer. Nothing else has stuff like that in it.

Positive anything is better than negative nothing.

Poverty is a condition with but one advantage, it doesn't take much to improve your lot.

Poverty within is as dangerous as poverty without.
— Rowan Swan

Power corrupts. Absolute power is kind of neat.
— John Lehman

Praise can be your most valuable asset as long as you don't aim it at yourself.

Prayer does not cause faith to work, faith causes prayer to work.
— Gloria Copeland

Preach the Gospel at all times; if necessary, use words.
—St. Francis of Assisi

Preconcieved notions are the locks on the door to wisdom.
— Merry Browne

Presence is more than just being there. If your absence doesn't make any difference, your presence won't either.

Pride is something we have. Vanity is something others have.

Problems are only opportunities in work clothes.
— Henry J. Kaiser

Professionals built the Titanic, amateurs built the ark.

Profound ignorance makes a man dogmatic. The man who knows nothing thinks he is teaching others what he has just learned himself; the man who knows a great deal cant imagine that what he is saying is not common knowledge, and speaks more indifferently.
— La Bruyere

Programming is like sex; one mistake and you have to support it for the rest of your life.
— Michael Sinz

Programming today is a race between software engineers striving to build bigger and better idiot—proof programs, and the

Proverbs 157

universe trying to produce bigger and better idiots. So far, the universe is winning.
— *Rich Cook*

Progress is a comfortable disease.
— *E.E. Cummings*

Promises are meant to be kept, for they are like precious pearls in an ocean, their value is high and quality genuine and true, and once they are made they can never be broken.

Proverbs contain within one or two lines the lessons of lifetime.

Provisions are assured by giving.

Punctuality is like having bad manners. You're sure of having lots of time to yourself.

Punishment without judgment is bearable. It has a name, besides, that guarantees our innocence: it is called misfortune.
— *Albert Camus*

Pure gold does not fear furnace.

Pure truth, like pure gold, has been found unfit for circulation because men have discovered that it is far more convenient to adulterate the truth than to refine themselves.
— *Charles Caleb Colton*

Put those that you love in a circle, not a heart Hearts can be broken, but circles go on forever.
— *Brian Littrell*

Put your eggs in one basket And watch the basket That's the way to make money.
— *Andrew Carnegie*

— *x* —

Q

Quality is an excuse for lack of quantity.

Quality is presence of value and not absence of mistake.

Quantum particles: The dreams that stuff is made of.

Quarrels would not last very long if the faults were only on one side.

Quite frankly, teachers are the only profession that teach our children.
— *Dan Quayle*

Quite often a motorist will knock a pedestrian down because his windshield is obscured by safety stickers.

Quote what the dead people said so you may be quoted some day and become famous.
— *Bernard Yen*

Quoting one is plagiarism. Quoting many is research.

— *x* —

Radio is a miraculous device which enables people who have nothing to say to talk to people who aren't listening.

Rain is something that, when you cany an umbrella, it doesn't.

Rain is what makes flowers grow and taxis disappear.

Rarely do we admire the virtues we do not possess.

Read, every day, something no one else is reading. Think, every day, something no one else is thinking. Do, every day, something no one else would be silly enough to do. It is bad for the mind to be always part of unanimity.
— *Christopher Mortey*

Real generosity is doing something nice for someone who will never find out.

Real joy comes not from ease or riches or from the praise of men, but from doing something worthwhile.

Real men don't ask directions.

Real programmers don't document. If it was hard to write, it should be hard to understand.

Real programmers never work from 9 to 5. If any real programmer is around at 9 a.m., it's because they were up all night.

Real wisdom comes from self-realization.
— *Chew Nai Chee*

Reality can destroy the dream; why shouldn't the dream destroy reality?
— *George Moore*

Reality is merely an illusion, albeit a very persistent one.
— *Albert Einstein*

Reality is nothing but a collective hunch.
— *Lily Tomlin*

Recipe: A series of step-by-step instructions for preparing ingredients you forgot to buy, in utensils you don't own, to make a dish the dog won't eat.

Reckless drivers may find they have plenty of hearse-power.

Reformers waste their time trying to dean up the horse races: it's the human race that needs cleaning up.

Refusing to have an opinion is a way of having one.

Regret can be deepest when you just stay silent

Reincarnation: Life sucks, then you die, then life sucks again.

Relationships are hard. It's like a full-time job, and we should treat it like one. If your boyfriend or girlfriend wants to leave you, they should give you two weeks' notice. There should be severance pay, and before they leave you, they should have to find you a temp.

— Bob Ettinger

Relatives are persons who come to visit us when the weather is too uncomfortable for them to do their own cooking at home.

Religion increasingly is tending to degenerate into a decent formula wherewith to embellish a comfortable life.

— Alfred North Whitehead

Religion is like a bank — neither one pays dividends unless we make deposits.

Religion is merely a path leading not to salvation, but rather, to slavery.

Remember that failure is an event, not a person.

Remember that the beauty of any dream is in never letting it go.

— Sarina

Remember that when you eat out in a swanky restaurant, the food may be plain, but the prices will be fancy.

Remember that you don't choose love. Love chooses you. All you can really do is accept it for all its mystery when it comes into your life. Feel the way it fills you to overflowing, then reach out and give it away.

— Kent Nurbum

Remember, don't put it off. Go ahead and do it. If you get to it and don't do it you may never get to it to do it again.

Remember, old folks are worth a fortune, with silver in their hair, gold in their teeth, stones in their kidneys, lead in their feet and gas in their stomachs.

Remember, the greatest gift is not found in a store nor under a tree, but in the hearts of true friends.

— Cindy Lew

Remember, worth and value are not wrapped up in what you do. You are not a human doing. You are a human being.

Remember, your relatives had no choice in the matter either.

Proverbs

Renunciation of thinking is a declaration of spiritual bankruptcy.
— *Albert Schweitzer*

Repentance is sorrow for the deed, not for getting caught.

Republicans understand the importance of bondage between a mother and child.
— *Dan Quayle*

Reputation is a large bubble which bursts when you try to blow it up yourself.

Reputation is character with whatever you've been caught doing subtracted.

Reputation is made in a moment character is built in a lifetime.

Research is what I'm doing when I don't know what I'm doing.
— *Wemher von Braun*

Resentment is like drinking poison and expecting someone else to die!

Respect cannot be learned, purchased or acquired; it can only be earned.

Respect is mutual: if you don't respect others viewpoints, chances are they wont acknowledge yours.

Retirement can be a great joy if you can figure out how to spend time without spending money.

Retirement is the time of life when you stop lying about your age and start lying about the house.

Retirement is when a man who figured he'd go fishing seven times a week finds himself washing the dishes three times a day.

Retirement is when the Irving is easy and the payments are hard.

Retirement is when your wife realizes she never gave your secretary enough sympathy.

Revenge has no more quenching effect on emotions, than salt water has on thirst.

Revenge is like biting a dog because the dog bites you.

Revenge may be sweet, but not when you are on the receiving end.

Revolutions are not about trifles, but they spring from trifles.
— *Aristotle*

Right is right is right, even if everyone is against it; and wrong is wrong, even if everyone is for it.
— *William Penn*

Right now I'm a freshman in my fourth year at UCLA but my goal is to become a veternarian, 'cause I love children.
— *Julie Brown*

Right now I'm having amnesia and deja vu at the same time. I think I've forgotten this before.

Rip Van Winkle slept for twenty years, but, of course, his neighbors didn't have a radio.

Run around in circles to discover centripetal acceleration. Jump out the window to discover gravitational acceleration.
— *Bernard Yen*

— x —

S

Salvation, whatever that may be, will not be found amidst the external; it awaits within.
— *Thanes*

Save time, see it my way.

Say what you mean, mean what you say, but don't say it mean.

Sayings remain meaningless until they are embodied in actions.
— *Kahlil Gibran*

School is a building with four walls, and tomorrow inside.

Science has proof without any certainty. Creationists have certainty without any proof.
— *Ashley Montague*

Science is a differential equation. Religion is a boundry condition.
— *Alan Turing*

Science is a wonderful thing if one does not have to earn one's living at it
— *Albert Einstein*

Science without religion is lame; religion without science is blind.
— *Albert Einstein*

Second place is the first loser.

See, when the government spends money, it creates jobs; whereas when the money is left in the hands of taxpayers, God only knows what they do with it Bake it into pies, probably. Anything to avoid creating jobs.
— *Dave Barry*

Seek first to understand and then to be understood.
— *Stephen R. Coyey*

Seek freedom and become captive of your desires. Seek discipline and find your liberty.
— *Frank Herbert*

Seek the wisdom of the ages, but look at the world through the eyes of a child.
— *Ron Wild*

Seen it all, done it all, cant remember most of it.

Seen on the back of a biker's vest If you can read this, my wife fell off.

Seen on the side of an East German factory: To the workers of the world, I am sorry.

—Karl Marx

Self confidence is to know your way around yourself so instinctively that you always have a strength to draw on. Somewhere inside, from the stillness, you always find something that can meet you need.

Serve locally, pray globally.

Setting a good example for the children takes all the tun out of middle age. Seven days without prayer makes one weak.

Sex is one of the nine reasons for reincarnation... the other eight are unimportant.

— Henry Miller

Sex without love is an empty experience, but, as empty experiences go, it's one of the best.

—Woody Allen

Share your smile with everyone, but save your kiss for only one.

She has a very sharp wit, and she wields it like a blunt instrument.

— Stone Phillips

She is an expert housekeeper Every time she gets divorced, she keeps the house.

Shoot for the moon. Even if you miss you'll end up in the stars.

— Les Brown

Should you shield the canyons from the windstorms, you would never see the beauty of their carvings.

— Elisabeth Kubler-Ross

Show me a man with both feet on the ground, and I'll show you a man who can't put on his pants.

Show me a sane man and I will cure him for you.

— Carl Jung

Sign on a church bulletin board: You aren't too bad to come in. You aren't good enough to stay out.

Silence is the only thing that cant be misquoted!

Silence is the ultimate weapon of power.

— Charles de Gaulle

Silence is wise if we are foolish, but foolish if we are wise.

Silent gratitude isn't much use to anyone.

— G.B. Stem

Silver's law: If Murphy's law can go wrong it will.

Proverbs 165

Since I have smashed my denominational glasses, I have a better vision of who Christ is.

Since you cannot do good to all, you are to pay special regard to those who, by the accidents of time, or place, or circumstances, are brought into closer connection with you.

— *St. Augustine*

Sipping a cup of tea, going for a morning walk, doing your work — all these small activities make up your living. And each part, each moment of living, is meaningful. You just have to be there; otherwise, who is going to experience the meaning? People go on drinking tea, but they never are there; their minds are wandering all over the world.

— *Osho Talks*

Sisyphus is the happiest man alive.

— *Albert Camus*

Sit next to a pretty girl for an hour, it seems like a minute. Sit on a red-hot stove for a minute, it seems like an hour. That's relativity.

— *Albert Einstein*

Six is a number perfect in itself, and not because God created the world in six days; rather the contrary is true. God created the world in six days because this number is perfect, and it would remain perfect, even if the work of the six days did not exist.

— *St. Augustine*

Skier One who pays an arm and a leg for the opportunity to break them.

Skip's law of office food: ft doesn't have to be good. It just has to be free.

Sky farms are fantastically beautiful, with their kilometer long networks of glass framed in grids of metal, and the sunlight shining through jungles of vegetation inside. When one of them catches the light you can see the refracted beauty for miles; they are life—giving stars on a desolate planet...gardens on the wing.

— *Deidre Skye*

Slander, like coffee, is usually handed to you without grounds.

Sleep away the years, sleep away the pain, wake tomorrow - a girl again.

— *Hal Summers*

Sleep is something that always seems more important the morning after than the night before.

Small minds are the first to condemn large ideas.

Smile! It increases your face value.

Smile. It makes others wonder what you're thinking.

So live that when death comes the mourners will outnumber the cheering section.

So many people will walk in and out of your life, but those who leave foot prints are true friends.

Software undergoes alpha testing as a first step in getting user feedback. Alpha is Latin for "doesn't work."

Some artists transform the sun with a yellow spot. Other artists transform a yellow spot into the sun.
— Pablo Picasso

Some cause happiness wherever they go; others whenever they go.
— Oscar Wilde

Some days you're the dog. Some days you're the hydrant.

Some fellows dream of worthy accomplishments, while others stay awake and do them.

Some folks get into the sea of matrimony on a wave of enthusiasm.

Some goals are so worthy, it's glorious even to fail.

Some have the wisdom of old age and the energy of youth. Most have the wisdom of youth, and the energy of old age.

Some men see things as they are and ask why. Others dream things that never were and ask why not.
— George Bernard Shaw

Some of the greatest writers this world has ever known have written their finest works while happily and blissfully drunk... and so shall I.

Some of the world's greatest feats were accomplished by people not smart enough to know they were impossible.
— Doug Larson

Some of us think holding on makes us strong, but sometimes it is letting go.

Some of us think holding on makes us strong, but sometimes it's letting go.
— Sam Ewing

Some people are alive only because it is illegal to kill them.

Some people are bitter, some sour, others are sweet Who you hang out with depends on your taste.

Proverbs

Some people are born mediocre, some people achieve mediocrity, and some people have mediocrity thrust upon them.
— *Joseph Heller*

Some people care too much. I think it's called love.
— *Pooh*

Some people come into our lives and quickly go. Some stay for a while and leave footprints on our hearts. And we are never, ever the same.

Some people dream at success while others wake up and work hard at it.

Some people grumble because roses have thorns. Be thankful instead that thorns have roses.

Some people just don't take advice; they have to hit their own head off the wall to believe it will hurt!

Some people say that cats are sneaky, evil, and cruel. True, and they have many other fine qualities as well.
— *Missy Dizick*

Some people take too much of vitamin "I".

Some people when they meet a successful rival, no matter in what, instantly shut their eyes to everything good in him and see only what is bad. Others, on the contrary, endeavour above all to discover in their fortunate rival the qualities which won him success and with an aching heart seek only the good in him.
— *Leo Tolstoy*

Some people who yearn for endless life don't know what to do with a rainy afternoon.
— *Harvey H. Potthoff*

Some people will believe anything if you tell them it's a rumor.

Some persons don't know the difference between thinking for yourself, and thinking of yourself.

Some say the world will end in fire, some say in ice. From what I've tasted of desire I hold with those who favor fire. But if the world should perish twice, I think I know enough of hate, to say that for destruction, ice is also great, and would suffice.
— *Robert Frost*

Some singers who have become teenage institutions belong in one.

Some sleep five hours; nature requires seven, laziness nine, and wickedness eleven.

Some stories are truth that never happened.
— *Elie Weisel*

Some succeed because they are destined to. But most succeed because they are determined to.

Some things that cost $5 to buy several years ago now costs $10 just to repair.

Someone who thinks logically is a nice contrast to the real world.

Sometimes God doesn't tell us His plan because we wouldn't believe it anyway.
— *Cariton Pearson*

Sometimes I lie awake at night, and I ask, "Where have I gone wrong?" Then a voice says to me, This is going to take more than one night"
— *Charlie Brown*

Sometimes I think the surest sign that intelligent life exists elsewhere in the universe is that none of it has tried to contact us.
— *Calvin and Hobbes*

Sometimes I think we're alone. Sometimes I think we're not in either case, the thought is staggering.
— *Buckminster Fuller*

Sometimes I wake up grumpy; other times I let her sleep.

Sometimes it costs more to do nothing than to do something.

Sometimes it's easier to ask forgiveness than permission.

Sometimes life can be as bitter as dragon tears. But whether dragon tears are bitter or sweet depends entirely on how each man perceives them.

Sometimes one pays most for the things one gets for nothing.
— *Albert Einstein*

Sometimes providences, like Hebrew letters, must be read backward.
— *John Flavel*

Sómetimes someone says something really small, and it just fits right into this empty place in your heart.

Sometimes the best helping hand you can give is a good, firm push.
— *Joann Thomas*

Sometimes the heart sees what is invisible to the eye.
— *H. Jackson Brown Jr.*

Sometimes to be headstrong, is to be brain—weak.
— *Bob Faravoni*

Sometimes virtue and prosperity have trouble Irving together.

Proverbs 169

Sometimes we learn more from a man's errors than from his virtues.

Sometimes when I am lonely, and the world just doesn't seem so right, I think of what you would say to cheer me up at night I feel your presence, hovering all around the air, your angelic ghostly hands dry my tears and you whisper, "I care."

Sometimes when I feel like killing someone, I do a little trick to calm myself down. I'll go over to the person's house and ring the doorbell. When the person comes to the door, I'm gone, but you know what I've left on the porch? A jack-o-lantern with a knife stuck in the side of its head with a note that says "You." After that, I usually feel a lot better, and no harm done.

Sometimes you gotta laugh through the tears, smite through the pain so that you can live through the sorrow...
— *Alex Tan*

Sometimes, after you've tried everything, breaking up is the best thing to do.

Sometimes, not matter how much faith we have, we lose people. But you never forget them. And sometimes, it's those memories that give us the faith to go on.

Somewhere on this globe, every ten seconds, there is a woman giving birth to a child. She must be found and stopped.
— *Sam Levenson*

Somewhere, something incredible is waiting to be known.
— *Carl Sagan*

Soul—winning and missions is the life blood of the church.

Sound is fifty percent of the motion picture experience.
— *George Lucas*

Sour, sweet, bitter, pungent all must be tasted.

Space is a dangerous place, especially if it's between your ears!

Speak only good of people and you will never have to whisper.

Speak when you're angry and you'll make the best speech you'll ever regret.
— *Henry Ward Beecher*

Speak, cousin, or if you cannot stop his mouth with a kiss and let not him speak neither.
— *Beatrice*

Spring is the time when youth dreams and old age remembers.

Stalinism begins at home.
— *Tom Neff*

Standard mathematics has recently been rendered obsolete by the discovery that for years we have been writing the numeral five backward. This has led to reevaluation of counting as a method of getting from one to ten. Students are taught advanced concepts of Boolean algebra, and formerly unsolvable equations are dealt with by threats of reprisals.
— *Woody Allen*

Start every day off with a smile and get it over with.
— *W.C. Fields*

Statistics is like a Bikini; what is revealed is suggestive, but what is concealed is vital.

Steal a bell with one's ears covered.

Sterilize: What you do to your first baby's pacifier by boiling it and to your last baby's pacifier by blowing on it.

Stewardesses is the longest word that is typed with only the left hand. Sticks and stones can break my bones, but words can shatter my soul.

Stress is when you wake up screaming and you realize you haven't fallen asleep yet.

Stupidity is NOT a handicap! PARK ELSEWHERE!

Style, like sheer silk, too often hides eczema.
— *Albert Camus*

Success always occurs in private, and failure in full view.

Success comes in cans, not cant's.

Success comes to those who become success conscience. Failure comes to those who indifferntly allow themselves to become failure conscience.
— *Napoleon Hill*

Success in Hollywood consists in having your name in the gossip columns and out of the phone book.

Success is a ladder that can not be dimbed with your hands in your pockets.

Success is never permanent. Failures are never final. The only thing that counts is to never, ever give up.

Success is not the result of spontaneous combustion. You have got to set yourself on fire for it

Success is relative — the more success, the more relatives.

Success is the best revenge.

Success is the result of perfection, hard work, learning from failure, loyalty, and persistence.
— *Colin Powell*

Proverbs

Success occurs when opportunity meets preparation.

Success requires no explanations. Failure permits no alibis.
— *Napoleon Hill*

Success: Its an never ending improvement in what you do.

Suddenly, quietly, you realize that — from this moment forth — you will no longer walk through this life alone. Like a new sun this awareness arises within you, freeing you from fear, opening your life. It is the beginning of love, and the end of all that came before.
— *Robert Frost*

Suffering well borne is better than suffering removed.

Sundial: An old timer.

Suppose you were an idiot And suppose you were a member of Congress. But I repeat myself.

Sure God created man before woman.. .but then you always make a rough draft before the final masterpiece.

Sure there are dishonest men in local government But there are dishonest men in national government too.
— *Richard Nixon*

— *x* —

T

Table manners must have been invented by people who were never hungry.

Tact is the ability to describe others as they see themselves.

Tact is the ability to say nice doggie, until you can find a big rock.

Tactics is what you do when there's something to do, strategy is what you do when there isn't.
— *Tartakower*

Take away love and earth is a tomb.
— *Robert Browning*

Take care of your character and your reputation will take care of itself.

Take care of your pennies and the pounds will take care of themselves.
— *Andrew Carnegie*

Take care that no one hates you justly.
— *Publilius Syrus*

Take inventory of yourself, see if any remnants of fear are standing in your way. Then you may grow... because nothing, absolutely nothing, can stand in your way.
— *Napoleon Hill*

Take nothing but pictures. Leave nothing but footprints. Kill nothing but time.
— *Baltimore Grotto*

Take time to laugh-it is the music of the soul.

Taking a new step...is what people fear most.
— *Dostoyevski*

Talent alone cannot make a writer. There must be a man behind the book.

Talk is cheap because supply exceeds demand.

Talk not of wasted affection; affection never was wasted.
— *Henry Wadsworth Longfellow*

Teachers open the doors; you enter by yourself.

Tear is a powerful weapon that can change the future of oneself or even the world. People living in the war, they cry. People love someone, they cry. Through that which is acquired without difficulty is dispersed with equal facility.

That which one man receives without working for, another must work for without receiving.

That which was hard to endure is sweet to remember.

That which you cannot give away, you don't possess; it possesses you.

That you may retain your self-respect, it is better to displease the people by doing what you know is right, than to temporarily please them by doing what you know is wrong.
— *William J.H. Boetcker*

That's kind of like my goal; to get naked with Robert Redford and to have a huge hit record.
— *Sheena Easton*

That's what learning is, after all; not whether we lose the game, but how we lose and how we've changed because of it and what we take away from it that we never had before, to apply to other games. Losing, in a curious way, is winning.
— *Richard Bach*

The 486 is to a modern CPU as a Jutes Verne reprint is to a modern SF novel.
— *Henry Spencer*

The absurd enlightens me on this point: there is no future.
— *Albert Camus*

The absurd is born of this confrontation between the human need and the unreasonable silence of the world.
— *Albert Camus*

The absurd man is he who never changes.
— *Auguste Barthelemy*

The act of putting pen to paper encourages pause for thought, this in turn makes us think more deeply about life, which helps us regain our equilibrium.
— *Norbet Platt*

The amount of sleep required by the average person is usually thirty minutes more.

The angry man will defeat himself in battle as well as in life.
— *Samurai Maxim*

The answers to life's problems aren't at the bottom of a bottle, they're on TV!
— *Homer Simpson*

The Army has carried the American... ideal to its logical conclusion. Not only do they prohibit discrimination on the grounds of race, creed and color, but also on ability.
— *T. Lehrer*

The arrow has to draw back to fly ahead.

The art of flying is to throw yourself at the ground and miss.
— *Douglas Adams*

The art of living lies less in eliminating our troubles than in growing with them.
— *Bernard M. Baruch*

The art of love... is largely the art of persistence.
— *Albert Ellis*

The attention span of a computer is only as long as its electrical cord.

The attitudes of your friends are like the buttons on an elevator. They will either take you up or they will take you down.
— *Alexander Lockhart*

The authority of Plato and Aristotle, of Zeno and Epicurus, still reigned in the schools; and their systems, transmitted with blind deference from one generation of disciples to another, precluded every generous attempt to exercise the powers, or enlarge the limits, of the human mind.
— *Edward Gibbon*

The average teenager still has all the faults his parents outgrew.

The basic principle of spiritual life is that our problems become the very place to discover wisdom and love.
— *Jack Kornfield*

The beginning and the end reach out their hands to each other.

The beginning of love is to let those we love be perfectly themselves, and not to twist them with our own image - otherwise, we love only the reflection of ourselves we find in them.

The beginning of wisdom is to call things by their right names.

The best and quickest way to appreciate other people is to try to do their job affirmative, if we accept it as one of the greatest eternal forms of life and transformation.
— *Hermann Hesse*

The common cold, if left untreated, lasts about two weeks. If treated with medication and rest, it lasts about fourteen days.

The computer only crashes when printing a document you haven't saved. The computing field is always in need of new cliches.
— *Alan Perlis*

Proverbs

The conventional view serves to protect us from the painful job of thinking.
— *John Kenneth Galbraith*

The country couldn't run without Prohibition. That is the industrial fact.
— *Henry Ford*

The course of true love never did run smooth.
— *William Shakespeare*

The creation of the universe was made possible by a grant from Texas Instruments.

The creator of the universe works in mysterious ways. But he uses a base ten counting system and likes round numbers.
— *Scott Adams*

The cross is easier to the Christian who takes it up than to the one who drags it along.

The cure for all ills and wrongs, the cares, the sorrows and the crimes of humanity, all lie in the one word 'love.' It is the divine vitality that everywhere produces and restores life.
— *Lydia Maria Child*

The cure for anything is salt-water - sweat, tears, or the sea.
— *Isak Dinesea*

The day we lose our need for dreams is the day the human race forfeits its soul.
— *John Chiam*

The deeper we look into nature the more we recognize that it is full of life, and the more profoundly we know that all life is a secret, and we are all united to all this life.
— *Albert Schweitzer*

The deepest human defeat suffered by human beings is constituted by the difference between what one was capable of becoming and what one has in fact become.
— *Ashley Montague*

The deepest rivers flow by most silently.
— *Victoria Richards*

The definition of virtue: insufficient temptation.
— *George Bernard Shaw*

The desire to forget the past is a form of suicide. I have come to believe that many of us would sooner die than remove our masks and stand barefaced before the world.
— *Richard Bode*

The difference between an rebel and a patriot is wether who is in power.

The difference between genius and stupidity is that genius has its limits.

The difference between literature and journalism is that journalism is unreadable and literature is not read.
— Oscar Wilde

The direct use of force is such a poor solution to any problem, it is generally employed only by small children and large nations.
— David Friedman

The dumber people think you are, the more surprised they're going to be when you kill them.
— William Clayton

The dying, the cripple, the mental, the unwanted, the unloved — they are Jesus in disguise.
— Mother Teresa

The easiest way to commit suicide is to take gas or step on it.

The easiest way to get a teenage boy to be quiet is to ask him where he's been when he gets home.

The empires of the future are the empires of the mind.
— Winston Churchill

The end is near, but we shall move on.
— Bernard Yen

The end of wisdom is to dream high enough to lose the dream in the seeking of it.
— William Faulkner

The essential sadness is to go through life without loving. But it would be almost equally sad to leave this world without ever telling those you loved that you love them.

The excuse for missing homework used to be "the dog ate it". Now it's "the disk was erased".

The expression often used by Mr. Herbert Spencer of the Survival of the Fittest is more accurate, and is sometimes equally convenient
— Charles Darwin

The fabric of a mighty state, which has been reared by the labours of successive ages, could not be overturned by the misfortune of a single day, if the fatal power of the imagination did not exaggerate the real measure of the calamity.
— Edward Gibbon

The fellow who is deeply in love with himself should get a divorce.

The fellow who is fired with enthusiasm for his work is seldom fired by his boss.

Proverbs

The first duty of a revolutionary is to get away with it
— *Abbie Hoffman*

The first man gets the oyster, the second man gets the shell.
— *Andrew Carnegie*

The first thing a child learns when he gets a drum is that he's never going to get another one.

The further the spiritual evolution of mankind advances, the more certain it seems to me that the path to genuine religiosity does not lie through the fear of life, and the fear of death, and blind faith, but through striving after rational knowledge.
— *Albert Einstein*

The future belongs to those who believe in the beauty of their dreams.
— *Eleanor Roosevelt*

The future holds something in store for the individual who keeps faith in it

The future will be better tomorrow.
— *Dan Quayle*

The gap between enthusiasm and indifference is filled with failures.

The gene pool could use a little chlorine.

The generation of random numbers is too important to be left to chance.
— *Robert R. Covevou*

The genius of you Americans is that you never make any clear-cut stupid moves, only complicated stupid moves that leave us scratching our heads wondering if we might possibly have missed something.
— *Gamel Abdel Nasser*

The goal of Computer Science is to build something that will last at least until we've finished building it.

The Gods cannot help those who do not seize opportunities.

The good Christian should beware of mathematicians, and all those who make empty prophecies. The danger already exists that the mathematicians have made a covenant with the devil to darken the spirit and to confine man in the bonds of Hell.
— *St. Augustine*

The good people sleep much better at night than the bad people. Of course, the bad people enjoy the waking hours much more.
—*Woody Allen*

The greatest act of faith takes place when a man finally decides that he is not God.

The greatest actions of love often got unnoticed. The greatest genius often lies concealed.

The greatest genius will never be worth much if he pretends to draw exclusively from his own resources.
— *Johann Wolfgang Goethe*

The greatest good is to preserve life, to promote life, to raise life to the highest value that it is capable of.

The greatest evil is to destroy life, to injure life, to repress life which is capable of development. We only become decent beings when we recognize this.
— *Albert Schweitzer*

The greatest happiness of life it the conviction that we are loved — loved for ourselves, or rather, loved in spite of ourselves.
—*Victor Hugo*

The greatest pain in the world is hurting the person who's closest to you. You cant fix it. You can't even look at it. So you leave.

The greatest pleasure in life is doing what people say you cannot do.
— *Waiter Bagehot*

The greatest test of courage on earth is to bear. defeat without losing heart
— *Robert G. Ingersoll*

The greatest wisdom doesn't know itself. The richest plan is not to have one.
— *Louise Erdrich*

The guardian angels of life sometimes fly so high as to be beyond our sight, but they are always looking down upon us.
— *Jean Paul Richter*

The happiest of people don't necessarily have the best of everything; they just make the most of everything that comes along their way.

The hardest of all is learning to be a well of affection, and not a fountain; to show them we love them not when we feel like it but when they do.
— *Nan Fairbrother*

The hardest thing in life is to know which bridge to cross and which to bum.
— *David Russell*

The hardest thing in the world to understand is the income tax.
— *Albert Einstein*

The headmaster governs. The schoolteacher teaches. And let the pupils exercise creativity.
— Chew Nai Chee

The heart has its reasons which reasons know nothing of.
— Blaise Pascal

The heart that loves is always young.

The highest compliment one can be paid by another human being is to be told: "Because of what you are, you are essential to my happiness."
— Nathaniel Branden

The highest proof of the Spirit is love. Love is the eternal thing which can already on earth possess as it really is.
— Albert Schweitzer

The Holocaust was an obscene period in our nation's history. I mean in this century's history. But we all lived in this century. I didn't live in this century.
— Dan Quayle

The hours I spend with you I look upon as sort of a perfumed garden, a dim twilight and a fountain singing to it. You and you alone make me feel that I am alive... Other men it is said have seen angels, but I have seen thee and thou art enough.
—George Moore

The idea is not responsible for the people who believe in it.

The important thing is not to stop questioning. Curiosity has its own reason for existing.
— Albert Einstein

The incidence of memory is like light from dead stars whose influence lingers long after the events themselves.
— David Horowitz

The income tax has made more liars out of the American people than golf has.
—Will Rogers

The influence of the clergy, in an age of superstition, might be usefully employed to assert the rights of mankind; but so intimate is the connection between the throne and the altar, that the banner of the church has very seldom been seen on the side of the people.
— Edward Gibbon

The inherent vice of capitalism is the unequal sharing of blessings; the inherent virtue of socialism is the equal sharing of miseries.
— Winston Churchill

The intellegence of the planet is constant and the population is growing.
— *Arthur C. Clarke*

The Internet is so big, so powerful and pointless that for some people it is a complete substitute for life.
— *Andrew Brown*

The Internet is the greatest tool our species has invented.

The kingdom of music is not the kingdom of this world; it will accept those whom breeding and intellect and culture have alike rejected. The commonplace person begins to play, and shoots into the empyrean without effort, whilst we look up, marvelling how he has escaped us, and thinking how we could worship him and love him, would he but translate his visions into human words, and his experiences into human actions. Perhaps he cannot; certainly he does not, or does so very seldom.
— *E.M. Forster*

The ladder of success is never crowded at the top.
— *Napoleon Hill*

The last day of school before summer vacation is the shortest day of a mother's year.
—*Dee Eldrige*

The life you have led doesn't need to be the only life you have.

The likelihood of a hard disk crash is in direct proportion to the value of the material that hasn't been backed up.

The longer I am out of office, the more infallible I appear to myself.
— *Henry Kissinger*

The longer I live the more I see that I am never wrong about anything, and that all the pains that I have so humbly taken to verify my notions have only wasted my time.
— *George Bernard Shaw*

The longer the night lasts, the more our dreams will be.

The Lord God is subtle, but malicious he is not
— *Albert Einstein*

The loss of life will be irreplaceable.
— *Dan Quayle*

The lottery is just a tax on people who are bad at math.

The magic of first love is our ignorance that it could ever end.
— *Isaac D'Israeli*

The main problem with teenagers is that they're just like their parents were at their age.

Proverbs

The man who dies rich dies disgraced.
— *Andrew Carnegie*

The man who removes a mountain begins by carrying away small stones.

The mathematical life of a mathematician is short. Work rarely improves after the age of twenty-five or thirty. If little has been accomplished by then, little will ever be accomplished.
— *Alfred Adler*

The mathematical sciences particularly exhibit order, symmetry, and limitation; and these are the greatest forms of the beautiful.
— *Aristotle*

The meaning of life is in the answer of death.
— *Emil Wenzzel*

The meaning of life is that it stops.
— *Franz Kafka*

The meeting of two personalities is like the contact of two chemical substances. If there is any reaction, both are transformed.
— *Cart Jung*

The middle of the road is not such a bad place; you don't fall off the edge.

The mind has exactly the same power as the hands; not merely to grasp the world, but to change it
— *Colin Wilson*

The mind I love must have wild places, a tangled orchard where dark damsons drop in the heavy grass, an overgrown little wood, the chance of a snake or two, a pool that nobody's fathomed the depth of, and paths threaded with flowers planted by the mind.
— *Katherine Mansfield*

The mind is not a vessel to be filled but a fire to be kindled.
— *Plutarch*

The mind of a poet begins. with an H and ends with a T, listening with an EAR in between.
— *Lori Herber*

The minute a man begins to feel his importance, his friends begin to doubt it

The misery and greatness of this world: It offers no truths, but only objects for love. Absurdity is. king, but love saves us from it
— *Albert Camus*

The moment of victory is much too short to live for that and nothing else.
— Martina Navratilova

The moment you have in your heart this extraordinary thing called love and feel the depth, the delight, the ecstasy of it, you will discover that for you the world is transformed.
— J. Krishnamurti

The more anger towards the past you carry in your heart, the less capable you are of loving in the present.
— Barbara De Angelis

The more arguments you win, the fewer friends you'll have.

The more corrupt a society, the more numerous its laws.

The more I study religions the more I am convinced that man never worshipped anything but himself.
— Sir Richard F. Burton

The more we team, the more we realize how little we know.

The more you sweat in peacetime. The less you bleed during war.

The more you use your brain, the more brain you will have to use.
— George A. Dorsey

The most beautiful thing we can experience is the mysterious. It is the source of all true art and all science. He to whom this emotion is a stranger, who can no longer pause to wonder and stand rapt in awe, is as good as dead: his eyes are closed.
— Albert Einstein

The most beautiful things in this world cannot be seen or touched — they are felt by the human heart.
— Helen Keller

The most efficient labor—saving device is still money.
— Franklin P. Jones

The most exciting phrase to hear in science, the one that heralds new discoveries, is not "Eureka!" but "That's funny..."
— Isaac Asimov

The most important thing in the programming language is the name. A language will not succeed without a good name. I have recently invented a very good name and now I am looking for a suitable language.
— Donald Knuth

The most incomprehensible thing about the world is that it is comprehensible.
— Albert Einstein

The most insane pride is that which oscillates between deifying oneself and despising oneself.

— *Kierkegaard*

The most likely way for the world to be destroyed, most experts agree, is by accident. That's where we come in; we're computer professionals. We cause accidents.

— *Nathaniel Borenstein*

The most lonely place in the world is the human heart when love is absent.

The most overlooked advantage to owning a computer is that if they foul up there's no law against wacking them around a little.

The most utterly lost of all days is the one in which you have not once laughed.

The most valuable knowledge we can have is how to deal with disappointments.

— *Albert Schweitzer*

The most wasted of all days is that during which one has not laughed.

The most wonderful of all things in life, I believe, is the discovery of another human being with whom one's relationship has a glowing depth, beauty, and joy as the years increase. This inner progressiveness of love between two human beings is a most marvelous thing, it cannot be found by looking for it or by passionately wishing for it. It is a sort of Divine accident.

— *Hugh Walpoe*

The myth of unlimited production brings war in its train as inevitably as clouds announce a storm.

— *Albert Camus*

The name of Poet was almost forgotten; that of Orator was usurped by the sophists. A cloud of critics, of compilers, of commentators, darkened the face of learning, and the decline of genius was soon followed by the corruption of taste.

— *Edward Gibbon*

The national budget must be balanced. The public debt must be reduced; the arrogance of the authorities must be moderated and controlled. Payments to foreign governments must be reduced, if the nation doesn't want to go bankrupt. People must again learn to work, instead of living on public assistance.

— *Marcus Tullius*

Tears will get you sympathy. Sweat will get you results.

Technological progress is like an axe in the hands of a pathological criminal.
— Albert Einstein

Ted Kennedy's car has killed more people than my gun.

Teenage boys will drive anything — except a lawn mower.

Teenager with nose rings, baggy clothing and spiked hair to a friend: "I don't really like dressing this way, but it keeps my parents from dragging me everywhere they go."

Teenagers express their burning desires to be different by dressing exactly alike.

Television — a medium. So called because it is neither rare nor well—done.
— Ernie Kovacs

Television ruins more minds than drugs.

Tell a man that there are 400 billion stars in the sky, and hell believe you. Tell him a bench has wet paint and he has to touch it

Tell me who admires you and loves you, and I will tell you who you are.
— Charles Auoustin Sainte-Beauve

Tell me, I'll forget Show me, I may remember, but involve me, and I'll understand.

Telling the boss what a good worker you are is worth 1%; showing him is worth 99%.

Telling the truth and making someone cry is just as bad as telling a lie and making someone smile!

Thank God for dirty dishes, they have a tale to tell. While others may go hungry, we've eaten very well. With home, health and happiness, I shouldn't want to fuss. By the stack of evidence, God's been very good to us.

That place is so crowded, nobody goes there anymore.
— Yogi Berra

That which does not kill us makes us stronger.

The best antique is an old friend.

The best kind of friend is the one you could sit on a porch, swing with, never saying a word, and then walk away feeling like that was best conversation you've had.

The best proof of love is trust
— Joyce Brothers

The best thing about the future is that it only comes one day at a time.
— Abraham Lincoln

Proverbs

The best thing to sleep on is a dear conscience. The best tranquilizer is a good conscience.

The best way of teaching is by being an example.

The best way to predict your future is to create it!

The better you know someone, the less there is to say. Or may be, there's less that needs to be said.

The biggest mistake people make in life is not trying to make a living at doing what they most enjoy.

— *Malcolm S. Forbes*

The biggest temptation is to settle for too little.

The books that the world calls immoral are the books that show the world it's own shame.

— *Oscar Wilde*

The brain is a wonderful organ; it starts working the moment you get up in the morning and does not stop until you get into the office.

— *Robert Frost*

The brightest future will always be based on a forgotten past you can't go on well in life until you let go of your past failures and heartaches.

The brute necessity of believing something so long as life lasts does not justify any belief in particular.

— *George Santayana*

The call of death is a call of love death can be sweet if we answer it.

— x —

U

Ulcers are caused not so much by what we eat as what's eating us.

Ulcers are contagious. You can get them from your boss.

Ulcers are something you get from mountain climbing over molehills. Uncle Sam has the whole world eating out of his hand.

Under a democratic government the citizens exercise the powers of sovereignty; and those powers will be first abused, and afterwards lost, if they are committed to an unwieldy multitude.
— *Edward Gibbon*

Unemployment takes the worry out of being late for work.

Unfortunately, an unfounded rumor isn't one that is lost.

Unless virtue guide us, our choice must be wrong.

Unless you are the lead sled dog, the view never changes.

Until the lions have their historians, tales of the hunt shall always glorify the hunter.

Use what talents you possess; the woods would be very silent if no birds sang there except those that sang best.

Usenet is a way of being annoyed by people you never would have met.

Usenet is like a herd of performing elephants with diarrhea — massive, difficult to redirect, awe—inspiring, entertaining, and a source of mind—boggling amounts of excrement when you least expect it.
— *Gene Spafford*

Usenet is like Tetris for people who still remember how to read.

— x —

Proverbs

Vacation is what you take when you can't take what you've been taking any longer.

Value is coextensive with reality.
— Whitehead

Verbosity leads to unclear, inarticulate things.
— Dan Quayle

Vicious as a tigress can be, she never eats her own cubs.

Victory begins with the name of Jesus on our lips, but it will not be consummated until the nature of Jesus is in our hearts.

Violence is the last refuge of the incompetent. Never let your morals stop you from doing what is right.
— Isaac Asimov

Virtue cannot separate itself from reality without becoming a principle of evil.
— Albert Camus

Virtue flourishes in misfortune.

Virtue has more admirers than followers.

Virtue never dwells alone; it always has neighbors.

Vision is not seeing things as they are, but as they will be.

Vision without action is merely a dream. Action without vision just passes time. Vision with action can change the world. A true leader must first see an idea as opportunity, then choose to act upon it.
— Joel Barker

Vital papers will demonstrate their vitality by spontaneously moving from where you left them to where you can't find them.

Voting by mail was conceived to encourage election fraud.

— x —

War never decides who is right, only who is left.

Warm fronds often freeze up at the mention of cash.

Watch your thoughts; they become words. Watch your words; they become actions. Watch your actions; they become habits. Watch your habits; they become character. Watch your character; for it becomes your destiny!

Watching a peaceful death of a human being reminds us of a falling star; one of a million lights in a vast sky that flares up for a brief moment only to disappear into the endless night forever.
— *Elisabeth Kibler–Ross*

We all agree that the nicest people in the world are those who minimize our faults and magnify our virtues.

We all carry within us our places of exile, our crimes, and our ravages. But our task is not to unleash them on the world; it is to fight them in ourselves and in others.
— *Albert Camus*

We all dream; we do not understand our dreams, yet we act as if nothing strange goes on in our sleep minds, strange at least by comparison with the logical, purposeful doings of our minds when we are awake.
— *Erich Fromm*

We all get heavier as we get older because there is a lot more information in our heads.
— *Vlade Divac*

We all sorely complain of the shortness of time, and yet have much more than we know what to do with. Our lives are either spent in doing nothing at all, or in doing nothing to the purpose, or in doing nothing that we ought to do. We are always complaining that our days are few, and acting as though there would be no end of them.
— *Seneca*

We all suffer from the preoccupation that there exists.. .in the loved one, perfection.
— *Sidney Poitier*

We always deceive ourselves twice about the people we love — first to their advantage, then to their disadvantage.
— *Albert Camus*

Proverbs

We Americans, we're a simple people.. .but piss us off, and we'll bomb your cities.
— *Robin Williams*

We are all born for love. It is the principle of existence, and its only end.
— *Benjamin Disraeli*

We are all mortal until the first kiss and second glass of wine.
— *Eduardo Galwano*

We are always getting ready to live, but never living.
— *Ralph Waldo Emerson*

We are here to add what we can to life, not to get what we can from it.
— *William Osler*

We are in danger of forgetting that we cannot do what God does, and that God will not do what we can do.
— *Oswald Chambers*

We are living in a world today where lemonade is made from artificial flavors and furniture polish is made from real lemons.
— *Alfred E. Neuman*

We are never defeated unless we give up.

We are not certain, we are never certain. If we were we could reach some conclusions, and we could, at last, make others take us seriously.
— *Albert Camus*

We are not here to live our lives in the best way possible; to perform to the highest standards of excellence; to leave a legacy that will stand the test of time; to make this world a better place for our children and their children, and their children; to amaze other worldly life with our unassailable morality. We are here cause God needed a comedy channel.
— *Young Liu*

We are not so much concerned if you are slow as when you come to a halt.

We are not without accomplishment. We have managed to distribute poverty equally.
— *Nguyen Co Thatch*

We are ready for any unforeseen event that may or may not occur.
— *Dan Quayle*

We are sometimes so interested in creating the machinery of the church that we let the fire go out in the boiler.

We are the center of our own universe. Do not let yourself into a tangle by letting the gravity of other cosmic bodies to distract your own.
— *Jerry Ru*

We are the hero of our own story.

We are what we repeatedly do. Excellence, therefore, is not an act but a habit.
— *Aristotle*

We are what we think. All that we are arises with our thoughts. With our thoughts, we make the world.
— *Buddha*

We are, each of us, angles with only one wing, and we can only fly embracing each other.
— *Luciano DeCrescenzo*

We call love what binds us to certain creatures only by reference to a collective way of seeing for which books and legends are responsible.
— *Albert Camus*

We call that person who has lost his father, an orphan; and a widower that man who has lost his wife. But that man who has known the immense unhappiness of losing a friend, by what name do we call him? Here every language is silent and holds its peace in impotence.
— *Joseph Roux*

We can admire what we see, but we can only love what we truly know.

We can be knowledgeable with other men's knowledge, but we cannot be wise with other men's wisdom.
— *Michel de Montaigne*

We can learn much from wise words, little from wisecracks, and less from wise guys.

We cannot assert the innocence of anyone, whereas we can state with certainty the guilt of all. Every man testifies to the crime of all the others — that is my faith and my hope.
— *Albert Camus*

We cherish our friends not for their ability to amuse us, but for ours to amuse them.
— *Evelyn Waugh*

We come into the world laden with the weight of an infinite necessity.
— *Albert Camus*

We could accomplish a lot more if we'd get rid of our it's and and's; and get off our butts.

We could all take a lesson from the weather. It pays no attention to criticism.

We do not believe in immortality because we can prove it, but we try to prove it because we cannot help believing it.
— Harriet Martineau

We do not need a reason to feel sad; nor do we need a reason to cry.
— Jason Q.

We don't stop playing because we grow old, we grow old because we stop playing.

We don't want to go back to tomorrow, we want to go forward.
— Dan Quayle

We don't have economical problems, yet we have political ones.
— Elimo Leite Cordeiro

We find confort among those who agree with us, growth among those who don't.

We find that the sexual instinct, when disappointed and unappeased, frequently seeks and finds a substitute in religion.
— Baron Richard Von Krafft-Ebing

We grow great by dreams. All big men are dreamers. They see things in the soft haze of a spring day or in the red fire of a long winter's evening. Some of us let these great dreams die, but others nourish and protect them; nurse them through bad days till they bring them to the sunshine and light which comes always to those who sincerely hope that their dreams will come true.
— Woodrow Wilson

We have a firm commitment to NATO, we are a part of NATO. We have a firm commitment to Europe. We are a part of Europe.
— Dan Quayle

We have all heard that a million monkeys banging on a million typewriters will eventually reproduce the entire works of Shakespeare. Now, thanks to the Internet, we know this is not true.
— Robert Silensky

We have invented many things, but we have no mastered the creation of life. We cannot even create an insect.
— Albert Schweitzer

We have never learned to support the things we support with the enthusiasm with which we oppose the things we oppose.

We have no more right to consume happiness without producing it than to consume wealth without producing it.

We have not inherited the earth from our ancestors, we have only borrowed it from our children.

We have not the reverent feeling for the rainbow that a savage has, because we know how it is made. We have lost as much as we gained by prying into that matter.
— Mark Twain

We have shared the incommunicable experience of war. In our youths, our hearts were touched by fire.
— Oliver Wendall Holmes

We learn from experience that people seldom learn from experience.

We learn more by looking for the answer to a question and not finding it than we do from learning the answer itself.
— Lloyd Alexander

We learn the rope of life by untying the knots.

We live in a dark frightening age. One reason for this is the part played by the ideology of inhumanity in our time.
— Albert Schweitzer

We live in a society where pizza gets to your house before the police.

We made too many wrong mistakes.
— Yogi Berra

We make a living by what we get, but we make a life by what we give.
— Winston Churchill

We make our friends; we make our enemies; but God makes our next-door neighbor.
— G. K. Chesterton

We must laugh before we are happy, for fear we die before we laugh at all.
— Jean de La Bruvere

We must learn to live together as brothers or perish together as fools.

We must one and for all admit that there is another side... that it is suffering and that we are behaving disgracefully.
— Avraham Shalom, on Israel's tough
military tactics toward the Palestinians

We need to be reminded more than we need to be educated.

We never see the target a man aims at in life; we see only the target he hits.

We occasionally stumble over the truth, but most of us pick ourselves up and hurry on as if nothing happened.

Proverbs

We often see further through a tear than through a telescope.

We ourselves feel that what we are doing is just a drop in the ocean, but the ocean would be less because of that missing drop.

— *Mother Teresa*

We rate ability in men by what they finish, not by what they attempt.

We should go forward, groping our way through the darkness, stumbling perhaps at whiles, and try to do what good lies in our power.

— *Albert Camus*

We should take care not to make the intellect our god; it has, of course, powerful muscles, but no personality.

— *Albert Einstein*

We spend more time working for our labor—saving machines than they do working for us.

We still can't understand how rumors without a leg to stand on get around so fast.

We the people, lest we forget who we are.

We the unwilling working for the ungrateful are doing the impossible.

We have done so much, for so long, with so little, we are now qualified to do anything with nothing.

We treat this world of ours as though we had a spare in the trunk.

We used to wonder where war lived, what it was that made it so vile.

And now we realize that we know where it lives, that it is inside ourselves.

— *Albert Camus*

We won't go far without enthusiasm, but neither will we go far if that's all we have.

We wonder why the dogs always drink out of our toilets, but look at it from their point of view: Why do humans keep peeing into their water bowls?

We would all like to vote for the best man but he is never a candidate.

We're all capable of mistakes, but I do not care to enlighten you on the mistakes we may or may not have made.

— *Dan Quayle*

We're bom to shimmer, we're bom to shine, we're bom to radiate, we're bom to live, we're bom to love, we're bom to never hate.
— Shawn Mullins

We're going to have the best—educated American people in the world.
— Dan Quayle

We're not lost We're locationally challenged.

We've got to pause and ask ourselves: How much clean air do we need?
— Lee Iacocca

Weakness of attitude becomes weakness of character.
— Albert Einstein

Wealth buys leisure, but not wisdom.

Weeping may endure for a night, but joy cometh in the morning.

Welcome to President Bush, Mrs. Bush, and my fellow astronauts.
— Dan Quayle

Well done is better than well said.
— Benjamin Franklin

Were we too strong to let our love die or were we just too weak to kill it?

What a dog I got. His favorite bone is in my arm!

What a peculiar privilege has this little agitation of the brain which we call 'thought'.
— Hume

What a person believes is not as important as how a person believes.
— Timothy Virkkala

What a waste it is to lose one's mind. Or not to have a mind is being very wasteful. How true that is.
— Dan Quayle

What a wonderful life I've had! I only wish I'd realized it sooner. What business has science and capitalism got bringing all these new inventions into the works, before society has produced a generation educated up to using them.
— Henrik Ibsen

What flowers grow between your nose and your chin? Tulips.

What has four legs and an arm? A happy pit bull.

What I like in a good author is not what he says, but what he whispers.
— Logan Pearsall Smith

What I'm looking for is a blessing that's not in disguise.
— Kitty O'Neil Collins

What if everything is an illusion and nothing exists? In that case, I definitely overpaid for my carpet.
— Woody Allen

What is a committee? A group of the unwilling, picked from the unfit, to do the unnecessary.
— Richard Harkness

What is a friend? A single soul dwelling in two bodies.
— Aristotle

What is a rebel? A man who says no.
— Albert Camus

What is called a reason for living is also an excellent reason for dying.
— Albert Camus

What is faith but to believe what you do not see?

What is life? A madness. What is life? An illusion, a shadow, a story, and the greatest good is little enough, for all life is a dream...
— Calderon de la Barca

What is life? It is the flash of a firefly in the night. It is the breath of a buffalo in the wintertime. It is the little shadow which runs across the grass and loses itself in the sunset.
— Crowfoot

What is moral is what you feel good after.
— Ernest Hemingway

What is right is often forgotten by what is convenient.

What is the difference between a Peeping Tom and someone who's just got out of the bath? One is aide and nosy, and the other's nude and rosy.

What is the most important thing to learn in chemistry? Never lick the spoon.

What kills a skunk is the publicity it gives itself.
— Abraham Lincoln

What lies behind us, and what lies before us are tiny matters compared to what lies within us.

What nature of being are we that even our dreams can be compromised?
— Alex Tan

What now is proved was once only imagined.
— William Blake

What passes as a womans intuition, is usually nothing more than a mans transparency.

What really matters is what happens in us, not to us.

What soap is for the body, tears are for the soul.

What some people mistake for the high cost of living, is really the cost of living high.

What sunshine is to flowers, smiles are to humanity.

What the caterpillar calls the end, the butterfly calls the beginning.

What we call human nature, is actually human habit.
— Jewel

What we need is a toy that picks itself off the floor.

What we see is mainly what we look for.

What you are is God's gift to you, what you become is your gift to God.

What you are will show in what you do.
— Thomas Edison

What you can't get out of, get into whole-heartedly.

What you do when you don't have to do it will determine what you are when its too late to do anything about it!

What you have done becomes the judge of what you are going to do, especially in other people's minds. When you are travelling, you are what you are right there and then. People don't have your past to hold against you. No yesterdays on the road.
— William Least Heat Moon

What you see and hear depends a good deal on where you are standing; it also depends on what sort of person you are.
— C.S. Lewis

What your laugh at tells, plainer than words, what you are.

What's another word for Thesaurus?
— Steven Wright

Whatever you do, or dream, begin it now. Boldness has genius, power and magic in it. Begin it now.
— Johann Wolfgang Goethe

Whatever your wages are, save a little.
— Andrew Carnegie

Proverbs

Whatsoever that be within us that feels, thinks, desires, and animates, is something celestial, divine, and, consequently, imperishable.
— *Aristotle*

When a finger points at the moon, the imbecile looks at the finger.

When a friend is in trouble, don't annoy him by asking if there is anything you can do. Think of something appropriate and do it.
— *E.W. Hobe*

When a man is in love or in debt, someone else has the advantage.
— *Bill Balance*

When a man is wrong and won't admit it, he always becomes angry.

When a man's best friend is his dog, that dog has a problem.
— *Edward Abbey*

When a person wants to believe something, it doesn't take much to convince them.

When a piece gets difficult, make faces.
— *Artur Schnabel*

When all men think alike, no one thinks very much.
— *Walter Lippmann*

When all of your wishes are granted, many of your dreams will be destroyed.
— *Marilyn Manson*

When beholding the tranquil beauty and brilliancy of the ocean's skin, one forgets the tiger heart that pants beneath it; and would not willingly remember that this velvet paw but conceals a remorseless fang.
— *Herman Melville*

When death knocks at your door, you must answer.

When dogs leap onto your bed, it's because they adore being with you. When cats leap onto your bed, it's because they adore your bed.
— *Alisha Everett*

When God allows a burden to be put upon you, He will put His arms underneath you to help you carry it.

When God closes a door He opens a window.

When God measures a person, he measures around the heart instead of the head.

When I consider the short duration of my life, swallowed up in the eternity before and after, the little space I fill, and even can see, engulfed in the infinite immensity of space of which I am ignorant, and which knows me not, I am frightened, and am astonished at being here rather than there, why now rather than then.
— *Blaise Pascal*

When I consider this carefully, I find not a single property which with certainty separates the waking state from the dream. How can you be certain that your whole life is not a dream?
— *Rene Descartes*

When I find myself fading, I close my eyes and realize my friends are my energy.

When I hold you like tomorrow you might die.. .well, that's because you might.

When I pray, coincidences happen, and when I don't pray, they don't.
— *William Temple*

When I see waste here, I feel angry on the inside. I don't approve of myself getting angry; but it's something you can't help after seeing Ethiopia.
— *Mother Teresa*

When I see you a blanket of stars covers me in my bed.

When I told you I loved you, I meant it, but only because I wanted to please you. When I touched you, and my eyes told you I loved you, I meant it because I'm bad at lying.
— *Claire Breaux*

When I was a boy of fourteen, my father was so ignorant I could hardly stand to have the old man around. But when I got to be twenty–one, I was astonished at how much he had learned in seven years.
— *Mark Twain*

When I was a kid, my favourite relative was Uncle Caveman. After school we'd all go play in his cave, and every once in awhile he would eat one of us. It wasn't until later that I found out that Uncle Caveman was a bear.

When I was young I used to pray for a bike. Then I realized that God doesn't work that way, so I stole a bike and prayed for forgiveness.

When I wash the cat, it takes me hours to get the hair off my tongue.

Proverbs

When in doubt, be vague.
— *Jenn Book*

When in doubt, tell the truth.
— *Mark Twain*

When in doubt, think!
— *George Shen*

When in doubt, use brute force.
— *Ken Thompson*

When it comes to music lessons, most kids make it a practice not to practice.

When it's dark the stars come out.

When life gives you lemons, squeeze out a smile.

When life gives you lemons, use them for lemonade!
—*Kwong*

When love ends, ask yourself, "Is it better to forgive than forget or is it better to forget than forgive?"

When one door of happiness closes, another opens: but often we look so long at the closed door that we do not see the one which has been opened for us.
— *Helen Keller*

When one eye is fixed upon your destination, there is only one eye left with which to see the way there.
— *Matthew Wallace*

When one robs another of virtue, he loses his own.

When people agree with me I always feel that I must be wrong.
— *Oscar Wilde*

When people are free to do as they please, they usually imitate each other.
— *Eric Hoffer*

When people stop laughing they grow old, but if you get a laugh out of life you'll always stay young.

When power leads man towards arrogance, poetry reminds him of his limitations. When power narrows the areas of man's concern, poetry reminds him of he richness and diversity of his existence. When power corrupts, poetry cleanses, for art establishes the basic human truths which must serve as the touchstone of our judgement.
— *John F. Kennedy*

When Satan reminds you of your past, remind him of his future.

When saving for old age, be sure to put away a few pleasant thoughts.

When signing a contract, it helps to remember "the big-type gives, and the small-type takes away."

When someone is having a bad day, be silent; sit close by and nuzzle them gently.

When someone says, "Do you want my opinion?" it's always a negative one.

When tempted to fight fire with fire, remember that the Fire Department usually uses water.

When the age of the Vikings came to a close, they must have sensed it Probably, they gathered together one evening, slapped each other on the back and said, "Hey, good job."

When the alarm clock rings the best part of the day is over.

When the bosses talk about improving productivity, they are never talking about themselves.

When the devil starts messing, God starts blessing.
— R.W. Schambach

When the game is over, the king and the pawn go into the same box.

When the leaves bum summer ends. Summers gone, you wasted every day.
— Buffalo Tom

When the mouth stumbles, it is worse than the foot.

When the people we love are stolen from us, the only way to keep them is to never stop loving them, people die, buildings bum, but eternal love lasts forever.

When the situation is desperate, it is too late to be serious. Be playful.

When the tide of life turns against you, and the current upsets your boat, don't waste time on what might have been; just lie on your back and float.

When the waves are round me breaking, as I pace the deck alone, and my eye in vain is seeking some green leaf to rest upon; what would not I give to wander where my old companions dwell? Absence makes the heart grow fonder, Isle of Beauty, fare thee well!
— John Milton

When there's a will, there's a way. When there's a won't, there isn't.

When they broke open molecules, they found they were only stuffed with atoms. But when they broke open atoms, they found them stuffed with explosions.

Proverbs

When things are going well, something will go wrong. When things just can't get any worse, they will. Anytime things appear to be going better, you have overlooked something.

When two people are under the influence of the most violent, most insane, most delusive, and most transient of passions, they are required to swear that they will remain in that excited, abnormal, and exhausting condition continuously until death do them part.

— *Georoe Bernard Shaw*

When we die we leave behind us all that we have and take with us all that we are.

When we die we leave behind us all that we have and take with us all that we are.

When we observe contemporary society one thing strikes us. We debate but make no progress. Why? Because as people we do not yet trust each other.

— *Albert Schweitzer*

When we seek to discover the best in others, we somehow bring out the best in ourselves.

— *William Arthur Ward*

When written in Chinese, the word crisis is composed of two characters. One represents danger and other represents opportunity.

— *John F. Kennedy*

When you aim for perfection you discover it is a moving target.

When you are arguing with an idiot, make sure the other person isn't doing the same thing.

When you are frustrated about love and want to abandon it, ask yourself firmly, "Will I regret it?"

— *Bernard Yen*

When you are not sure where you are going, you are on the road to opportunity.

— *Alan Bauermiester*

When you are standing on the edge of a cliff a step forward is not progress.

When you are through changing, you are through.

— *Bruce Barton*

When you bow, bow low.

When you cease to use your faith, you lose it.

When you come to a fork in the road, take it!

— *Yogi Berra*

When you don't know what to do, walk fast and look worried.

When you fall in a dream, sometimes you die, sometimes you wake up, and sometimes you learn to fly.
— Neil Gaiman

When you finally go back to your old hometown, you find it wasn't the old home you missed but your childhood.
— Sam Ewing

When you fool a fool you strike a blow for intelligence.
— Giacomo de Seingalt

When you forgive it takes you from the place of the victim to that of a victor.

When you have once seen the glow of happiness on the face of a beloved person, you know that a man can have no vocation but to awaken that light on the faces surrounding him; and you are torn by the thought of the unhappiness and night you cast by the mere fact of living, in the hearts you encounter.
— Albert Camus

When you hear a kind word spoken about a friend, tell her so.

When you judge another, you do not define them, you define yourself.
— Wayne Dyer

When you laugh at something that happens to somebody else, that's a sense of humor. If it happens to you, that's an outrage.

When you live in a cookie—cutter world being different is a sin. So you don't stand out and you don't fit in.
— Hanson

When you live in the shadow of insanity, the appearance of another mind that thinks and talks as yours does is something dose to a blessed event
— Robert Pirsig

When you long with all your heart for someone to love you, a madness grows there that shakes all sense from the trees and the water and the earth. And nothing lives for you, except the long deep bitter want And this is what everyone feels from birth to death.
— Denton Welch

When you reach the end of your rope, tie a knot in it and hang on.
— Thomas Jefferson

When you squeeze an orange, orange juice comes out — because that's what's inside. When you are squeezed, what comes out is what is inside.
— Wayne Dyer

When you teach your son, you teach your son's son.
— *Talmud Kidskin*

When you think that you have lost someone, look into your heart and often you will their footprints, footprints they have left you so you will never truly lose them.

When you were born, you cried and the world rejoiced. Live your life in such a manner that when you die the world cries and you rejoice.

When your conscious becomes unconscious, you are drunk. When your unconscious becomes conscious, you are stoned.

When your dreams turn to dust, vacuum.

When your mother dies.. .that is when you know everybody dies.
— *Jeanne Beskrone*

Whenever I have to decide between two evils, I always choose the one I haven't tried before.
— *Mae West*

Whenever we fan the flames of a rumor, we're likely to get burned ourselves.

Whenever you find that you are on the side of the majority, it is time to reform.
— *Mark Twain*

Where God guides, He provides. Where love leads, happiness follows.

Where there is great love, there are always wishes.
— *Willa Cather*

Where there is love there is life.
— *Mahatma Gandhi*

Where there is music, there can be no harm.

Where we love is home, home that our feet may leave, but not our hearts.
— *Oliver Wendall Holmes*

Where will you be sitting in eternity, smoking or non-smoking? Where you're going is more important then where you stand.

Wherever you are, be all there.
— *Jim Elliot*

Which comes first Chicken or Egg? Egg, because animals have been laying eggs before the coming of chicken AND chicken eggs.

Which dreams indeed are ambition, for the very substance of the ambitious is merely the shadow of a dream.
— *William Shakespeare*

While hunting in Africa, I shot an elephant in my pajamas. How an elephant got into my pajamas I'll never know.
— *Groucho Marx*

While one person hesitates because he feels inferior, the other is busy making mistakes and becoming superior.
— *Henry C. Link*

While the law of competition may be sometimes hard for the individual, it is best for the race, because it ensures the survival of the fittest in every department.
— *Andrew Carnegie*

While we stop to think, we often miss our opportunity.
— *Publilius Syrus*

While we try to teach our children all about life, our children teach us what life is all about.
— *Angela Schwindth*

While you are away, movie stars are taking your women. Robert Redford is dating your girlfriend, Tom Selleck is kissing your lady, Bart Simpson is making love to your wife.

Who controls the past controls the future; who controls the present controls the past.
— *George Orwell*

Who do you turn to when the only person in the world who can stop you from crying is the exact person who is making you cry?

Who got it, did get it; and who left it, did regret it.

Who says nothing is impossible, I have been doing nothing for years.

Who travels for love finds a thousand miles not longer than one.

Who will tell whether one happy moment of love or the joy of breathing or walking on a bright morning and smelling the fresh air, is not worth all the suffering and effort which life implies...
— *Erich Fromm*

Whoever claimed that love is like a roller coaster, didn't know what they were talking about because love has no safety belts in case you fall out.
— *Becky Meynell*

Whoever follows a crowd will never be followed by a crowd.

Whoever gossips to you will gossip about you.

Whoever is happy will make others happy too.

Whoever loved that loved not at first sight?
— *Christopher Marlow*

Whoever said you cant buy happiness forgot about puppies.
— *Gene Hill*

Whoever serves his country well has no need of ancestors.

Whoever thinks of going to bed before twelve o'clock is a scoundrel.
— *Samuel Johnson*

Whoever today speaks of human existence in terms of power, efficiency, and 'historical tasks' is an actual or potential assassin.
— *Albert Camus*

Whoever undertakes to set himself up as a judge of Truth and Knowledge is shipwrecked by the laughter of the gods.
— *Albert Einstein*

Whom we love best to them we can say least.
— *Ray*

Why is it that our memory is good enough to retain the least triviality that happens to us, and yet not good enough to recollect how often we have told it to the same person?
— *La Rouchefoucauld*

Why is it that we rejoice at a birth and grieve at a funeral? It is because we are not the person involved.
— *Mark Twain*

Why not make friends before you need them?

Will power is eating just one salted peanut. Win with humility; lose with grace.

Winning isn't everything, but losing isn't anything.

Winter is in my head, but Spring is in my heart.

Wisdom is a comb given to a man once he is bald.

Wisest is he who knows he does not know.

With every passing hour our solar system comes forty-three thousand miles closer to globular cluster 13 in the constellation Hercules, and still there are some misfits who continue to insist that there is no such thing as progress.
— *Ransom K. Perm*

With memory set smarting like a reopened wound, a man's past is not simply a dead history, an outworn preparation of the present. It is not a repented error shaken loose from the life. It is a still quivering part of himself, bringing shudders and bitter flavors and the tinglings of a merited shame.
— *George Eliot*

With money you are a dragon; with no money, a worm.

With prayer as with other gifts from God, it is not what you get that counts, it's what you do with it.

Within you I lose myself Without you I find myself, wanting to be lost again.

Without culture, and the relative freedom it implies, society, even when perfect, is but a jungle. This is why any authentic creation is a gift to the future.
— Albert Camus

Without music, life would be a mistake.
— Friedrich Nietzsche

Without realizing it, the individual composes his life according to the laws of beauty even in times of greatest distress.
— Milan Kundera

Without respect, love cannot go far.
— Alexander Dumas

Without rice, even the cleverest housewife cannot cook.

Without risk there is no opportunity for gain.

Without sorrow, we would never recognize happiness.

Woman absent is woman dead.
— Ambrose Bierce

Women and cats will do as they please, and men and dogs should relax and get used to the idea.
— Robert A. Heinlein

Women would be more charming if one could fall into her arms without falling into her hands.
— Ambrose Bierce

Women's creed: Men are like linoleum. If you lay them right the first time, you can walk on them for 20 years.

Words may lie; music can not
— Frank Damrosch

Work harder, millions on welfare depends on you.

Work is the refuge of people who have nothing better to do.
— Oscar Wilde

Wrinkles should merely indicate where smiles have been.

Writing free verse is like playing tennis with the net down.
— Robert Frost

Writing is a socially acceptable form of schizonhrenia

— x —

Y

Years wrinkle the skin, but lack of enthusiasm wrinkles the soul.

Yes, children are deductible, but they also can be taxing.

Yesterday I was a dog. Today I'm a dog. Tomorrow I'll probably still be a dog. Sigh! There's so little hope for advancement.
— *Snoopy*

Yesterday is a cancelled cheque. Tomorrow is a promised note. Today is ready cash, use it!

Yesterday is but a dream, and tomorrow is only a vision... But today well-lived makes every yesterday a dream of happiness and every tomorrow a vision of hope.

Yesterday is history, tomorrow is a mystery, today is a gift of God, which is why we call it the present.
— *Bill Keane*

You always find something in the last place you look.

You always have to give up something you want for something you want more.

You always write it's bombing, bombing, bombing. It's not bombing, it's air support.
— *David Opfer*

You are never a loser until you quit trying.
— *Mike Ditka*

You are never fully dressed until you wear a smile.

You are only hurting yourself by hating, since often times the person you hate doesn't know it, and the others don't care.

You are young only once, but you can be immature all your life.

You ask whether I have ever been in love: fool as I am, I am not such a fool as that But if one is only to talk from first-hand experience, conversation would be a very poor business. But though I nave no personal experience of the things they call love, I have what is better - the experience of Sappho, of Euripides, of Catallus, of Shakespeare, of Spenser, of Austen, of Bronte, of anyone else I have read.
— *C.S. Lewis*

You better think about the future, for it's where you will spend the rest of your life.

You can always get someone to love you — even if you have to do it yourself.

You can always tell a cat, but you cant tell him much.

You can blow out a candle, but you can't blow out a fire, once the flame begins to catch, the wind will blow it higher.
— *Peter Gabriel*

You can call it madness, but i call it love.
— *Don Byas*

You can chain me, you can torture me, you can even destroy this body, but you will never imprison my mind.
— *Mahatma Gandhi*

You can discover more about a person in an hour of play than in a year of conversation.
— *Plato*

You can discover what your enemy fears most by observing the means he uses to frighten you.
— *Eric Hoffer*

You can get more with a kind word and a gun than you can with a kind word atone.
— *Al Capone*

You can give without loving, but you cant love without giving.

You can go anywhere you want if you look serious and carry a clipboard.

You can kill a thousand; you can bring an end to life; you cannot kill an idea.
— *Shimon Peres*

You can leave home, but home never leaves you.

You can listen to thunder after lightening and tell how dose you came to getting hit. If you don't hear it you got hit so never mind.

You can measure a programmer's perspective by noting his attitude on the continuing viability of FORTRAN.
— *Alan Pertis*

You can never understand the true value of something until you don't have it anymore.

You can observe a lot by just watching.

You can send a message around the world in 1/7 of a second; yet it may take several years to move a simple idea through a 1/4 inch of human skull.

Proverbs

You can survive on charm for about 5 minutes. After that, you'd better know something!

You can think negatively or positively. If you are a positive thinker, you will base your decisions on faith rather than fear

You can win more friends with your ears than you can with your mouth!

You can't always control the circumstances in life, but you can control your attitude toward those circumstances.
— *Alexander Lockhart*

You can't build character and courage by taking away men's initiative and independence.

You can't do anything, if you believe you cant. You cant get to the top by sitting on your bottom.

You can't have everything. Where would you put it?
— *Steven Wright*

You can't help the poor man by destroying the rich.

You can't save your ass and your face at the same time.

You can't shake hands with a clenched fist
— *Indira Gandhi*

You can't strengthen the weak by weakening the strong.

You can't tell which way the train went by looking at the track.
— *Jeanne Thevaites*

You can't test courage cautiously.

You can't train a horse with shouts, and expect it to obey a whisper.

You can't trample infidels when you're a tortoise. I mean, all you could do is give them a meaningful look.
— *Terry Pratchett*

You can't turn back the dock but you can wind it up again.

You can't walk with God, and hold hands with Satan.

You cannot acquire experience by making experiments.

You cannot create experience. You must undergo it
— *Albert Camus*

You cannot always wait for the perfect time. Sometimes you must dare to jump.
— *Yasmeen Bleeth*

You cannot control the length of your life, but you can control its breadth, depth, and height.

You cannot make a deal with honor, valor cannot be bought, magic cannot be caught, love cannot be taught.

You cannot push anyone up a ladder unless he is willing to climb a little.
— *Andrew Carnegie*

You cannot step twice into the same river, for other waters are continually flowing on.
— *Heraclitus of Ephesus*

You cannot undermine police authority and then complain about rising crime.

You did touch me but didn't feel my pain. Jesus came and touched me and I don't feel the pain any more.

You don't become a missionary by crossing the sea but by seeing the cross. You don't have to agree with me, but its quicker.

You don't know what you know until you know what you don't know!
— *John F. Kennedy*

You don't look at a picture of a Chevy when you drive a Cadillac.

You don't love a woman because she is beautiful, but she is beautiful because you love her.

You either have to be first, best, or different.
— *Loretta Lynn*

You enter into a certain amount of madness when you marry a person with pets.
— *Nora Ephron*

You get education by reading the fine print. .and experience by not reading it.

You have to do your own growing no matter how tall your grandfather was.
— *Abraham Lincoln*

You have to protect the privacy of the advice you get, or you'll never get the advice you need.
— *Richard Nixon*

You know children are growing up when they start asking questions that have answers.
— *John J. Plomp*

You know what would make a good story? Something about a down who makes people happy, but inside he's real sad. Also, he has severe diarrhea.

You know what's the most terrifying thing about admitting that you're in love? You're just naked. You put yourself in harm's way and you lay down all your defences. No clothes, no

Proverbs

weapons. Nowhere to hide, completely vulnerable. The only thing that makes it tolerable is to believe the other person loves you back and you can trust him not to hurt you.

— *Mary Doria Russell*

You know you are getting old when you get your annual dental check-up by mail.

You know you love someone when you want them to be happy even if their happiness means that you're not a part of it.

You know you're getting old when you know your way around, but you don't feel like going.

You know your children are growing up when they stop asking you where they came from and refuse to tell you where they're going.

— *P. J. O'Rourke*

You know, a heart can be broken, but it still keeps a-beatin' just the same.

— *Fried Green Tomatoes*

You long for success? Start at the bottom; dig down.

You may glean knowledge by reading, but you must separate the chaff from the wheat by thinking.

You may not realize it when it happens, but a kick in the teeth may be the best thing in the world for you.

— *Walt Disney*

You may pass violets looking for roses and contentment looking for victory.

You may say that I'm a dreamer, but I'm not the only one.

— *John Lennon*

You must be tired, because you've been running through my mind all day!

You must continue to gain expertise, but avoid thinking like an expert.

— *Denis Waitley*

You must first be a believer if you would be an achiever.

You need to recognize and sweep aside certain weaknesses which stand between you and your goals. Your persistence develops into a respected, proved, progressive power.

— *Napoleon Hill*

You need to start worrying about health if you can't sleep when it's time to get up.

You never asked me to write this email to you, so sue me for sending unsolicited email.

— *Kenny Huang*

You never really understand a person until you consider things from his point of view.

You only have one chance to make a first impression.

You satisfy the hungry heart with gift of finest wheat Now give to us, O saving Lord, the bread of life to eat.

You say that I have no power? Perhaps you speak truly, but you say that Dreams have no power here? Tell me — what power would hell have if those here imprisoned were not able to dream of heaven?
— Morpheus

You see, wire telegraph is a kind of a very, very long cat You pull his tail in New York and his head is meowing in Los Angeles. Do you understand this? And radio operates exactly the same way: you send signals here, they receive them mere. The only difference is that there is no cat.
— Albert Einstein

You should always go to a vet who is also a taxidermist. Either way, you get your dog back.

You should never have your best trousers on when you turn out to fight for freedom and truth.
— Henrik Ibsen

You should not confuse your career with your life.

You spend your whole life believing that you're on the right track, only to discover that you're on the wrong train.

You will always be lucky if you know how to make friends with strange cats.

You will face many defeats in your life, but never let yourself be defeated.
— Mava Anoelou

You will find as you look back upon your life that the moments when you have truly lived are the moments when you have done things in the spirit of love.
— Henry Drummond

You will never be happy if you continue to search for what happiness consists of. You will never live if you are looking for the meaning of life.
— Albert Camus

You will scon break the bow if you keep it always stretched.
— Phaedrus

You win more friends in life by being interested in others than trying to get others interested in you.
— Dale Carnegie

Proverbs

You would make a ship sail against the winds and currents by lighting a bon-fire under her deck... I have no time for such nonsense.
— *Napoleon*

You wouldn't care what people thought of you if you realized how seldom they do.

You wrote me a beautiful letter, I wonder if you meant it to be as beautiful as it was. I think you did; for somehow I know that your feeling for me, however slight it is, is of the nature of love... When you tell me to come, I will come, by the next train, just as I am. This is not meekness, be assured; I do not come naturally by meekness; know that it is a proud surrender to You.
— *Edna St. Vincent Millay*

You'd better start giving me mouth to mouth, because you just took my breath away!

You're in middle age when you realize you have more on your mind and less on your head.

You're not old until it takes you longer to rest than it does to get tired.

You've been in love with someone for a decade - someone who barely knows you're alive. You've done everything, tried everything to make this person see that you're a valuable, estimable person, and that your love is worth something. Then one day you open the paper and glance at the Personals column, and there you see that your loved one has placed an ad...seeking someone worthwhile to love and be loved by.
— *Daniel Quinn*

You've got a lot of choices. If getting out of bed in the morning is a chore and you're not smiling on a regular basis, try another choice.
— *Steven D. Woodhull*

You've got to dance like nobody's watching, and Jove like it's never going to hurt.
— *Kathy Mattea*

You've never been as old as you are this minute, and you'll never be as young again.

You've reached middle age when all you exercise is caution.

You've reached middle age when the phone rings on Saturday night, you pray it isn't for you.

You've seen one nuclear holocaust, you've seen them all.

You, yourself, as much as anybody in the entire universe, deserve your love and affection.
— *Buddha*

Young love is a flame; very pretty, often very hot and fierce, but still only light and flickering. The love of the older and disciplined heart is as coals, deep burning, unquenchable.
— Henry Ward Beecher

Your actions speak so loud that I cant hear what you're saying.

Your attitude is the librarian of your past, the speaker of your present, and the prophet of your future!

Your brain is that bodily organ which starts working the moment you awake and does not stop until you get into the office.

Your dreams can be realities. They are the stuff that leads us through life toward great happiness.
— Deborah Norville

Your food stamps will be stopped effective March 1932 because we received notice that you passed away. May God bless you. You may reapply if there is a change in your circumstances.

Your getting old when you get the same sensation from a rocking chair that you once got from a roller coaster

Your life and my life flow into each other as wave flows into wave, and unless there is peace and joy and freedom for you, there can be no real peace or joy or freedom for me. To see reality - not as we expect it to be but as it is - is to see that unless we live for each other and in and through each other, we do not really live very satisfactorily; that there can really be life only where there really is, in just this sense, love.
— Frederick Buechner

Your life would be very empty if you had nothing to regret. Your temper is the only thing you can lose and still have.

Your tongue is in a wet place, take care it doesn't slip.
— Teri Nutton

Your true friends are those who can pick on you and you seem really pissed off but you always laugh at their harmless jokes in the end.
— Charles J. Duncan

Your vision will become dear only when you look into your heart... Who looks outside, dreams. Who looks inside, awakens.
— Carl Jung

Your words are my food, your breath my wine. You are everything to me.
— Sarah Bernhardt

Your worst days are never so bad that you are beyond the reach of God's grace. And your best days are never so good that you are beyond the need of God's grace.
— *Jerry Bridges*

Youth is easily deceived, because it is quick to hope.
— *Aristotle*

— x —

Z

Zeal is fit only for wise men, but is found mostly in fools.

Zeal without knowledge is fanaticism

— xx —

PROVERBS BY SUBJECTS

1. ART

(i) Literature

Literature always anticipates life. It does not copy it, but moulds it to its purpose. The nineteenth century, as we know it, is largely an invention of Balzac.
— *Wilde, Oscar*

The difference between literature and journalism is that journalism is unreadable and literature is not read.
— *Wilde, Oscar*

Anybody can write a three-volume novel. It merely requires a complete ignorance of both life and literature.
— *Wilde, Oscar*

In literature the ambition of the novice is to acquire the literary language: the struggle of the adept is to get rid of it.
— *Shaw, George Bernard*

Leisure without literature is death and burial alive.
— *Seneca, Lucius Annaeus*

The atmosphere of orthodoxy is always damaging to prose, and above all it is completely ruinous to the novel, the most anarchical of all forms of literature.
— *Orwell, George*

The existence of good bad literature - the fact that one can be amused or excited or even moved by a book that one's intellect simply refuses to take seriously - is a reminder that art is not the same thing as cerebration.
— *Orwell, George*

Literature is a toil and a snare, a curse that bites deep.
— *Lawrence, D. H.*

The decline in literature indicates a decline in the nation. The two keep pace in their downward tendency.
— *Goethe, Johann Wolfgang Von*

People do not deserve to have good writings; they are so pleased with the bad.
— *Emerson, Ralph Waldo*

Literature always anticipates life. It does not copy it, but moulds it to its purpose. The nineteenth century, as we know it, is largely an invention of Balzac.
— *Wilde, Oscar*

The difference between literature and journalism is that journalism is unreadable and literature is not read.
— Wilde, Oscar

Anybody can write a three-volume novel. It merely requires a complete ignorance of both life and literature.
— Wilde, Oscar

In literature the ambition of the novice is to acquire the literary language: the struggle of the adept is to get rid of it.
— Shaw, George Bernard

Leisure without literature is death and burial alive.
— Seneca, Lucius Annaeus

The atmosphere of orthodoxy is always damaging to prose, and above all it is completely ruinous to the novel, the most anarchical of all forms of literature.
— Orwell, George

The existence of good bad literature - the fact that one can be amused or excited or even moved by a book that one's intellect simply refuses to take seriously - is a reminder that art is not the same thing as cerebration.
— Orwell, George

Literature is a toil and a snare, a curse that bites deep.
— Lawrence, D. H.

The decline in literature indicates a decline in the nation. The two keep pace in their downward tendency.
Goethe, Johann Wolfgang Von

People do not deserve to have good writings; they are so pleased with the bad.
Emerson, Ralph Waldo

(ii) Writers

I never know what I think about something until I read what I've written on it.
— Faulkner, William

To write well, express yourself like common people, but think like a wise man. Or, think as wise men do, but speak as the common people do.
— Aristotle

The greatest part of a writer's time is spent in reading, in order to write; a man will turn over half a library to make one book.
— Johnson, Samuel

Every author in some degree portrays himself in his works, even if it be against his will.
— Goethe, Johann Wolfgang Von

Proverbs by Subjects

He who does not expect a million readers should not write a line.
— *Goethe, Johann Wolfgang Von*

If any man wishes to write a clear style, let him first be clear in his thoughts.
— *Goethe, Johann Wolfgang Von*

Either write something worth reading or do something worth writing.
— *Franklin, Benjamin*

I have the conviction that excessive literary production is a social offence.
— *Eliot, George*

In all pointed sentences, some degree of accuracy must be sacrificed to conciseness.
— *Johnson, Samuel*

Writing is a dreadful labor, yet not so dreadful as Idleness.
— *Carlyle, Thomas*

Composition is, for the most part, an effort of slow diligence and steady perseverance, to which the mind is dragged by necessity or resolution, and from which the attention is every moment starting to more delightful amusements.
— *Johnson, Samuel*

If I had not existed, someone else would have written me, Hemingway, Dostoevski, all of us.
— *Faulkner, William*

The tools I need for my work are paper, tobacco, food, and a little whiskey.
— *Faulkner, William*

There is no luck in literary reputation. They who make up the final verdict upon every book are not the partial and noisy readers of the hour when it appears; but a court as of angels, a public not to be bribed, not to be entreated, and not to be overawed, decides upon every man's title to fame.
— *Emerson, Ralph Waldo*

If I don't write to empty my mind, I go mad. As to that regular, uninterrupted love of writing, I do not understand it. I feel it as a torture, which I must get rid of, but never as a pleasure. On the contrary, I think composition a great pain.
— *Lord Byron*

Nothing so fretful, so despicable as a Scribbler, see what I am, and what a parcel of Scoundrels I have brought about my ears,

and what language I have been obliged to treat them with to deal with them in their own way; - all this comes of Authorship.
— *Lord Byron*

To withdraw myself from myself has ever been my sole, my entire, my sincere motive in scribbling at all.
— *Lord Byron*

In general I do not draw well with literary men — not that I dislike them but I never know what to say to them after I have praised their last publication.
— *Lord Byron*

An author who speaks about his own books is almost as bad as a mother who talks about her own children.
— *Disraeli, Benjamin*

How vain it is to sit down to write when you have not stood up to live.
— *Thoreau, Henry David*

A writer must teach himself that the basest of all things is to be afraid.
— *Faulkner, William*

A writer is congenitally unable to tell the truth and that is why we call what he writes fiction.
— *Faulkner, William*

This morning I took out a comma and this afternoon I put it back in again.
— *Wilde, Oscar*

His style is chaos illumined by flashes of lightning. As a writer he has mastered everything except language.
— *Wilde, Oscar*

From the point of view of literature Mr. Kipling is a genius who drops his aspirates. From the point of view of life, he is a reporter who knows vulgarity better than any one has ever known it.
— *Wildem Oscar*

As to the adjective, when in doubt strike it out.
— *Twain, Mark*

Most writers regard the truth as their most valuable possession, and therefore are economical in its use.
— *Twain, Mark*

I know not, Madam, that you have a right, upon moral principles, to make your readers suffer so much.
— *Johnson, Samuel*

A perfectly healthy sentence, it is true, is extremely rare. For the most part we miss the hue and fragrance of the thought; as

if we could be satisfied with the dews of the morning or evening without their colors, or the heavens without their azure.
— Thoreau, Henry David

A writer needs three things, experience, observation, and imagination, any two of which, at times any one of which, can supply the lack of the others.
— Faulkner, William

The man who writes about himself and his own time is the only man who writes about all people and about all time.
— Shaw, George Bernard

You must not suppose, because I am a man of letters, that I never tried to earn an honest living.
— Shaw, George Bernard

When an author is too meticulous about his style, you may presume that his mind is frivolous and his content flimsy.
— Seneca, Lucius Annaeus

It is excellent discipline for an author to feel that he must say all that he has to say in the fewest possible words, or his readers is sure to skip them.
— Ruskin, John

For a creative writer possession of the "truth" is less important than emotional sincerity.
— Orwell, George

Of all that is written, I love only what a person has written with his own blood.
— Nietzsche, Friedrich

I write in order to attain that feeling of tension relieved and function achieved which a cow enjoys on giving milk.
— Mencken, Henry Louis

Write without pay until somebody offers to pay you. If nobody offers within three years, sawing wood is what you were intended for.
— Twain, Mark

(iii) Critics

The person of analytic or critical intellect finds something ridiculous in everything. The person of synthetic or constructive intellect, in almost nothing.
— Goethe, Johann Wolfgang Von

Critics are already made.
— Lord Byron

A man must serve his time to every trade save censure - critics all are ready made.
— Lord Byron

The covers of this book are too far apart.
— Bierce, Ambrose

No sadder proof can be given of a person's own tiny stature, than their disbelief in great people.
— Cartyle, Thomas

The artist doesn't have time to listen to the critics. The ones who want to be writers read the reviews, the ones who want to write don't have the time to read reviews.
— Faulkner, William

If all printers were determined not to print anything till they were sure it would offend nobody, there would be very little printed.
— Franklin, Benjamin

It is much easier to be critical than to be correct.
— Disraeli, Benjamin

Critics are those who have failed in literature and art.
— Disraeli, Benjamin

If I care to listen to every criticism, let alone act on them, then this shop may as well be closed for all other businesses. I have learned to do my best, and if the end result is good then I do not care for any criticism, but if the end result is not good, then even the praise of ten angels would not make the difference.
— Lincoln, Abraham

If the end brings me out all right, what is said against me won't amount to anything. If the end brings me out wrong, then ten angels swearing I was right would make no difference.
— Lincoln, Abraham

Blame is safer than praise.
— Emerson Ralph, Waldo

Criticism should not be querulous and wasting, all knife and root-puller, but guiding, instructive, inspiring.
— Emerson Ralph Waldo

Their is no defense against criticism except obscurity.
— Addison, Joseph

Strike the dog dead, it's but a critic!
— Goethe, Johann Wolfgang Von

On an occasion of this kind it becomes more than a moral duty to speak one's mind, it becomes a pleasure.
— Wilde, Oscar

To avoid criticism, do nothing, say nothing, be nothing.
— Hubbard, Elbert

Criticism, as it was first instituted by Aristotle, was meant as a standard of judging well.

— *Johnson, Samuel*

Criticism is a study by which men grow important and formidable at very small expense. He whom nature has made weak, and idleness keeps ignorant, may yet support his vanity by the name of a critic.

— *Johnson, Samuel*

I would rather be attacked than unnoticed. For the worst thing you can do to an author is to be silent as to his works. An assault upon a town is a bad thing; but starving it is still worse.

— *Johnson, Samuel*

Prolonged, indiscriminate reviewing of books is a quite exceptionally thankless, irritating and exhausting job. It not only involves praising trash but constantly inventing reactions towards books about which one has no spontaneous feeling whatever.

— *Orwell, George*

It is impossible to think of a man of any actual force and originality, universally recognized as having those qualities, who spent his whole life appraising and describing the work of other men.

— *Mencken, Henry Louis*

Criticism is prejudice made plausible.

— *Mencken, Henry Louis*

I am sorry to think that you do not get a man's most effective criticism until you provoke him. Severe truth is expressed with some bitterness.

— *Thoreau, Henry David*

The public is the only critic whose opinion is worth anything at all.

— *Twain, Mark*

Temperament is the primary requisite for the critic — a temperament exquisitely susceptible to beauty, and to the various impressions that beauty gives us.

— *Wilde, Oscar*

The critic has to educate the public; the artist has to educate the critic.

— *Wilde, Oscar*

The true critic is he who bears within himself the dreams and ideas and feelings of myriad generations, and to whom no form of thought is alien, no emotional impulse obscure.

— *Wilde. Oscar*

Men over forty are no judges of a book written in a new spirit.
— *Emerson, Ralph Waldo*

(iv) Music

Without music, life would be a mistake.
— *Nietzsche, Friedrich*

Music, the greatest good that mortals know, and all of heaven we have below.
— *Addison, Joseph*

Hell is full of musical amateurs: music is the brandy of the damned.
— *Shaw, George Bernard*

Music causes us to think eloquently.
— *Emerson, Ralph Waldo*

If you look deep enough you will see music; the heart of nature being everywhere music.
— *Carlyle, Thomas*

Music is well said to be the speech of angels; in fact, nothing among the utterances allowed to man is felt to be so divine. It brings us near to the infinite.
— *Carlyle, Thomas*

Song is the heroics of speech.
— *Carlyle, Thomas*

One is hardly sensible of fatigue while he marches to music.
— *Carlyle, Thomas*

The effects of good music are not just because it's new; on the contrary music strikes us more the more familiar we are with it.
— *Goethe, Johann Wolfgang Von*

It is the only sensual pleasure without vice.
— *Johnson, Samuel*

Difficult do you call it, Sir? I wish it were impossible.
— *Johnson, Samuel*

Nothing is capable of being well set to music that is not nonsense.
— *Addison, Joseph*

Only sick music makes money today.
— *Nietzsche, Friedrich*

Musical people are so absurdly unreasonable. They always want one to be perfectly dumb at the very moment when one is longing to be absolutely deaf.
— *Wilde, Oscar*

The opera is to music what a bawdy house is to a cathedral.
— *Mencken, Henry Louis*

Music when healthy, is the teacher of perfect order, and when depraved, the teacher of perfect disorder.
— *Ruskin, John*

The man that hath no music in himself, nor is not moved with concord of sweet sounds, is fit for treasons, stratagems, and spoils. The motions of his spirit are dull as night, and his affections dark as Erebus. Let no such man be trusted.
— *Shakespeare, William*

Is it not strange that sheep's guts should hale souls out of men's bodies?
— *Shakespeare, William*

If music be the food of love; play on.
— *Shakespeare, William*

The pleasure we feel in music springs from the obedience which is in it.
— *Thoreau, Henry David*

There are German songs which can make a stranger to the language cry.
— *Twain, Mark*

If one hears bad music, it is one's duty to drown it by one's conversation.
— *Wilde, Oscar*

Without music, life would be an error. The German imagines even God singing songs
— *Nietzsche, Friedrich*

— x —

2. DEFECTS

(i) Jealousy

Jealousy contains more of self-love than of love.
— *La Rochefoucauld, Francois de*

Jealously is always born with love but it does not die with it.
— *La Rochefoucauld, Francois de*

Who surpasses or subdues mankind, must look down on the hate of those below.
— *Lord, Byron*

The disease of jealously is so malignant that is converts all it takes into its own nourishment.
— Addison, Joseph

Plain women are always jealous of their husbands. Beautiful women never are. They are always so occupied with being jealous of other women's husbands.
— Wilde, Oscar

Never waste jealousy on a real man: it is the imaginary man that supplants us all in the long run.
— Shaw, George Bernard

I had rather be a toad, and live upon the vapor of a dungeon than keep a corner in the thing I love for others uses.
— Shakespeare, William

Live on doubts; it becomes madness or stops entirely as soon as we pass from doubt to certainty.
— La Rochefoucauld, Francois de

Jealousy is never satisfied with anything short of an omniscience that would detect the subtlest fold of the heart.
— Eliot, George

There is a sort of jealousy which needs very little fire; it is hardly a passion, but a blight bred in the cloudy, damp despondency of uneasy egoism.
— Eliot, George

(ii) Ignorance

I would rather have my ignorance than another man's knowledge, because I have so much of it.
— Twain, Mark

When I was fourteen, my father was so ignorant I could hardly stand to have him around. When I got to be twenty-one,! was astonished at how much he had learned in seven years.
— Twain, Mark

Ignorance is like a delicate fruit; touch it, and the bloom is gone.
— Wilde, Oscar

There is no darkness, but ignorance.
— Shakespeare, William

Being ignorant is not so much a shame as being unwilling to learn.
— Franklin, Benjamin

Nothing is more terrible than to see ignorance in action.
— Goethe, Johann Wolfgang Von

To be conscience that you are ignorant is a great step to knowledge.
— *Disraeli, Benjamin*

He was so learned that he could name a horse in nine languages; so ignorant that he bought a cow to ride on.
— *Franklin, Benjamin*

A learned blockhead is a greater blockhead than an ignorant one.
— *Franklin, Benjamin*

I do not believe in the collective wisdom of individual ignorance.
— *Cartyle, Thomas*

(iii) Envy

Man will do many things to get himself loved; he will do all things to get himself envied.
— *Twain, Mark*

The sure mark of one born with noble qualities is being born without envy.
— *La Rochefoucauld, Francois de*

It is not enough to succeed, others must fail.
— *La Rochefoucauld, Francois de*

There is no sweeter sound than the crumbling of ones fellow man.
— *Groucho, Marx*

Envy is more irreconcilable than hatred.
— *La Rochefoucauld, Francois de*

Oh, what a bitter thing it is to look into happiness through another man's eyes.
— *Shakespeare, William*

His scorn of the great is repeated too often to be real; no man thinks much of that which he despises.
— *Johnson, Samuel*

Men are so constituted that every one undertakes what he sees another successful in, whether he has aptitude for it or not.
— *Goethe, Johann Wolfgang Von*

Envy is the tax which all distinction must pay.
— *Emerson, Ralph Waldo*

None of the affections have been noted to fascinate and bewitch but envy.
— *Bacon, Francis*

(iv) Madness

Madness is something rare in individuals — but in groups, parties, peoples, ages it is the rule.
— *Nietzsche, Friedrich*

No excellent soul is exempt from a mixture of madness.
— *Aristotle*

We want a few mad people now. See where the sane ones have landed us!
— *Shaw, George Bernard*

No great genius has ever existed without some touch of madness.
— *Aristotle*

O, let me not be mad, not mad, sweet heaven I Keep me in temper. I would not be mad.
— *Shakespeare, William*

What can you do against the lunatic who is more intelligent than yourself, who gives your arguments a fair hearing and then simply persists in his lunacy?
— *Orwell, George*

— x —

3. FEELINGS

(i) Love

To be able to say how much love, is love but little.
— *Petrarch, Francesco*

The way to love anything is to realize that it might be lost.
— *Chesterton, Gilbert Keith*

The magic of first love is our ignorance that it can never end.
— *Disraeli, Benjamin*

Love and you shall be loved. All love is mathematically just, as much as the two sides of an algebraic equation.
— *Emerson, Ralph Waldo*

Keep love in your heart. A life without it is like a sunless garden when the flowers are dead.
— *Wilde, Oscar*

Love possesses not nor will it be possessed, for love is sufficient unto love.
— *Gibran, Kahlil*

Who loves, raves.
— *Lord Byron*

When we are in love we seem to ourselves quite different from what we were before.
— Pascal, Blaise

Frustrated love has been the incentive for many great works.
— Mitchell, John Newton

Love is the delusion that one man or woman differs from another.
— Mencken, Henry Louis

Love is a state in which a man sees things most decidedly as the are not.
— Nietzsche, Friedrich

There is no living with thee, nor without thee.
— Marcus Valerius, Martial

Love means to love that which is unlovable; or it is no virtue at all.
— Chesterton, Gilbert Keith

Love is the triumph of imagination over intelligence.
— Mencken, Henry Louis

If we are to judge of love by its consequences, it more nearly resembles hatred than friendship.
— La Rochefoucauld, Francois de

It is with true love as it is with ghosts; everyone talks about it, but few have seen it.
— La Rochefoucauld, Francois de

Love makes everything that is heavy light.
— Kempis, Thomas

Love is the wisdom of the fool and the folly of the wise.
— Johnson, Samuel

Love's like the measles; all the worse when it comes late in life.
— Jerrold, Douglas William

Love gives itself; it is not bought.
— Longfellow, Henry Wadsworth

Nuptial love makes mankind; friendly love perfects it; but wanton love corrupts and debases it.
— Bacon, Francis

Love sought is good, but given unsought is better.
— Shakespeare, William

Love must be as much a light, as it is a flame.
— Thoreau, Henry David

There is no remedy for love than to love more.
— Thoreau, Henry David

Love is made by two people, in different kinds of solitude. It can be in a crowd, but in an oblivious crowd.
— *Aragon, Louis*

In love, there is always one who kisses and one who offers the cheek.
— *French Proverb*

Love: A temporary insanity curable by marriage.
— *Bierce, Ambrose*

All mankind loves a lover.
— *Emerson, Ralph Waldo*

There is always something ridiculous about the emotions of people whom one has ceased to love.
— *Wilde, Oscar*

When one is in love, one always begins by deceiving one's self, and one always ends by deceiving others. That is what the world calls a romance.
— *Wilde, Oscar*

To be in love is merely to be in a perpetual state of anesthesia.
— *Mencken, Henry Louis*

Yet each man kills the thing he loves from all let this be heard some does it with a bitter look some with a flattering word the coward does it with a kiss the brave man with the sword.
— *Wilde, Oscar*

It is difficult to know at what moment love begins; it is less difficult to know that it has begun.
— *Longfellow, Henry Wadsworth*

People who are not in love fail to understand how an intelligent man can suffer because of a very ordinary woman. This is like being surprised that anyone should be stricken with cholera because of a creature so insignificant as the comma bacillus.
— *Proust, Marcel*

Many people when they fall in love look for a little haven of refuge from the world, where they can be sure of being admired when they are not admirable, and praised when they are not praiseworthy.
— *Russell, Bertrand*

Love is an emotion that is based on an opinion of women that is impossible for those who have had any experience with them.
— *Mencken, Henry Louis*

Love is swift, sincere, pious, joyful, generous, strong, patient, faithful, prudent, long-suffering, courageous, and never seeking

its own; for wheresoever a person seeketh his own, there he falleth from love.
— Kempis, Thomas

The spiritualization of sensuality is called love: it is a great triumph over Christianity.
— Nietzsche, Friedrich

To an ordinary human being, love means nothing if it does not mean loving some people more than others.
— Orwell, George

Accept the things to which fate binds you, and love the people with whom fate brings you together, but do so with all your heart.
— Marcus Aureiius

Wicked men obey from fear; good men, from love.
— Aristotle

For a crowd is not company; and faces are but gallery of pictures, and talk but a tinkling cymbal, where there is no love.
Bacon, Francis

Love is a better teacher than duty.
— Einstein, Albert

They do not love that do not show their love. The course of true love never did run smooth. Love is familiar. Love is a devil. There is no evil angel but Love.
— Shakespeare, William

True love makes the throught of death frequent, easy, without teoors; it merely becomes the standard of comparison, the price one would pay for many things.
— Stendhal

For what is love itself, for the one we love best? An enfolding of immeasurable cares which yet are better than and joys outsides our love.
— Eliot, George

A supreme love, a motive that gives a sublime rhythm to a woman's life, and exalts habit into partnership with the soul's highest needs, is not to be had where and how she wills.
— Eliot, George

I like not only to be loved, but also to be told that I am loved. I am not sure that you are of the same kind. But the realm of silence is large enough beyond the grave. This is the world of literature and speech and I shall take leave to tell you that you are very dear.
— Eliot, George

Love is not altogether a delirium, yet it has many points in common therewith.
— Carlyle, Thomas

Man's love is of man's life a part; it is a woman's whole existence. In her first passion, a woman loves her lover, in all the others all she loves is love.
— Lord Byron

Like the measles, love is most dangerous when it comes late in life.
— Lord Byron

We are all born for love. It is the principle of existence, and its only end.
— Disraeli, Benjamin

The power of love, as the basis of a State, has never been tried.
— Emerson, Ralph Waldo

We love those who admire us, but not those whom we admire.
— La Rochefoucauld, Francois de

If you wish to be loved; Love!
— Seneca, Lucius Annaeus

First love is only a little foolishness and a lot of curiosity: no really self-respecting woman would take advantage of it.
— Shaw, George Bernard

The fickleness of the women I love is only equaled by the infernal constancy of the women who love me.
— Shaw, George Bernard

Love bears it out even to the edge of doom.
— Shakespeare, William

But love is blind, and lovers cannot see What petty follies they themselves commit
— Shakespeare, William

Love is a smoke made with the fume of sighs. Being purged, a fire sparkling in lovers eyes. Being vexed, a sea nourished with lovers tears. What is it else? A madness most discreet, a choking gall and a preserving sweet.
— Shakespeare, William

When love begins to sicken and decay it uses an enforced ceremony. [Julius Caesar]
— Shakespeare, William

To say the truth, reason and love keep little company together now-a-days.
— Shakespeare, William

Love is too young to know what conscience is.
— Shakespeare, William

True love is like ghosts, which everybody talks about and few have seen.
— *La Rochefoucauld, Francois de*

Those whom true love has held, it will go on holding.
— *Seneca, Lucius Annaeus*

He who is in love is wise and is becoming wiser, sees newly every time he looks at the object beloved, drawing from it with his eyes and his mind those virtues which it possesses.
— *Emerson, Ralph Waldo*

We are nearer loving those who hate us than those who love us more than we wish.
— *La Rochefoucauld, Francois de*

Women wish to be loved not because they are pretty, or good, or well bred, or graceful, or intelligent, but because they are themselves.
— *Amiel, Henri Frederic*

There is no disguise that can for long conceal love where it exists or simulate it where it does not.
— *La Rochefoucauld, Francois de*

That is the true season of love; when we believe that we alone can love, that no one could ever have loved as much before, and that no one will ever love in the same way again.
— *Goethe, Johann Wolfgang Von*

We are shaped and fashioned by what we love.
— *Goethe, Johann Wolfgang Von*

If I love you, what business is it of yours?
— *Goethe, Johann Wolfgang Von*

Love is an ideal thing, marriage a real thing; a confusion of the real with the ideal never goes unpunished.
— *Goethe, Johann Wolfgang Von*

He that falls in love with himself will have no rivals.
— *Franklin, Benjamin*

Men have died from time to time, and worms have eaten them, but not for love.
— *Shakespeare, William*

(ii) Love Ended

When a man has once loved a woman, he will do anything for her, except continue to love her.
— *Wilde, Oscar*

She's gone. I am abused, and my relief must be to loathe her.
— *Shakespeare, William*

There are few people who are not ashamed of their love affairs when the infatuation is over.
— La Rochefoucauld, Francois de

But that intimacy of mutual embarrassment, in which each feels that the other is feeling something, having once existed, its effect is not to be done away with.
— Eliot, George

The best way will be to avoid each other without appearing to do so — or if we jostle, at any rate not to bite.
— Lord Byron

(iii) Lovers

What makes lovers never tire of one another is that they talk always about themselves.
— La Rochefoucauld, Francois de

Lovers are fools, but Nature makes them so.
— Hubbard, Elbert

It is a beautiful trait in the lovers character, that they think no evil of the object loved.
— Longfellow, Henry Wadsworth

There's nothing in the world like the devotion of a married woman. It's a thing no married man knows anything about.
— Wilde, Oscar

Age cannot wither her, nor custom stale her infinite variety. Other women cloy the appetites they feed, but she makes hungry where most she satisfies.
— Shakespeare, William

We that are true lovers run into strange capers.
— Shakespeare, William

The more one loves a mistress, the more one is ready to hate her.
— La Rochefoucauld, Francois de

Lovers may be — and indeed generally are — enemies, but they never can be friends, because there must always be a spice of jealousy and a something of Self in all their speculations.
— Lord Byron

In every loving woman there is a priestess of the past — a pious guardian of some affection, of which the object has disappeared.
— Amiel, Henri Frederic

(iv) Friendship

The ornament of a house is the friends who frequent it.
— Emerson, Ralph Waldo

A true friend is somebody who can make us do what we can.
— Emerson, Ralph Waldo

Am I not destroying my enemies when I make friends of them?
— Lincoln, Abraham

To the query, "What is a friend?" his reply was "A single soul dwelling in two bodies."
— Aristotle

Without friends, no one would want to live, even if he had all other goods.
— Aristotle

Suspicion is the cancer of friendship.
— Petrarch, Francesco

I didn't find my friends; the good Lord gave them to me.
— Emerson, Ralph Waldo

Those that are a friend to themselves are sure to be a friend to all.
— Seneca, Lucius Annaeus

A woman may very well form a friendship with a man, but for this to endure, it must be assisted by a little physical antipathy.
— Nietzsche, Friedrich

The worst solitude is to have no real friendships.
— Bacon, Francis

Friendship improves happiness, and abates misery, by doubling our joys, and dividing our grief.
— Addison, Joseph

The most I can do for my friend is simply be his friend.
—Thoreau, Henry David

Friendships, in general, are suddenly contracted; and therefore it is no wonder they are easily dissolved.
— Addison, Joseph

The friendships of the world are oft confederacies in vice, or leagues of pleasures.
— Addison, Joseph

Friendship is essentially a partnership.
— Aristotle

Friends, such as we desire, are dreams and fables.
— Emerson, Ralph Waldo

Go oft to the house of thy friend, for weeds choke the unused path.
— Emerson, Ralph Waldo

The glory of friendship is not in the outstretched hand, nor the kindly smile, nor the joy of companionship; it is in the spiritual inspiration that comes to one when he discovers that someone else believes in him and is willing to trust him.
— Emerson, Ralph Waldo

We talk of choosing our friends, but friends are self-elected.
— Emerson, Ralph Waldo

Every man passes his life in the search after friendship.
— Emerson, Ralph Waldo

He who has a thousand friends has not a friend to spare, And he who has one enemy will meet him everywhere.
— Emerson, Ralph Waldo

A friend is a person with whom I may be sincere. Before him, I may think aloud.
— Emerson, Ralph Waldo

I do then with my friends as I do with my books. I would have them where I can find them, but I seldom use them.
— Emerson, Ralph Waldo

It is one of the blessings of old friends that you can afford to be stupid with them.
— Emerson, Ralph Waldo

The greatest good you can do for another is not just to share your riches but to reveal to him his own.
— Disraeli, Benjamin

Best friend, my well-spring in the wilderness!
— Eliot, George

Without friends no one would choose to live.
— Aristotle

Friendships begin with liking or gratitude roots that can be pulled up.
— Eliot, George

Perhaps the most delightful friendships are those in which there is much agreement, much disputation, and yet more personal liking.
— Eliot, George

The only way to have a friend is to be one.
— Emerson, Ralph Waldo

I look upon every day to be lost, in which I do not make a new acquaintance.
— Johnson, Samuel

I have always laid it down as a maxim - and found it justified by experience —that a man and a woman make far better friendships than can exist between two of the same sex but then with the condition that they never have made or are to make love to each other.

— *Lord Byron*

In poverty and other misfortunes of life, true friends are a sure refuge. The young they keep out of mischief; to the old they are a comfort and aid in their weakness, and those in the prime of life they incite to noble deeds.

— *Aristotle*

I have had, and may have still, a thousand friends, as they are called, in life, who are like one's partners in the waltz of this world —not much remembered when the ball is over.

— *Lord Byron*

A mistress never is nor can be a friend. While you agree, you are lovers; and when it is over, anything but friends.

— *Lord Byron*

Friendship is Love without his wings.

— *Lord Byron*

Without friends the world is but a wilderness. There is no man that imparteth his joys to his friends, but he joyeth the more; and no man that imparteth his grieves to his friend, but he grieveth the less.

— *Bacon, Francis*

Wishing to be friends is quick work, but friendship is a slow-ripening fruit.

— *Aristotle*

A day for toil, an hour for sport, but for a friend is life too short.

— *Emerson, Ralph Waldo*

A man cannot be said to succeed in this life who does not satisfy one friend.

— *Thoreau, Henry David*

Friendship always benefits; love sometimes injures.

— *Seneca, Lucius Annaeus*

The friends thou hast, and their adoption tried, grapple them to thy soul with hoops of steel, but do not dull thy palm with entertainment of each new-hatched unfledged comrade.

— *Shakespeare, William*

Friendship is constant in all other things, Save in the office and affairs of love.

— *Shakespeare, William*

A friend should bear a friends infirmities, But Brutus makes mine greater than they are.
— Shakespeare, William

A friend is one that knows you as you are, understands where yo have been, accepts what you have become, and still gently allows you to grow.
— Shakespeare, William

Words are easy, like the wind; Faithful friends are hard to find.
— Shakespeare, William

There are three faithful friends, an old wife, an old dog, and ready money.
— Franklin, Benjamin

But a lifetime of happiness! No man alive could bear it: it would be hell on earth.
— Shaw, George Bernard

"A drop of honey catches more flies than a gallon of gal." So with men. If you would win a man to your cause, first convince him that you are his sincere friend. Therein is a drop of honey which catches his heart, which, say what he will, is the highroad to his reason.
— Lincoln, Abraham

One may discover a new side to his most intimate friend when for the first time he hears him speak in public. He will be stranger to him as he is more familiar to the audience. The longest intimacy could not foretell how he would behave then
— Thoreau, Henry David

The language of friendship is not words but meanings.
— Thoreau, Henry David

True friendship can afford true knowledge. It does not depend on darkness and ignorance.
— Thoreau, Henry David

We have not so good a right to hate any as our Friend.
— Thoreau, Henry David

The holy passion of friendship is of so sweet and steady and loyal and enduring a nature that it will last through a whole lifetime, if not asked to lend money.
— Twain, Mark

Laughter is not at all a bad beginning for a friendship, and it is far the best ending for one.
— Wilde, Oscar

The only service a friend can really render is to keep up your courage by holding up to you a mirror in which you can see a noble image of yourself.
— Shaw, George Bernard

In the misfortunes of our best friends we always find something not altogether displeasing to us.
— *La Rochefoucauld, Francois de*

The greatest sweetener of human life is Friendship. To raise this to the highest pitch of enjoyment, is a secret which but few discover.
— *Addison, Joseph*

In comradeship is danger countered best.
— *Goethe, Johann Wolfgang Von*

An acquaintance that begins with a compliment is sure to develop into a real friendship.
— *Wilde, Oscar*

If a man does not make new acquaintances as he advances through life, he will soon find himself left alone; one should keep his friendships in constant repair.
— *Johnson, Samuel*

Never, my dear Sir, do you take it into your head that I do not love you; you may settle yourself in full confidence both of my love and my esteem; I love you as a kind man, I value you as a worthy man, and hope in time to reverence you as a man of exemplary piety.
— *Johnson, Samuel*

The endearing elegance of female friendship.
— *Johnson, Samuel*

Men are more evanescent than pictures, yet one sorrows for lost friends, and pictures are my friends, I have none others. I am never long enough with men to attach myself to them; and whatever feelings of attachment I have are to material things.
— *Ruskin, John*

To let friendship die away by negligence and silence is certainly not wise. It is voluntarily to throw away one of the greatest comforts of the weary pilgrimage.
— *Johnson, Samuel*

The lonely one offers his hand too quickly to whomever he encounters.
— *Nietzsche, Friedrich*

What men have called friendship is only a social arrangement, a mutual adjustment of interests, an interchange of services given and received; it is, in sum, simply a business from which those involved propose to derive a steady profit for their own self-love.
— *La Rochefoucauld, Francois de*

A true friend is the greatest of all blessings, and that which we take the least care to acquire.
— *La Rochefoucauld, Francois de*

It is more shameful to distrust our friends than to be deceived by them.
— *La Rochefoucauld, Francois de*

However rare true love may be, it is less so than true friendship.
— *La Rochefoucauld, Francois de*

I don't like that man. I'm going to have to get to know him better.
— *Lincoln, Abraham*

I desire to so conduct the affairs of this administration that if at the end, when I come to lay down the reins of power, I have lost every other friend on earth, I shall at least have one friend left, and that friend shall be down inside of me.
— *Lincoln, Abraham*

A friend may well be reckoned the masterpiece of nature.
— *Emerson, Ralph Waldo*

The most fatal disease of friendship is gradual decay, or dislike hourly increased by causes too slender for complaint, and too numerous for removal.
— *Johnson, Samuel*

(v) Happiness

Happiness is an agreeable sensation, arising from contemplating the misery of others.
— *Bierce, Ambrose*

Happiness is a perfume which you cannot pour on someone without getting some on yourself.
— *Emerson, Ralph Waldo*

Three grand essentials to happiness in this life are something to do, something to love, and something to hope for.
— *Addison, Joseph*

For who is pleased with himself.
— *Johnson, Samuel*

Happiness is a ball after which we run wherever it rolls, and we push it with our feet when it stops.
— *Goethe, Johann Wolfgang Von*

The highest happiness of man is to have probed what is knowable and quietly to revere what is unknowable.
— *Goethe, Johann Wolfgang Von*

A person is never happy till their vague strivings has itself marked out its proper limitations.
— *Goethe, Johann Wolfgang Von*

What makes people happy is activity; changing evil itself into good by power, working in a God like manner.
— *Goethe, Johann Wolfgang Von*

The most happy man is he who knows how to bring into relation the end and beginning of his life.
— *Goethe, Johann Wolfgang Von*

The man who is born with a talent which he was meant to use finds his greatest happiness in using it.
— *Goethe, Johann Wolfgang Von*

Happiness consists more in small conveniences of pleasures that occur every day, than in great pieces of good fortune that happen but seldom to a man in the course of his life.
— *Franklin, Benjamin*

There are two ways of being happy: We must either diminish our wants or augment our means — either may do - the result is the same and it is for each man to decide for himself and to do that which happens to be easier.
— *Franklin, Benjamin*

Sir, that all who are happy, are equally happy, is not true. A peasant and a philosopher may be equally satisfied, but not equally happy. Happiness consists in the multiplicity of agreeable consciousness.
— *Johnson, Samuel*

I look on that man as happy, who, when there is question of success, looks into his work for a reply.
— *Emerson, Ralph Waldo*

To strive with difficulties, and to conquer them, is the highest human felicity.
— *Johnson, Samuel*

Happiness is a mystery, like religion, and should never be rationalized.
— *Chesterton, Gilbert Keith*

The only happiness a brave person ever troubles themselves in asking about, is happiness enough to get their work done.
— *Carlyle, Thomas*

To have joy one must share it. Happiness was born a twin.
— *Lord Byron*

Happiness is a sort of action.
— *Aristotle*

Happiness depends upon ourselves.
— Aristotle

If happiness is activity in accordance with excellence, it is reasonable that it should be in accordance with the highest excellence.
— Aristotle

To live we must conquer incessantly, we must have the courage to be happy.
— Amiel, Henri Frederic

True happiness arises, in the first place, from the enjoyment of one's self, and in the next, from the friendship and conversation of a few select companions.
— Addison, Joseph

Many persons have a wrong idea of what constitutes true happiness. It is not attained through self-gratification but through fidelity to a worthy purpose.
— Addison, Joseph

To fill the hour — that is happiness.
— Emerson, Ralph Waldo

If one only wished to be happy, this could be easily accomplished; but we wish to be happier that other people, and this is always difficult, for we believe others to be happier than they are.
— Montesquieu, Charles-Louis de Secondat

Some cause happiness wherever they go; others whenever they go.
— Wilde, Oscar

There are people who can do all fine and heroic things but one: keep from telling their happiness to the unhappy.
— Twain, Mark

Happiness ain't a thing in itself -it's only a contrast with something that ain't pleasant. And so, as soon as the novelty is over and the force of the contrast dulled, it ain't happiness any longer, and you have to get something fresh.
— Twain, Mark

We are made happy when reason can discover no occasion for it. The memory of some past moments is more persuasive than the experience of present ones. There have been visions of such breadth and brightness that these motes were invisible in their light.
— Thoreau, Henry David

Man is the artificer of his own happiness.
— Thoreau, Henry David

A lifetime of happiness? No man alive could bear it; it would be hell on earth.
— Shaw, George Bernard

Give a man health and a course to steer; and he'll never stop to trouble about whether he's happy or not.
— Shaw, George Bernard

Life at its noblest leaves mere happiness far behind; and indeed cannot endure it. Happiness is not the object of life: life has no object: it is an end in itself; and courage consists in the readiness to sacrifice happiness for an intenser quality of life.
— Shaw, George Bernard

We have no more right to consume happiness without producing it than to consume wealth without producing it.
— Shaw, George Bernard

I had rather have a fool make me merry, than experience make me sad.
— Shakespeare, William

Happiness is not a state to arrive at, rather, a manner of traveling.
— Johnson, Samuel

True happiness is to enjoy the present, without anxious dependence upon the future, not to amuse ourselves with either hopes or fears but to rest satisfied with what we have, which is sufficient, for he that is so wants nothing. The great blessings of mankind are within us and within our reach. A wise man is content with his lot, whatever it may be, without wishing for what he has not.
— Seneca, Lucius Annaeus

When we are happy we are always good, but when we are good we are not always happy.
— Wilde, Oscar

False happiness renders men stem and proud, and that happiness is never communicated. True happiness renders them kind and sensible, and that happiness is always shared.
— Montesquieu, Charles-Louis de Secondat

We wish to be happier than other people; and this is difficult, for we believe others to be happier than they are.
— Montesquieu, Charles-Louis de Secondat

Ask yourself whether you are happy, and you cease to be so.
— Mill, John Stuart

Happiness is not a possession to be prized. It is a quality of thought, a state of mind.
— du Maurier, Dame Daphne

Happy the man whose wish and care a few paternal acres bound, content to breathe his native air in his own ground.
— Pope, Alexander

Men can only be happy when they do not assume that the object of life is happiness.
— Orwell, George

A person will be just about as happy as they make up their minds to be.
— Lincoln, Abraham

We are never so happy nor so unhappy as we imagine.
— La Rochefoucauld, Francois de

We are more interested in making others believe we are happy than in trying to be happy ourselves.
— La Rochefoucauld, Francois de

We are long before we are convinced that happiness is never to be found; and each believes it possessed by others, to keep alive the hope of obtaining it for himself.
— Johnson, Samuel

But O, how bitter a thing it is to look into happiness through another man's eyes.
— Shakespeare, William

(vi) Fear

Shame arises from the fear of men, conscience from the fear of God.
— Johnson, Samuel

It is a miserable state of mind to have few things to desire and many things to fear.
— Bacon, Francis

Fear is the mother of morality.
— Nietzsche, Friedrich

People die of fright and live of confidence.
— Thoreau, Henry David

The best safety lies in fear.
— Shakespeare, William

In time we hate that which we often fear.
— Shakespeare, William

The first duty of man is to conquer fear; he must get rid of it, he cannot act till then.
— Carlyle, Thomas

Men fear death as children fear to go in the dark; and as that natural fear in children is increased with tales, so is the other.
— Bacon, Francis

You mistake me, my dear. I have a high respect for your nerves. They are my old friends. I have heard you mention them with consideration these twenty years at least.
— *Austen, Jane*

The timidity of the child or the savage is entirely reasonable; they are alarmed at this world, because this world is a very alarming place. They dislike being alone because it is verily and indeed an awful idea to be alone. Barbarians fear the unknown for the same reason that Agnostics worship it - because it is a fact.
— *Chesterton, Gilbert Keith*

Fear defeats more people than any other one thing in the world.
— *Emerson, Ralph Waldo*

Fear always springs from ignorance.
— *Emerson, Ralph Waldo*

Do the thing we fear, and the death of fear is certain.
— *Emerson, Ralph Waldo*

Always do what you are afraid to do.
— *Seneca, Lucius Annaeus*

Where the fear is, happiness is not.
— *Seneca, Lucius Annaeus*

A person's fears are lighter when the danger is at hand.
— *Seneca, Lucius Annaeus*

Fearless minds climb soonest into crowns.
— *Shakespeare, William*

— x —

5. MEDIA

(i) Journalism

Bad manners make a journalist.
— *Wilde, Oscar*

In the real world, nothing happens at the right place at the right time. It is the job of journalists and historians to correct that.
— *Twain, Mark*

Journalism consists largely in saying "Lord James is dead" to people who never knew Lord James was alive.
— *Chesterton, Gilbert Keith*

Journalism is popular, but it is popular mainly as fiction. Life is one world, and life seen in the newspapers another.
— *Chesterton, Gilbert Keith*

(ii) Television

TV is chewing gum for the eyes.
— Wright, Frank Lloyd

I find television very educational. Every time someone switches it on I go into another room and read a good book.
— Groucho, Marx

(iii) Newspapers

Newspapers have degenerated. They may now be absolutely relied upon.
— Wilde, Oscar

Early in life I had noticed that no event is ever correctly reported in a newspaper.
— Orwell, George

— x —

5. NATURE

(i) Life

And in the end, it's not the years in your life that count. It's the life in your years.
— Lincoln, Abraham

The tragedy of life is not so much what men suffer, but rather what they miss.
— Carlyle, Thomas

Not how long, but how well you have lived is the main thing.
— Seneca, Lucius Annaeus

What is important in life is life, and not the result of life.
— Goethe, Johann Wolfgang Von

There is no wealth but life.
— Ruskin, John

If we live truly, we shall see truly.
— Emerson, Ralph Waldo

The golden moments in the stream of life rush past us, and we see nothing but sand; the angels come to visit us, and we only know them when they are gone.
— Eliot, George

What do we live for; if it is not to make life less difficult to each other?
— Eliot, George

Life is a perpetual instruction in cause and effect.
— Emerson, Ralph Waldo

Proverbs by Subjects

Life is a succession of lessons which must be lived to be understood.
— *Emerson, Ralph Waldo*

Life too near paralyses art.
— *Emerson, Ralph Waldo*

Like bees, they must put their lives into the sting they give.
— *Emerson, Ralph Waldo*

The life of man is the true romance, which when it is valiantly conduced, will yield the imagination a higher joy than any fiction.
— *Emerson, Ralph Waldo*

Nothing is beneath you if it is in the direction of your life.
— *Emerson, Ralph Waldo*

It is not length of life, but depth of life.
— *Emerson, Ralph Waldo*

Live, let live, and help live Emerson.
— *Ralph Waldo*

The three great essentials to achieve anything worth while are: Hard work, Stick-to-itiveness, and Common sense.
— *Edison, Thomas Alva*

Life is the childhood of our immortality.
— *Goethe, Johann Wolfgang Von*

Life is too short to be little. Man is never so manly as when he feels deeply, acts boldly, and expresses himself with frankness and with fervor.
— *Disraeli, Benjamin*

When it comes to life the critical thing is whether you take things for granted or take them with gratitude.
— *Chesterton, Gilbert Keith*

The ideals which have always shone before me and filled me with the joy of living are goodness, beauty, and truth.
— *Einstein, Albert*

Life... It is a tale told by an idiot, full of sound and fury; signifying nothing.
— *Shakespeare, William*

The man who says he has exhausted life generally means that life has exhausted him.
— *Wilde, Oscar*

To live is the rarest thing in the world. Most people exist, that is all.
— *Wilde, Oscar*

We quaff the cup of life with eager haste without draining it, instead of which it only overflows the brim — objects press around us, filling the mind with the throng of desires that wait upon them, so that we have no room for the thoughts of death.
— Wilde, Oscar

Let us so live that when we come to die even the undertaker will be sorry.
— Twain, Mark

Life does not consist mainly, or even largely, of facts and happenings. It consists mainly of the storm of thought that is forever flowing through one's head.
— Twain, Mark

Most men lead lives of quiet desperation and go to the grave with the song still in them.
— Thoreau, Henry David

If I shall sell both my forenoons and afternoons to society, as most appear to do, I'm sure that, for me, there would be nothing left worth living for.
— Thoreau, Henry David

However mean your life is, meet it and live it; do not shun it and call it hard names. It is not so bad as you are. It looks poorest when you are the richest.
— Thoreau, Henry David

Life is a little gleam of time between two eternity s.
— Cariyle, Thomas

In private life I never knew anyone interfere with other people's disputes but he heartily repented of it.
— Carlyle, Thomas

Life's enchanted cup sparkles near the brim.
— Lord Byron

When one subtracts from life infancy (which is vegetation), sleep, eating and swilling, buttoning and unbuttoning — how much remains of downright existence? The summer of a dormouse.
— Lord Byron

Between two worlds life hovers like a star, twixt night and morn, upon the horizon's verge.
— Lord Byron

It is very certain that the desire of life prolongs it.
— Lord Byron

Don't be afraid of death so much as an inadequate life.
— Brecht, Bertolt

Life, A spiritual pickle preserving the body from decay.
— *Bierce, Ambrose*

Life, an age to the miserable, and a moment to the happy.
— *Bacon, Francis*

The energy of the mind is the essence of life.
— *Aristotle*

Life is no brief candle to me. It is a sort of splendid torch which I have got a hold of for the moment, and I want to make it burn as brightly as possible before handing it on to future generations.
— *Shaw, George Bernard*

Life is a disease; and the only difference between one man and another is the stage of the disease at which he lives. You are always at the crisis: I am always in the convalescent stage.
— *Shaw, George Bernard*

Life does not cease to be funny when people die any more than it ceases to be serious when people laugh.
— *Shaw, George Bernard*

Life's tragedy is that we get old too soon and wise too late
— *Franklin, Benjamin*

Life is as tedious as a twice-told tale.
— *Shakespeare, William*

I should have no objection to go over the same life from its beginning to the end: requesting only the advantage authors have, of correcting in a second edition the faults of the first.
— *Franklin, Benjamin*

So live with men as if God saw you and speak to God, as if men heard you.
— *Seneca, Lucius Annaeus*

Life is warfare.
— *Seneca, Lucius Annaeus*

I will govern my life and thoughts as if the whole world were to see the one and read the other, for what does it signify to make anything a secret to my neighbor, when to God, who is the searcher of our hearts, all our privacies are open?
— *Seneca, Lucius Annaeus*

It is advisable that a person know at least three things, where they are, where they are going, and what they had best do under the circumstances.
— *Ruskin, John*

Life is a dead-end street.
— *Mencken, Henry Louis*

If you believed more in life you would fling yourself less to the moment.
— *Nietzsche, Friedrich*

I love those who do not know how to live for today.
— *Nietzsche, Friedrich*

He that embarks on the voyage of life will always wish to advance rather by the impulse of the wind than the strokes of the oar; and many fold in their passage; while they lie waiting for the gale."
— *Johnson, Samuel*

Plunge boldly into the thick of life, and seize it where you will, it is always interesting.
— *Goethe, Johann Wolfgang Von*

Life! Life! Don't let us go to life for our fulfillment or our experience. It is a thing narrowed by circumstances, incoherent in its utterance, and without that fine correspondence of form and spirit which is the only thing that can satisfy the artistic
— *Wilde, Oscar*

Were it offered to my choice, I should have no objection to a repetition of the same life from its beginning, only asking the advantages authors have in a second edition to correct some faults in the first.
— *Franklin, Benjamin*

Life is short and we have never too much time for gladdening the hearts of those who are travelling the dark journey with us. Oh be swift to love, make haste to be kind.
— *Amiel, Henri Frederic*

Simply the thing I am shall make me live.
— *Shakespeare, William*

(ii) Death

One should die proudly when it is no longer possible to live proudly.
— *Nietzsche, Friedrich*

Death is the king of this world: Tis his park where he breeds life to feed him. Cries of pain are music for his banquet
— *Eliot, George*

See in what peace a Christian can die.
— *Addison, Joseph*

One who does not know when to die, does not know how to live.
— *Ruskin, John*

Proverbs by Subjects 251

One has to pay dearly for immortality; one has to die several times while one is still alive.

— Nietzsche, Friedrich

Die when I may, I want it said of me by those who knew me best, that I always plucked a thistle and planted a flower where I thought a flower would grow.

— Lincoln, Abraham

Neither the sun nor death can be looked at with a steady eye.

— La Rochefoucauld, Francois de

I will be conquered; I will not capitulate.

— Johnson, Samuel

It matters not how a man dies, but how he lives. The act of dying is not of importance, it lasts so short a time.

— Johnson, Samuel

A useless life is an early death.

— Goethe, Johann Wolfgang Von

Death is a commingling of eternity with time; in the death of a good man, eternity is seen looking through time.

— Goethe, Johann Wolfgang Von

The final hour when we cease to exist does not itself bring death; it merely of itself completes the death-process. We reach death at that moment, but we have been a long time on the way.

— Seneca, Lucius Annaeus

Our dead are never dead to us, until we have forgotten them.

— Eliot, George

A punishment to some, to some a gift, and to many a favor.

— Seneca, Lucius Annaeus

He who can no longer pause to wonder and stand rapt in awe is as good as dead; his eyes are closed.

— Einstein, Albert

I look upon death to be as necessary to our constitution as sleep. We shall rise refreshed in the morning.

— Franklin, Benjamin

Many people die at twenty five and aren't buried until they are seventy five.

— Franklin, Benjamin

I do not believe that any man fears to be dead, but only the stroke of death.

— Bacon, Francis

It is as natural to die as to be born; and to a little infant, perhaps, the one is as painful as the other.

— Bacon, Francis

It is natural to die as to be born.
— Bacon, Francis

For the sword outwears its sheath, and the soul wears out the breast. And the heart must pause to breathe, and love itself have rest.
— Lord Byron

I have seen a thousand graves opened, and always perceived that whatever was gone, the teeth and hair remained of those who had died with them. Is not this odd? They go the very first things in youth and yet last the longest in the dust.
— Lord Byron

Death, so called, is a thing which makes men weep, and yet a third of life is passed in sleep.
— Lord Byron

The fear of death often proves mortal, and sets people on methods to save their Lives, which infallibly destroy them.
— Addison, Joseph

When death comes it is never our tenderness that we repent from, but our severity.
— Eliot, George

Life levels all men. Death reveals the eminent.
— Shaw, George Bernard

I am dying beyond my means.
— Wilde, Oscar

Alas, I am dying beyond my means.
— Wilde, Oscar

For he who lives more lives than one: More deaths than one must die.
— Wilde, Oscar

Whoever has lived long enough to find out what life is, knows how deep a debt of gratitude we owe to Adam, the first great benefactor of our race. He brought death into the world.
— Twain, Mark

Why is it that we rejoice at birth and grieve at a funeral? It is because we are not the person involved.
— Twain, Mark

We owe a deep debt of gratitude to Adam, the first great benefactor of the human race: he brought death into the world.
— Twain, Mark

We never become really and genuinely our entire and honest selves until we are dead — and not then until we have been dead years and years. People ought to start dead and then they would be honest so much earlier.
— Twain, Mark

Proverbs by Subjects

All say, How hard it is that we have to die — a strange complaint to come from the mouths of people who have had to live.

— Twain, Mark

Let us endeavor so to live that when we come to die even the undertaker will be sorry.

— Twain, Mark

Live your life, do your work, then take your hat.

— Thoreau, Henry David

Death is the wish of some, the relief of many, and the end of all.

— Seneca, Lucius Annaeus

I want to be all used up when I die.

— Shaw George Bernard

Once can survive everything nowadays, except death.

— Wilde, Oscar

I come to bury Caesar, not to praise him. The evil that men do lives after them; the good is oft interred with their bones.

— Shakespeare, William

After life's fitful fever he sleeps well. Treason has done his worst. Nor steel nor poison, malice domestic, foreign levy, nothing can touch him further.

— Shakespeare, William

All that live must die, passing through nature to eternity.

— Shakespeare, William

But I will be a bridegroom in my death, and run into a lover's bed.

— Shakespeare, William

I care not, a man can die but once; we owe God and death.

— Shakespeare. William

Nothing in his life became him like the leaving it.

— Shakespeare, William

Our remedies oft in ourselves do lie, which we ascribe to heaven.

— Shakespeare, William

The undiscovered country form whose born no traveler returns. [Hamlet]

— Shakespeare, William

Men must endure, their going hence even as their coming hither. Ripeness is all.

— Shakespeare, William

The weariest and most loathed worldly life, that age, ache, penury and imprisonment can lay on nature is a paradise, to what we fear of death.
— *Shakespeare, William*

Dying is a troublesome business: there is pain to be suffered, and it wrings one's heart; but death is a splendid thing - a warfare accomplished, a beginning all over again, a triumph. You can always see that in their faces.
— *Shaw, George Bernard*

(iii) Humankind

We cannot despair of humanity, since we ourselves are human beings.
— *Einstein, Albeit*

Man is a beautiful machine that works very badly.
— *Mencken, Henry Louis*

Have you ever watched a crab on the shore crawling backward in search of the Atlantic Ocean, and missing? That's the way the mind of man operates.
— *Mencken, Henry Louis*

Man is by nature a political animal.
— *Aristotle*

Our humanity is a poor thing, except for the divinity that stirs within us.
— *Bacon, Francis*

There are times when one would like to hang the whole human race, and finish the farce.
— *Twain, Mark*

If man had created man, he would be ashamed of his performance.
— *Twain, Mark*

The brotherhood of man is not a mere poet's dream: it is a most depressing and humiliating reality.
— *Wilde, Oscar*

The basic fact about human existence is not that it is a tragedy, but that it is a bore. It is not so much a war as an endless standing in line.
— *Mencken, Henry Louis*

Man... knows only when he is satisfied and when he suffers, and only his sufferings and his satisfactions instruct him concerning himself, teach him what to seek and what to avoid. For the rest, man is a confused creature; he knows not whence

Proverbs by Subjects

he comes or whither he goes, he knows little of the world, and above all, he knows little of himself.
— *Goethe, Johann Wolfgang Von*

The end of the human race will be that it will eventually die of civilization.
— *Emerson, Ralph Waldo*

Considered logically this concept is not identical with the totality of sense impressions referred to; but it is an arbitrary creation of the human (or animal) mind.
— *Einstein, Albert*

I hate mankind, for I think of myself as one of the best of them, and I know how bad I am.
— *Johnson, Samuel*

Man is an exception, whatever else he is. If he is not the image of God, then he is a disease of the dust. If it is not true that a divine being fell, then we can only say that one of the animals went entirely off its head.
— *Chesterton, Gilbert Keith*

Man is emphatically a proselytizing creature.
— *Cartyle, Thomas*

Man is born passionate of body, but with an innate though secret tendency to the love of Good in his main-spring of Mind. But God help us all! It is at present a sad jar of atoms.
— *Lord Byron*

The best security for civilization is the dwelling, and upon properly appointed and becoming dwellings depends, more than anything else, the improvement of mankind.
— *Disraeli, Benjamin*

God must love the common man, he made so many of them.
— *Lincoln, Abraham*

Either a beast or a god.
— *Aristotle*

I teach you the Superman. Man is something that should be overcome.
— *Nietzsche, Friedrich*

Man's only true happiness is to live in hope of something to be won by him. Reverence something to be worshipped by him, and love something to be cherished by him, forever.
— *Ruskin, John*

What a piece of work is a man! How noble in reason, how infinite in faculty, in form and moving how express and admirable, in action how like an angel, in apprehension how like a god — the beauty of the world, the paragon of animals!
— *Shakespeare, William*

Physically there is nothing to distinguish human society from the farm-yard except that children are more troublesome and costly than chickens and calves and that men and women are not so completely enslaved as farm stock.
— Shaw, George Bernard

Human beings are the only animals of which I am thoroughly and cravenly afraid.
— Shaw, George Bernard

The human race was always interesting and we know by its past that it will always continue so, monotonously.
— Twain, Mark

Such is the human race. Often it does seem such a pity that Noah and his party did not miss the boat.
— Twain, Mark

Man is a creature made at the end of the week's work when God was tired.
— Twain, Mark

I sometimes think that God in creating man somewhat overestimated his ability.
— Wilde, Oscar

It is because Humanity has never known where it was going that it has been able to find its way.
— Wilde, Oscar

Man is no longer an artist, he has become a work of art.
— Nietzsche, Friedrich

(iv) Men and Women

If women were as fastidious as men, morally or physically, there would be an end of the race.
— Shaw, George Bernard

Girls we love for what they are; men for what they promise to be.
— Goethe, Johann Wolfgang Von

A man can be happy with any woman, as long as he does not love her.
— Wilde, Oscar

But there certainly are not so many men of large fortune in the world as there are of pretty woman to deserve them.
— Austen, Jane

For the woman, the man is a means: the end is always the child.
— Nietzsche, Friedrich

Proverbs by Subjects

When men and woman die, as poets sung, his heart's the last part moves, her last, the tongue.

— *Franklin, Benjamin*

So it is naturally with the male and the female; the one is superior, the other inferior; the one governs, the other is governed; and the same rule must necessarily hold good with respect to all mankind.

— *Aristotle*

With men he can be rational and unaffected, but when he has ladies to please, every feature works.

— *Austen, Jane*

There is something to me very softening in the presence of a woman, some strange influence, even if one is not in love with them, which I cannot at all account for, having no very high opinion of the sex. But yet, I always feel in better humor with myself and every thing else, if there is a woman within ken.

— *Lord Byron*

I think the worst woman that ever existed would have made a man of very passable reputation — they are all better than us and their faults such as they are must originate with ourselves.

— *Lord Byron*

But as to women, who can penetrate the real sufferings of their she condition? Man's very sympathy with their estate has much of selfishness and more suspicion. Their love, their virtue, beauty, education, but form good housekeepers, to breed a nation.

— *Lord Byron*

A woman who gives any advantage to a man may expect a lover — but will sooner or later find a tyrant.

— *Lord Byron*

What a strange thing man is; and what a stranger thing woman.

— *Lord Byron*

And when a woman's will is as strong as the man's who wants to govern her, half her strength must be concealment.

— *Eliot, George*

Where women love each other, men learn to smother their mutual dislike.

— *Eliot, George*

I tell you there isn't a thing under the sun that needs to be done at all, but what a man can do better than a woman, unless it's bearing children, and they do that in a poor make-shift way; it had better has been left to the men.

— *Eliot, George*

As vivacity is the gift of women, gravity is that of men. Addison, Joseph

Let us treat the men and women well: treat them as if they were real: perhaps they are.
— Emerson, Ralph Waldo

The fact is, you have fallen lately, Cecily, into a bad habit of thinking for yourself. You should give it up. It is not quite womanly... men don't like it.
— Wilde, Oscar

Men know that women are an over-match for them, and therefore they choose the weakest or most ignorant. If they did not think so, they never could be afraid of women knowing as much as themselves.
— Johnson, Samuel

Man weeps to think that he will die so soon; woman, that she was born so long ago.
— Mencken, Henry Louis

Men have a much better time of it than women. For one thing, they marry later, for another thing, they die earlier.
— Mencken, Henry Louis

Man is always looking for someone to boast to; woman is always looking for a shoulder to put her head on.
— Mencken, Henry Louis

He is half of a blessed man. Left to be finished by such as she; and she a fair divided excellence, whose fullness of perfection lies in him.
— Shakespeare, William

Women love us for our defects. If we have enough of them, they will forgive us everything, even our gigantic intellects.
— Wilde, Oscar

Between men and women there is no friendship possible. There is passion, enmity, worship, love, but no friendship.
— Wilde, Oscar

I should like to know what is the proper function of women, if it is not to make reasons for husbands to stay at home, and still stronger reasons for bachelors to go out.
— Eliot, George

— x —

6. SCIENCE
(i) Philosophy

Plato was a bore.
— *Nietzsche, Friedrich*

Philosophy when superficially studied, excites doubt, when thoroughly explored, it dispels it.
— *Bacon, Francis*

All are lunatics, but he who can analyze his delusion is called a philosopher.
— *Bierce, Ambrose*

Philosophy: A route of many roads leading from nowhere to nothing.
— *Bierce, Ambrose*

Pythagoras, Locke, Socrates — but pages might be filled up, as vainly as before, with the sad usage of all sorts of sages, who in his life-time, each was deemed a bore! The loftiest minds outrun their tardy ages.
— *Lord Byron*

A new philosophy generally means in practice the praise of some old vice.
— *Chesterton, Gilbert Keith*

The most dangerous criminal now is the entirely lawless modern philosopher. Compared to him, burglars and bigamists are essentially moral men.
— *Chesterton, Gilbert Keith*

Out of Plato come all things that are still written and debated about among men of thought.
— *Emerson, Ralph Waldo*

The philosopher must station themselves in the middle.
— *Goethe, Johann Wolfgang Von*

We are much beholden to Machiavel and others, that write what men do, and not what they ought to do.
— *Bacon, Francis*

Every philosophy is the philosophy of some stage of life.
— *Nietzsche, Friedrich*

If He Tom Sawyer had been a great and wise philosopher, like the writer of this book, he would now have comprehended that Work consists of whatever a body is obliged to do and Play consists of whatever a body is not obliged to do.
— *Twain, Mark*

Philosophy consists very largely of one philosopher arguing that all others are jackasses. He usually proves it, and I should

add that he also usually proves that he is one himself.
— Mencken, Henry Louis

There is no record in history of a happy philosopher.
— Mencken, Henry Louis

Philosophy does not regard pedigree, she received Plato not as a noble, but she made him one.
— Seneca, Lucius Annaeus

There are more things in Heaven and Earth, Horatio, than are dreamt of in your philosophies.
— Shakespeare, William

Every philosophy is the philosophy of some stage of life.
— Nietzsche, Friedrich

If He Tom Sawyer had been a great and wise philosopher, like the writer of this book, he would now have comprehended that work consists of whatever a body is obliged to do and Play consists of whatever a body is not obliged to do.
— Twain, Mark

Philosophy consists very largely of one philosopher arguing that all others are jackasses. He usually proves it, and I should add that he also usually proves that he is one himself.
— Mencken, Henry Louis

There is no record in history of a happy philosopher.
— Mencken, Henry Louis

Philosophy does not regard pedigree, she received Plato not as a noble, but she made him one.
— Seneca, Lucius Annaeus

There are more things in Heaven and Earth, Horatio, than are dreamt of in your philosophies.
— Shakespeare, William

For there was never yet philosopher that could endure the toothache patiently.
— Shakespeare, William

The philosopher is Nature's pilot. And there you have our difference: to be n hell is to drift: to be in heaven is to steer.
— Shaw, George Bernard

To be a philosopher is not merely to have subtle thoughts, nor even to found a school, but so to love wisdom as to live according to its dictates a life of simplicity, independence, magnanimity, and trust. It is to solve some of the problems of life, not only theoretically, but practically.
— Thoreau, Henry David

What sort of philosophers are we, who know absolutely nothing about the origin and destiny of cats?
— Thoreau, Henry David

If he really thinks there is no distinction between vice and virtue, when he leaves our houses let us count our spoons.
— Johnson, Samuel

(ii) Architecture

When we build, let us think that we build for ever.
— Ruskin, John

No architecture is so haughty as that which is simple.
— Ruskin, John

No person who is not a great sculptor or painter can be an architect. If he is not a sculptor or painter, he can only be a builder.
— Ruskin, John

An architect should live as little in cities as a painter. Send him to our hills, and let him study there what nature understands by a buttress, and what by a dome.
— Ruskin, John

A doctor can bury his mistakes, but an architect can only advise his clients to plant vines.
— Wright, Frank Lloyd

All fine architectural values are human values, else not valuable.
— Wright, Frank Lloyd

Form ever follows function.
— Sullivan, Louis Henry

Believe me, that was a happy age, before the days of architects, before the days of builders.
— Seneca, Lucius Annaeus

We may live without her, and worship without her, but we cannot remember without her. How cold is all history, how lifeless all imagery, compared to that which the living nation writes, and the uncorrupted marble bears!
— Ruskin, John

I don't think of form as a kind of architecture. The architecture is the result of the forming. It is the kinesthetic and visual sense of position and wholeness that puts the thing into the realm of art.
— Lichtenstein, Roy

(iii) Technology

Our inventions are wont to be pretty toys, which distract our attention from serious things. They are but improved means to an unimproved end.
— Thoreau, Henry David

In health of mind and body, men should see with their own eyes, hear and speak without trumpets, walk on their feet, not on wheels, and work and war with their arms, not with engine-beams, nor rifles warranted to kill twenty men at a shot before you can see them.
— Ruskin, John

Men are only as good as their technical development allows them to be.
— Orwell, George

The press, the machine, the railway, the telegraph are premises whose thousand-year conclusion no one has yet dared to draw.
— Nietzsche, Friedrich

Technological progress is like an ax in the hands of a pathological criminal.
— Einstein, Albert

When we can drain the Ocean into mill-ponds, and bottle up the Force of Gravity, to be sold by retail, in gas jars; then may we hope to comprehend the infinitudes of man's soul under formulas of Profit and Loss; and rule over this too, as over a patent engine, by checks, and valves, and balances.
— Carlyle, Thomas

— x —

7. SOCIETY

(i) Marriage

The best friend is likely to acquire the best wife, because a good marriage is based on the talent for friendship.
— Nietzsche, Friedrich

One should always be in love. That is the reason one should never marry.
— Wilde, Oscar

Marriage: The state or condition of a community consisting of a master, a mistress and two slaves, making in all, two.
— Bierce, Ambrose

To marry unequally is to suffer equally.
— Amiel, Henri Frederic

Happiness in marriage is entirely a matter of chance.
— Austen, Jane

The world has suffered more from the ravages of ill-advised marriages than from virginity.
— Bierce, Ambrose

Marriage is an adventure, like going to war.
— Chesterton, Gilbert Keith

Both marriage and death ought to be welcome: The one promises happiness, doubtless the other assures it.
— Twain, Mark

Keep your eyes wide open before marriage, and half-shut afterwards.
— Franklin, Benjamin

An undutiful daughter will prove an unmanageable wife.
— Franklin, Benjamin

Where there is marriage without love, there will be love without marriage.
— Franklin, Benjamin

One good husband is worth two good wives, for the scarcer things are, the more they are valued.
— Franklin, Benjamin

The betrothed and accepted lover has lost the wildest charms of his maiden by her acceptance. She was heaven while he pursued her, but she cannot be heaven if she stoops to one such as he!
— Emerson, Ralph Waldo

Is not marriage an open question, when it is alleged, from the beginning of the world, that such as are in the institution wish to get out, and such as are out wish to get in?
— Emerson, Ralph Waldo

Marriage must be a relation either of sympathy or of conquest.
— Eliot, George

When a wife has a good husband it is easily seen in her face.
— Goethe, Johann Wolfgang Von

All tragedies are finished by a death, all comedies by a marriage.
— Lord Byron

There is, indeed, nothing that so much seduces reason from vigilance, as the thought of passing life with an amiable woman.
— Johnson, Samuel

Though women are angels, yet wedlock's the devil.
— Lord Byron

I have great hopes that we shall love each other all our lives as much as if we had never married at all.
— Lord Byron

Incompatibility: In matrimony a similarity of tastes, particularly the taste for domination.
— Bierce, Ambrose

Wives are young men's mistresses; companions for middle age, and old men's nurses.

— Bacon, Francis

It is always incomprehensible to a man that a woman should ever refuse an offer of marriage.

— Austen, Jane

It destroys one's nerve to be amiable every day to the same human being.

— Disraeli, Benjamin

If I ever marry it will be on a sudden impulse, as a man shoots himself.

— Mencken, Henry Louis

Long engagements give people the opportunity of finding out each other's character before marriage, which is never advisable.

— Wilde, Oscar

On the whole, the great success of marriage in the States is due partly to the fact that no American man is ever idle, and partly to the fact that no American wife is considered responsible for the quality of her husband's dinners.

— Wilde, Oscar

Men marry because they are tired; women, because they are curious; both are disappointed.

— Wilde, Oscar

They flaunt their conjugal felicity in one's face, as if it were the most fascinating of sins.

— Wilde, Oscar

When a woman marries again it is because she detested her first husband. When a man marries again it is because he adored his first wife. Women try their luck; men risk theirs.

— Wilde, Oscar

When two people are under the influence of the most violent, most insane, most delusive, and most transient of passions, they are required to swear that they will remain in that excited, abnormal, and exhausting condition continuously until death do them part.

— Shaw, George Bernard

There is no subject on which more dangerous nonsense is talked and thought than marriage.

— Shaw, George Bernard

Marriage is popular because it combines the maximum of temptation with the maximum of opportunity.

— Shaw, George Bernard

By taking a second wife he pays the highest compliment to the first, by showing that she made him so happy as a married man, that he wishes to be so a second time.
— *Johnson, Samuel*

The world must be peopled. When I said I would die a bachelor, I did not think I should live till I were married.
— *Shakespeare, William*

A woman seldom asks advice before she has bought her wedding clothes.
— *Addison, Joseph*

For it is mutual trust, even more than mutual interest that holds human associations together. Our friends seldom profit us but they make us feel safe. Marriage is a scheme to accomplish exactly that same end.
— *Mencken, Henry Louis*

Whenever a husband and wife begin to discuss their marriage they are giving evidence at a coroner's inquest.
— *Mencken, Henry Louis*

It is obvious that all sense has gone out of modern marriage: which is, however, no objection to marriage but to modernity.
— *Nietzsche, Friedrich*

I have come to the conclusion never again to think of marrying, and for this reason, I can never be satisfied with anyone who would be blockhead enough to have me.
— *Lincoln, Abraham*

Marriage is neither heaven nor hell, it is simply purgatory.
— *Lincoln, Abraham*

Marriage has many pains, but celibacy has no pleasures.
— *Johnson, Samuel*

Marriage is the best state for man in general, and every man is a worst man in proportion to the level he is unfit for marriage.
— *Johnson, Samuel*

It is not from reason and prudence that people marry, but from inclination.
— *Johnson, Samuel*

It is a woman's business to get married as soon as possible, and a man's to keep unmarried as long as he can.
— *Shaw, George Bernard*

(ii) Money

The world is his who has money to go over it.
— *Emerson, Ralph Waldo*

Cash-payment never was, or could except for a few years be, the union-bond of man to man. Cash never yet paid one man fully his deserts to another; nor could it, nor can it, now or henceforth to the end of the world.
— Carlyle, Thomas

Business, you know, may bring you money, but friendship hardly ever does.
— Austen, Jane

Money has never made man happy, nor will it, there is nothing in its nature to produce happiness. The more of it one has the more one wants.
— Franklin, Benjamin

If you know how to spend less than you get, you have the philosopher's stone.
— Franklin, Benjamin

He that is of the opinion money will do everything may well be suspected of doing everything for money.
— Franklin, Benjamin

Money, which represents the prose of life, and which is hardly spoken of in parlors without an apology, is, in its effects and laws, as beautiful as roses.
— Emerson, Ralph Waldo

Money often costs too much.
— Emerson, Ralph Waldo

Money is the representative of a certain quantity of corn or other commodity. It is so much warmth, so much bread.
— Emerson, Ralph Waldo

Many people take no care of their money till they come nearly to the end of it, and others do just the same with their time.
— Goethe, Johann Wolfgang Von

Many of the things you can count, don't count. Atony of the things you can't count, really count.
— Einstein, Albert

Whatever you have spend less.
— Johnson, Samuel

I have imbibed such a love for money that I keep some sequins in a drawer to count, and cry over them once a week.
— Lord Byron

Ready money is Aladdin's lamp.
— Lord Byron

Yes! Ready money is Aladdin's lamp.
— Lord Byron

Money is like muck, not good except it be spread.
— *Bacon, Francis*

Money makes a good servant, but a bad master.
— *Bacon, Francis*

If money be not they servant, it will be thy master. The covetous man cannot so properly be said to possess wealth, as that may be said to possess him.
— *Bacon, Francis*

Be not penny-wise. Riches have wings. Sometimes they fly away of themselves, and sometimes they must be set flying to bring in more.
— *Bacon, Francis*

No man's fortune can be an end worthy of his being.
— *Bacon, Francis*

It requires a great deal of boldness and a great deal of caution to make a great fortune, and when you have it, it requires ten times as much skill to keep it.
— *Emerson, Ralph Waldo*

Money is indeed the most important thing in the world; and all sound and successful personal and national morality should have this fact for its basis.
— *Shaw, George Bernard*

There is only one class in the community that thinks more about money than the rich, and that is the poor. The poor can think of nothing else.
— *Wilde, Oscar*

His money is twice tainted: taint yours and taint mine.
— *Twain, Mark*

The lack of money is the root of all evils.
— *Twain, Mark*

I am opposed to millionaires, but it would be dangerous to offer me the position.
— *Twain, Mark*

Almost any man knows how to earn money, but not one in a million knows how to spend it.
— *Thoreau, Henry David*

Money is not required to buy one necessity of the soul.
—*Thoreau, Henry David*

The only wealth is life.
— *Thoreau, Henry David*

The way by which you may get money almost without exception leads downward.
— *Thoreau, Henry David*

The use of money is all the advantage there is in having money.
— Franklin, Benlamin

Money is the most important thing in the world. It represents health, strength, honor, generosity, and beauty as conspicuously as the want of it represents illness, weakness, disgrace, meanness, and ugliness.
— Shaw, George Bernard

When I was young I used to think that money was the most important thing in life; now that I am old, I know it is.
— Wilde, Oscar

Lack of money is the root of all evil.
— Shaw, George Bernard

A miser grows rich by seeming poor. An extravagant man grows poor by seeming rich.
— Shakespeare, William

A great fortune is a great slavery.
— Seneca, Lucius Annaeus

But it is a pretty thing to see what money will do!
— Seneca, Lucius Annaeus

It is not how much one makes but to what purpose one spends.
— Ruskin, John

The most valuable of all human possessions, next to a superior and disdainful air, is the reputation of being well-to-do.
— Mencken, Henry Louis

The chief value of money lies in the fact that one lives in a world in which it is overestimated.
— Mencken, Henry Louis

There are few ways in which a man can be more innocently employed than in getting money.
— Johnson, Samuel

The universal regard for money is the one hopeful fact in our civilization. Money is the most important thing in the world. It represents health, strength, honor, generosity and beauty. Not the least of its virtues is that it destroys base people as certainly as it fortifies and dignifies noble people.
— Shaw, George Bernard

(iii) Politicians

An empty stomach is not a good political advisor.
— Einstein, Albert

Therefore, the good of man must be the end of the science of politics.
— Aristotle

Politics is far more complicated than physics.
— Einstein, Albert

A majority is always better than the best repartee.
— Disraeli, Benjamin

It is as hard and severe a thing to be a true politician as to be truly moral.
— Bacon, Francis

A politician is one that would circumvent God.
— Shakespeare, William

Suppose you were an idiot. And suppose you were a member of Congress. But I repeat myself.
— Twain, Mark

What is a democrat? One who believes that the republicans have ruined the country. What is a republican? One who believes that the democrats would ruin the country.
— Bierce, Ambrose

A sophistical rhetorician, inebriated with the exuberance of his own verbosity, and gifted with an egotistical imagination that can at all times command an interminable and inconsistent series of arguments to malign an opponent and to glorify himself.
— Disraeli, Benjamin

A Conservative government is an organized hypocrisy.
— Disraeli, Benjamin

There is no gambling like politics. Nothing in which the power of circumstance is more evident.
— Disraeli, Benjamin

Things must be done by parties, not by persons using parties as tools.
— Disraeli, Benjamin

No man is regular in his attendance at the House of Commons until he is married.
— Disraeli, Benjamin

What the statesman is most anxious to produce is a certain moral character in his fellow citizens, namely a disposition to virtue and the performance of virtuous actions.
— Aristotle

In politics, nothing is contemptible.
— Disraeli, Benjamin

In politics, as on the sickbed, people toss from side to side, thinking they will be more comfortable.
— Goethe, Johann Wolfgang Von

The art of governing mankind by deceiving them.
— *Disraeli, Benjamin*

The world is weary of statesmen whom democracy has degraded into politicians.
— *Disraeli, Benjamin*

Half a truth is better than no politics.
— *Chesterton, Gilbert Keith*

Little other than a red tape Talking-machine, and unhappy Bag of Parliamentary Eloquence.
— *Carlyle, Thomas*

It is a vain hope to make people happy by politics.
— *Carlyle, Thomas*

Finality is not the language of politics.
— *Disraeli, Benjamin*

The courts of kings are full of people, but empty of friends.
— *Seneca, Lucius Annaeus*

Only people who look dull ever get into the House of Commons, and only people who are dull ever succeed there.
— *Wilde, Oscar*

I adore political parties. They are the only place left to us where people don't talk politics.
Wilde, Oscar

In statesmanship get the formalities right, never mind about the moralities.
— *Twain, Mark*

Fleas can be taught nearly anything that a Congressman can.
— *Twain, Mark*

Politics is the gizzard of society, full of gut and gravel.
— *Thoreau, Henry David*

He knows nothing; and he thinks he knows everything. That points clearly to a political career.
— *Shaw, George Bernard*

We mustn't be stiff and stand-off, you know. We must be thoroughly democratic, and patronize everybody without distinction of class.
— *Shaw, George Bernard*

There is a certain satisfaction in coming down to the lowest ground of politics, for we get rid of cant and hypocrisy.
— *Emerson, Ralph Waldo*

Get thee glass eyes, and like a scurvy politician, seem to see the things thou dost not.
— *Shakespeare, William*

The first mistake in public business is going into it.
— *Franklin, Benjamin*

Political speech and writing are largely the defense of the indefensible.
— *Orwell, George*

The whole aim of practical politics is to keep the populace alarmed [and Hence Clamorous To Be Led To Safety] by an endless series of hobgoblins.
— *Mencken, Henry Louis*

Nothing is so abject and pathetic as a politician who has lost his job, save only a retired stud-horse.
— *Mencken, Henry Louis*

A good politician is quite as unthinkable as an honest burglar.
— *Mencken, Henry Louis*

The newspaper reader says: this party will ruin itself if it makes errors like this. My higher politics says: a party which makes errors like this is already finished - it is no longer secure in its instincts.
— *Nietzsche, Friedrich*

Honest statesmanship is the wise employment of individual meanness for the public good.
— *Lincoln, Abraham*

Politics are now nothing more than means of rising in the world. With this sole view do men engage in politics, and their whole conduct proceeds upon it.
— *Johnson, Samuel*

He thinks like a Tory, and talks like a Radical, and that's so important nowadays.
— *Wilde, Oscar*

There have been many great men that have flattered the people who never loved them.
— *Shakespeare, William*

(iv) Power

Nearly all men can stand adversity, but if you want to test a man's character, give him power.
— *Lincoln, Abraham*

Every man has enough power left to carry out that of which he is convinced.
— *Goethe, Johann Wolfgang Von*

Nothing destroys authority more than the unequal and untimely interchange of power stretched too far and relaxed too much.
— *Bacor, Francis*

It is a strange desire, to seek power, and to lose liberty; or to seek power over others, and to lose power over a man's self.
— *Bacon, Francis*

Power has only one duty —to secure the social welfare of the People.
— *Disraeli, Benlamin*

The attempt to combine wisdom and power has only rarely been successful and then only for a short while.
— *Einstein, Albert*

The stupidity of men always invites the insolence of power.
— *Emerson, Ralph Waldo*

There is no knowledge that is not power.
— *Emerson, Ralph Waldo*

What lies behind you and what lies in front of you, pales in comparison to what lies inside of you.
— *Emerson, Ralph Waldo*

Wherever there is power there is age.
— *Emerson, Ralph Waldo*

Do the thing and you will have the power. But they that do not the thing, had not the power.
— *Emerson, Ralph Waldo*

The creation of a thousand forest in one acorn.
— *Emerson, Ralph Waldo*

Nature arms each man with some faculty which enables him to do easily some feat impossible to any other.
— *Emerson, Ralph Waldo*

Our duty is to be useful, not according to our desires, but according to our powers.
— *Amiel, Henri Frederic*

Napoleon for the sake of a good name broke in pieces half the world.
— *Goethe, Johann Wolfgang Von*

Power does not corrupt men; fools, however, if they get into a position of power, corrupt power.
— *Shaw, George Bernard*

Must a government be too strong for the liberties of its people or too weak to maintain its own existence?
— *Lincoln, Abraham*

Not necessity, not desire —no, the love of power is the demon of men. Let them have everything -health, food, a place to live, entertainment —they are and remain unhappy and low-spirited: for the demon waits and waits and will be satisfied.
— *Nietzsche, Friedrich*

The urge to save humanity is almost always only a false face for the urge to rule it.
— Mencken, Henry Louis

Power-worship blurs political judgment because it leads, almost unavoidably, to the belief that present trends will continue. Whoever is winning at the moment will always seem to be invincible.
— Orwell, George

Power is not a means, it is an end. One does not establish a dictatorship in order to safeguard a revolution; one makes the revolution in order to establish the dictatorship.
— Orwell, George

Most powerful is he who has himself in his own power.
— Seneca, Lucius Annaeus

If you sit in judgment, investigate, if you sit in supreme power, sit in command.
— Seneca, Lucius Annaeus

Authority founded on injustice is never of long duration.
— Seneca, Lucius Annaeus

He is the most powerful who has himself, in his power.
— Seneca, Lucius Annaeus

Madness in great ones must not unwatched go.
— Shakespeare, William

You cannot have power for good without having power for evil too. Even mother's milk nourishes murderers as well as heroes.
— Shaw, George Bernard

A good indignation brings out all one's powers.
— Emerson, Ralph Waldo

(v) Education

Men are born ignorant, not stupid; they are made stupid by education.
— Russell, Bertrand

Education is the period during which you are being instructed by somebody you do not know, about something you do not want to know.
— Chesterton, Gilbert Keith

Those who trust us educate us.
— Eliot, George

According to this conception, the sole function of education was to open the way to thinking and knowing, and the school,

as the outstanding organ for the people's education, must serve that end exclusively.
— *Einstein, Albert*

Education is the progressive realization of our ignorance.
— *Einstein, Albert*

It should be possible to explain the laws of physics to a barmaid.
— *Einstein, Albert*

Talk to a man about himself and he will listen for hours.
— *Disraeli, Benjamin*

On the education of the people of this country the fate of the country depends.
— *Disraeli, Benjamin*

What sculpture is to a block of marble, education is to an human soul.
— *Addison, Joseph*

Upon the education of the people of this country the fate of this country depends.
— *Disraeli, Benjamin*

The secret in education lies in respecting the student.
— *Emerson, Ralph Waldo*

If a man empties his purse into his head, no man can take it away from him. An investment in knowledge always pays the best interest.
— *Franklin, Benjamin*

Education is that which discloses to the wise and disguises from the foolish their lack of understanding.
— *Bierce, Ambrose*

Those who educate children well are more to be honored than they who produce them; for these only gave them life, those the art of living well.
— *Aristotle*

The roots of education are bitter, but the fruit is sweet.
— *Aristotle*

The educated differ from the uneducated as much as the living from the dead.
— *Aristotle*

Education is the best provision for old age.
— *Aristotle*

Education is an ornament in prosperity and a refuge in adversity.
— *Aristotle*

There is no education like adversity.

— Disraeli, Benjamin

The child who desires education will be bettered by it; the child who dislikes it disgraced.

— Ruskin, John

Education is an admirable thing, but it is well to remember from time to time that nothing that is worth knowing can be taught.

— Wilde, Oscar

I have never let my schooling interfere with my education.

— Twain, Mark

Soap and education are not as sudden as a massacre, but they are more deadly in the long run. Training is everything. The peach was once a bitter almond; cauliflower is nothing but cabbage with a college education.

— Twain, Mark

Education is the path from cocky ignorance to miserable uncertainty.

— Twain, Mark

What does education often do? It makes a straight-cut ditch of a free, meandering brook.

— Thoreau, Henry David

How could youths better learn to live than by at once trying the experiment of living?

— Thoreau, Henry David

Upon the subject of education, not presuming to dictate any plan or system respecting it, I can only say that I view it as the most important subject which we as a people may be engaged in. That everyone may receive at least a moderate education appears to be an objective of vital importance.

— Lincoln, Abraham

The first condition of education is being able to put someone to wholesome and meaningful work.

— Ruskin, John

There is a time in every man's education when he arrives at the conviction that envy is ignorance; that imitation is suicide.

— Emerson, Ralph Waldo

Modern education has devoted itself to the teaching of impudence, and then we complain that we can no longer control our mobs.

— Ruskin, John

In large states public education will always be mediocre, for the same reason that in large kitchens the cooking is usually bad.

— Nietzsche, Friedrich

They teach in academies far too many things, and far too much that is useless.

— *Goethe, Johann Wolfgang Von*

We are shut up in schools and college recitation rooms for ten or fifteen years, and come out at last with a belly-full of words and do not know a thing. The things taught in schools and colleges are not an education, but the means of education.

— *Emerson, Ralph Waldo*

I pay the schoolmaster, but it is the school boys who educate my son.

— *Emerson, Ralph Waldo*

Respect the child. Be not too much his parent. Trespass not on his solitude.

— *Emerson, Ralph Waldo*

The whole theory of modem education is radically unsound. Fortunately in England, at any rate, education produces no effect whatsoever. If it did, it would prove a serious danger to the upper classes, and probably lead to acts of violence.

— *Wilde, Oscar*

What we call education and culture is for the most part nothing but the substitution of reading for experience, of literature for life, of the obsolete fictitious for the contemporary real.

— *Shaw, George Bernard*

— x —

8. TIME

(i) Age

To know how to grow old is the master work of wisdom, and one of the most difficult chapters in the great art of living.

— *Amiel, Henri Frederic*

Old wood best to burn, old wine to drink, old friends to trust, and old authors to read.

— *Bacon, Francis*

If you wouldn't live long, live well; for folly and wickedness shorten life.

— *Franklin, Benjamin*

Youth is a blunder, manhood is a struggle and old age a regret.

— *Disraeli, Benjamin*

Perfection of means and confusion of goals seem - in my opinion — to characterize our age.

— *Einstein, Albert*

Few women, I fear, have had such reason as I have to think the long sad years of youth were worth living for the sake of middle age.

— *Eliot, George*

In the multitude of middle-aged men who go about their vocations in a daily course determined for them much in the same way as the tie of their cravats, there is always a good number who once meant to shape their own deeds and alter the world a little.

— *Eliot, George*

We do not count a man's years until he has nothing else to count.

— *Emerson, Ralph Waldo*

Nature is full of freaks, and now puts an old head on young shoulders, and then takes a young heart heating under fourscore winters.

— *Emerson, Ralph Waldo*

The disappointment of manhood succeeds the delusion of youth.

— *Disraeli, Benjamin*

An old young man, will be a young old man.

— *Franklin, Benjamin*

Old age is not a matter for sorrow. It is matter for thanks if we have left our work done behind us.

— *Carlyle, Thomas*

Many foxes grow gray but few grow good.

— *Franklin, Benjamin*

Those who love deeply never grow old; they may die of old age, but they die young.

— *Franklin, Benjamin*

Rejoice that you have still have a long time to live, before the thought comes to you that there is nothing more in the world to see.

— *Goethe, Johann Wolfgang Von*

It is only necessary to grow old to become more charitable and even indulgent. I see no fault committed by others that I have not committed myself.

— *Goethe, Johann Wolfgang Von*

At twenty years of age the will reigns; at thirty, the wit; and at forty, the judgment.

— *Franklin, Benlamin*

I always looked to about thirty as the barrier of any real or fierce delight in the passions, and determined to work them

out in the younger ore and better veins of the mine -and I flatter myself (perhaps) that I have pretty well done so - and now the dross is coming.
— Lord Byron

Age will not be defied.
— Bacon, Francis

People of age object too much, consult too long, adventure too little, repent too soon and seldom drive business home to it's conclusion, but content themselves with a mediocrity of success.
— Bacon, Francis

Discern of the coming on of years, and think not to do the same things still; for age will not be defied.
— Bacon, Francis

Men of age object too much, consult too long, adventure too little, repent too soon, and seldom drive business home to the full period, but content themselves with a mediocrity of success.
— Bacon, Francis

Age. That period of life in which we compound for the vices that remain by reviling those we have no longer the vigor to commit.
— Bierce, Ambrose

Youth is the period in which a man can be hopeless. The end of every episode is the end of the world. But the power of hoping through everything, the knowledge that the soul survives its adventures, that great inspiration comes to the middle-aged.
— Chesterton, Gilbert Keith

A lady of a "certain age," which means certainly aged.
— Lord Byron

He who would pass his declining years with honor and comfort, should, when young, consider that he may one day become old, and remember when he is old, that he has once been young.
— Addison, Joseph

I shall soon be six-and-twenty. Is there anything in the future that can possibly console us for not being always twenty-five?
— Lord Byron

My time has been passed viciously and agreeably; at thirty-one so few years months days hours or minutes remain that "Carpe Diem" is not enough. I have been obliged to crop even the seconds - for who can trust to tomorrow?
— Lord Byron

Of all the barbarous middle ages, that which is most barbarous is the middle age of man! it is —I really scarce know what; but

when we hover between fool and sage, and don't know justly what we would be at — a period something like a printed page, black letter upon foolscap, while our hair grows grizzled, and we are not what we were.
— Lord Byron

What is the worst of woes that wait on age? What stamps the wrinkle deeper on the brow? To view each loved one blotted from life's page, And be alone on earth, as I am now.
— Lord Byron

We must not take the faults of our youth with us into old age, for age brings along its own defects.
— Goethe, Johann Wolfgang Von

The outer passes away; the innermost is the same yesterday, today, and forever.
— Cartyle, Thomas

It was one of the deadliest and heaviest feelings of my life to feel that I was no longer a boy. From that moment I began to grow old in my own esteem —and in my esteem age is not estimable.
— Lord Byron

The older we grow the greater becomes our wonder at how much ignorance one can contain without bursting one's clothes.
— Twain, Mark

Age does not make us childish, as some say; it finds us true children.
— Goethe, Johann Wolfgang Von

Have you not a moist eye, a dry hand, a yellow cheek, a white beard, a decreasing leg, an increasing belly? Is not your voice broken, your wind short, your chin double, your wit single, and every part about you blasted with antiquity?
— Shakespeare, William

Old men are dangerous: it doesn't matter to them what is going to happen to the world.
— Shaw, George Bernard

Every man over forty is a scoundrel.
— Shaw, George Bernard

The youth gets together his materials to build a bridge to the moon, or, perchance, a palace or temple on the earth, and, at length, the middle-aged man concludes to build a woodshed with them.
— Thoreau, Henry David

None are so old as those who have outlived enthusiasm
— Thoreau, Henry David

Youth is full of sport, age's breath is short; youth is nimble, age is lame; Youth is hot and bold, age is weak and cold; Youth is wild, and age is tame.

— Shakespeare, William

Methuselah lived to be 969 years old . You boys and girls will see more in the next fifty years than Methuselah saw in his whole lifetime.

— Twain, Mark

My age is as a lusty winter, frosty but kindly.

— Shakespeare, William

When your friends begin to flatter you on how young you look, it's a sure sign you're getting old.

— Twain, Mark

Let us not be too particular; it is better to have old secondhand diamonds than none at all."

— Twain, Mark

Life would be infinitely happier if we could only be born at the age of eighty and gradually approach eighteen.

— Twain, Mark

I delight in men over seventy. They always offer one the devotion of a lifetime.

— Wilde, Oscar

No woman should ever be quite accurate about her age. It looks so calculating.

— Wilde, Oscar

The tragedy of old age is not that one is old, but that one is young.

— Wilde, Oscar

How earthy old people become —moldy as the grave! Their wisdom smacks of the earth. There is no foretaste of immortality in it. They remind me of earthworms and mole crickets.

— Thoreau, Henry David

The older I grow the more I distrust the familiar doctrine that age brings wisdom.

— Mencken, Henry Louis

Thirty-five is a very attractive age. London society is full of women of the highest birth who have, of their own free choice, remained thirty-five for years.

— Wilde, Oscar

When I was as you are now, towering in the confidence of twenty-one, little did I suspect that I should be at forty-nine, what I now am.

— Johnson, Samuel

At seventy-seven it is time to be in earnest.
— *Johnson, Samuel*
Old people love to give good advice to console themselves for no longer being able to set a bad example.
— *La Rochefoucauld, Francois de*
Old men are fond of giving good advice to console themselves for their inability to give bad examples.
— *La Rochefoucauld, Francois de*
Few people know how to be old. La Rochefoucauld.
— *Francois de*
I have lived long enough. My way of life is to fall into the sere, the yellow leaf, and that which should accompany old age, as honor, love, obedience, troops of friends I must not look to have.
— *Shakespeare, William*
Old age is a tyrant, who forbids, under pain of death, the pleasures of youth.
— *La Rochefoucauld, Francois de*
The older we get the more we must limit ourselves if we wish to be active.
— *Goethe, Johann Wolfgang Von*
How people keep correcting us when we are young! There is always some bad habit or other they tell us we ought to get over. Yet most bad habits are tools to help us through life.
— *Nietzsche, Friedrich*
Lord, Lord, how subject we old men are to this vice of lying!
— *Shakespeare, William*
There is nothing more despicable than an old man who has no other proof than his age to offer of his having lived long in the world.
— *Seneca, Lucius Annaeus*
As for old age, embrace and love it. It abounds with pleasure if you know how to use it. The gradually declining years are among the sweetest in a man's life, and I maintain that, even when they have reached the extreme limit, they have their pleasure still.
— *Seneca, Lucius Annaeus*
With mirth and laughter let old wrinkles come. [Merchant of Venice]
— *Shakespeare, William*
Though I look old, yet 1 am strong and lusty; for in my youth I never did apply hot and rebellious liquors in my blood; and did

not, with unbashful forehead, woo the means of weakness and debility: therefore my age is as a lusty winter, frosty but kindly.
— Shakespeare, William

As one grows older, one becomes wiser and more foolish.
— La Rochefoucauld, Francois de

(ii) Youth

Do you set down your name in the scroll of youth, that are written down old with all the characters of age?
— Shakespeare, William

Young people are fitter to invent than to judge; fitter for execution than for counsel; and more fit for new projects than for settled business.
— Bacon, Francis

Youth is to all the glad season of life; but often only by what it hopes, not by what it attains, or what it escapes.
— Carlyle, Thomas

No man knows he is young while he is young.
— Chesterton, Gilbert Keith

We live in an age when to be young and to be indifferent can be no longer synonymous. We must prepare for the coming hour. The claims of the Future are represented by suffering millions; and the Youth of a Nation are the trustees of Posterity.
— Disraeli, Benjamin

Youth is the trustee of prosperity.
— Disraeli, Benjamin

The Youth of a Nation are the trustees of posterity.
— Disraeli, Benjamin

Great endowments often announce themselves in youth in the form of singularity and awkwardness.
— Goethe, Johann Wolfgang Von

So different are the colors of life, as we look forward to the future, or backward to the past; and so different the opinions and sentiments which this contrariety of appearance naturally produces, that the conversation of the old and young ends generally with contempt or pity on either side.
— Johnson, Samuel

Youth enters the world with very happy prejudices in her own favor. She imagines herself not only certain of accomplishing every adventure, but of obtaining those rewards which the accomplishment may deserve. She is not easily persuaded to believe that the force of merit can be resisted by obstinacy and avarice, or its luster darkened by envy and malignity.
— Johnson, Samuel

Proverbs by Subjects

The young are permanently in a state resembling intoxication.
— Aristotle

A man loves the meat in his youth that he cannot endure in his age.
— Shakespeare, William

Youth is a quality, not a matter of circumstances.
— Wright, Frank Lloyd

Youth is such a wonderful thing. What a crime to waste it on children.
— Shaw, George Bernard

It is all that the young can do for the old, to shock them and keep them up to date.
— Shaw, George Bernard

Even the youngest of us may be wrong sometimes.
— Shaw, George Bernard

Youth, which is forgiven everything, forgives itself nothing: age, which forgives itself everything, is forgiven nothing.
Shaw, George Bernard

Youth gets together with their materials to build a bridge to the moon or maybe a palace on earth; then in middle age they decide to build a woodshed with them instead.
— Thoreau, Henry David

It is better to be a young June-bug than an old bird of paradise.
— Twain, Mark

Those whom the gods love grow young.
— Wilde, Oscar

Youth! There is nothing like youth. The middle-aged are mortgaged to Life. The old are in Life's lumber-room. But youth is the Lord of Life. Youth has a kingdom waiting for it. Every one is born a king, and most people die in exile.
— Wilde, Oscar

In America the young are always ready to give to those who are older than themselves the full benefits of their inexperience.
— Wilde, Oscar

It is the failing of youth not to be able to restrain its own violence.
— Seneca, Lucius Annaeus

(iii) Past

One's past is what one is. It is the only way by which people should be judged.
— Wilde, Oscar

What is past is prologue.
— Shakespeare, William

We have seen better days.
— Shakespeare, William

Things without remedy, should be without regard; what is done, is done.
— Shakespeare, William

Who controls the past controls the future: who controls the present controls the past.
— Orwell, George

Man... cannot learn to forget, but hangs on the past: however far or fast he runs, that chain runs with him.
— Nietzsche, Friedrich

Because men really respect only that which was founded of old and has developed slowly, he who wants to live on after his death must take care not only of his posterity but even more of his past.
— Nietzsche, Friedrich

There is no past that we can bring back by longing for it. There is only an eternally new now that builds and creates itself out of the Best as the past withdraws.
— Goethe, Johann Wolfgang Von

With memory set smarting like a reopened wound, a man's past is not simply a dead history, an outworn preparation of the present: it is not a repented error shaken loose from the life: it is a still quivering part of himself, bringing shudders and bitter flavors and the tinglings of a merited shame.
— Eliot, George

The distinction between the past, present and future is only a stubbornly persistent illusion.
— Einstein, Albert

The past is all holy to us; the dead are all holy; even they that were wicked when alive.
— Carlyle, Thomas

Antiquities are history defaced, or some remnants of history which have casually escaped the shipwreck of time.
— Bacon, Francis

(iv) Maturity

My experience is that as soon as people are old enough to know better, they don't know anything at all.
— Wilde, Oscar

Proverbs by Subjects

Your lordship, though not clean past your youth, have yet some smack of age in you, some relish of the saltiness of time.
— *Shakespeare, William*

Maturity is often more absurd than youth and very frequently is most unjust to youth.
— *Edison, Thomas Alva*

— x —

9. UNCLASSIFIED

(i) Thoughts

A man thinks as well through his legs and arms as this brain.
— *Thoreau, Henry David*

Thoughts are the shadows of our sensations — always darker, emptier, simpler than these.
— *Nietzsche, Friedrich*

Thought is the sculptor who can create the person you want to be.
— *Thoreau, Henry David*

Having each some shingles of thought well dried, we sat and whittled them.
— *Thoreau, Henry David*

Associate reverently, as much as you can, with your loftiest thoughts.
— *Thoreau, Henry David*

To him whose elastic and vigorous thought keeps pace with the sun, the day is a perpetual morning.
— *Thoreau, Henry David*

We shall require a substantially new manner of thinking if mankind is to survive.
— *Einstein, Albert*

Our virtues are dearer to us the more we have had to suffer for them. It is the same with our children. All profound affection entertains a sacrifice. Our thoughts are often worse than we are, just as they are often better.
— *Eliot, George*

Each thought is a nail that is driven in structures that cannot decay; And the mansion at last will be given To us as we build it each day.
— *Eliot, George*

The key to every man is his thought. Sturdy and defying though he look, he has a helm which he obeys, which is the idea after

which all his facts are classified. He can only be reformed by showing him a new idea which commands his own.
— *Emerson, Ralph Waldo*

What your heart thinks is great, is great. The soul's emphasis is always right.
— *Emerson, Ralph Waldo*

A man's what he thinks about all day long
— *Emerson, Ralph Waldo*

Life consists in what a person is thinking of all day.
— *Emerson, Ralph Waldo*

Nurture your mind with great thoughts, for you will never go any higher than you think.
— *Disraeli, Benjamin*

The revelation of Thought takes men out of servitude into freedom.
— *Emerson, Ralph Waldo*

The soul of God is poured into the world through the thoughts of men.
— *Emerson, Ralph Waldo*

A sect or party is an incognito devised to save man from the vexation of thinking.
— *Emerson, Ralph Waldo*

There is no thought in any mind, but it quickly tends to convert itself into power.
— *Emerson, Ralph Waldo*

It is astonishing what an effort it seems to be for many people to put their brains definitely and systematically to work.
— *Edison, Thomas Alva*

Beware when the great God lets loose a thinker on this planet.
— *Emerson, Ralph Waldo*

How you think when you lose determines how long it will be until you win.
— *Chesterton, Gilbert Keith*

Thought is the parent of the deed.
— *Carlyle, Thomas*

Thought once awakened does not again slumber; unfolds itself into a System of Thought; grows, in man after man, generation after generation, - till its full stature is reached, and such System of Thought can grow no farther, but must give place to another.
— *Carlyle, Thomas*

The power of thought, the magic of the mind.
— *Lord Byron*

For in itself a thought, a slumbering thought, is capable of years, and curdles a long life into one hour.
— Lord Byron

Think twice before you speak to a friend in need.
— Bierce, Ambrose

In thinking, if a person begins with certainties, they shall end in doubts, but if they can begin with doubts, they will end in certainties.
— Bacon, Francis

There is no expedient to which a man will not resort to avoid the real labor of thinking.
— Edison, Thomas Alva

When I'm getting ready to reason with a man, I spend one-third of my time thinking about myself and what I am going to say and two-thirds thinking about him and what he is going to say.
— Lincoln, Abraham

We like a man to come right out and say what he thinks, if we agree with him.
— Twain, Mark

Each thought that is welcomed and recorded is a nest egg by the side of which more will be laid.
— Thoreau, Henry David

How can they expect a harvest of thought who have not had the seed time of character.
— Thoreau, Henry David

Few people think more than two or three times a year. I have made an international reputation for myself thinking once or twice a week.
— Shaw, George Bernard

It is difficult, if not impossible, for most people to think otherwise than in the fashion of their own period.
— Shaw, George Bernard

I was a freethinker before I knew how to think.
— Shaw, George Bernard

Thought is free.
— Shakespeare, William

There is nothing good or bad, but thinking makes it so.
— Shakespeare, William

Make not your thoughts you prisons.
— Shakespeare, William

We are ashamed of our thoughts and often see them brought forth by others.
— Emerson, Ralph Waldo

When we talk in company we lose our unique tone of voice, and this leads us to make statements which is no way correspond to our real thoughts.

— *Nietzsche, Friedrich*

Thought makes every thing fit for use.

— *Emerson, Ralph Waldo*

Thought expands, but paralyzes; action animates, but narrows.

— *Goethe, Johann Wolfgang Von*

Thinking is more interesting than knowing, but less interesting than looking.

— *Goethe, Johann Wolfgang Von*

All truly wise thoughts have been thoughts already thousands of times; but to make them truly ours, we must think them over again honestly, till they take root in our personal experience.

— *Goethe, Johann Wolfgang Von*

If a man sits down to think, he is immediately asked if has a headache.

— *Emerson, Ralph Waldo*

Some thoughts always find us young, and keep us so. Such a thought is the love of the universal and eternal beauty.

— *Emerson, Ralph Waldo*

Thinking is the most unhealthy thing in the world, and people die of it just as they die of any other disease. Fortunately, in England at any rate, thought is not catching. Our splendid physique as a people is entirely due to our national stupidity.

— *Wilde, Oscar*

What is the hardest thing in the world? To think.

— *Emerson, Ralph Waldo*

Thought is a kind of opium; it can intoxicate us, while still broad awake; it can make transparent the mountains and everything that exists.

— *Amiel, Henri Frederic*

To think is to act.

— *Emerson, Ralph Waldo*

Many a man fails as an original thinker simply because his memory it too good.

— *Nietzsche, Friedrich*

(ii) Truth

Truth is always strange, stranger than fiction.

— *Lord Byron*

If you are out to describe the truth, leave elegance to the tailor.
— Einstein, Albert

Plato is dear to me, but dearer still is truth.
— Aristotle

All necessary truth is its own evidence.
— Emerson, Ralph Waldo

Every mind has a choice between truth and repose. Take which you please you can never have both.
— Emerson, Ralph Waldo

The greatest homage we can pay truth is to use it.
— Emerson, Ralph Waldo

Truth is beautiful, without doubt; but so are lies.
— Emerson, Ralph Waldo

Truth is the property of no individual but is the treasure of all men.
— Emerson, Ralph Waldo

Truth is the summit of being; justice is the application of it to affairs.
— Emerson, Ralph Waldo

Whoever undertakes to set himself up as judge in the eld of truth and knowledge is shipwrecked by the laughter of the Gods.
— Einstein, Albert

Anyone who doesn't take truth seriously in small matters cannot be trusted in large ones either.
— Einstein, Albert

I am not bound to win, but I am bound to be true. I am not bound to succeed but I am bound to live the best life that I have. I must stand with anybody that stands right and part from him when he goes wrong.
— Lincoln, Abraham

All these constructions and the laws connecting them can be arrived at by the principle of looking for the mathematically simplest concepts and the link between them.
— Einstein, Albert

Let the people know the truth and the country is safe.
— Lincoln, Abraham

Something unpleasant is coming when men are anxious to tell the truth.
— Disraeli, Benjamin

Time is precious, but truth is more precious than time.
— Disraeli, Benjamin

Never apologize for showing feeling. When you do so you apologize for truth.

— Disraeli, Benjamin

Truth must necessarily be stranger than fiction, for fiction is the creation of the human mind and therefore congenial to it.

— Chesterton, Gilbert Keith

You can only find truth with logic if you have already found truth without it.

— Chesterton, Gilbert Keith

Truth: An ingenious compound of desirability and appearance.

— Bierce, Ambrose

Truth arises more readily from error than from confusion.

— Bacon, Francis

The least initial deviation from the truth is multiplied later a thousandfold.

— Aristotle

The pursuit of truth and beauty is a sphere of activity in which we are permitted to remain children all our lives.

— Einstein, Albert

Rather than love, than money, than fame, give me truth.

— Thoreau, Henry David

if one tells the truth, one is sure, sooner or later, to be found out.

— Wilde, Oscar

The pure and simple truth is rarely pure and never simple.

— Wilde, Oscar

A thing is not necessarily true because a man dies for it.

— Wilde, Oscar

Truth is neither alive nor dead; it just aggravates itself all the time.

— Twain, Mark

Often the surest way to convey misinformation is to tell the strict truth.

— Twain, Mark

If you tell the truth, you don't have to remember anything.

— Twain, Mark

Truth is stranger than fiction, but it is because Fiction is obliged to stick to possibilities; Truth isn't.

— Twain, Mark

No real gentleman will tell the naked truth in the presence of ladies.

— Twain, Mark

Proverbs by Subjects

Never tell the truth to people who are not worthy of it.
— *Twain, Mark*

It is easier to perceive error than to find truth, for the former lies on the surface and is easily seen, while the latter lies in the depth, where few are willing to search for it.
— *Goethe, Johann Wolfgang Von*

It takes two to speak truth — one to speak, and another to hear.
— *Thoreau, Henry David*

Man is least himself when he talks in his own person. Give him a mask, and he will tell you the truth.
— *Wilde, Oscar*

Between whom there is hearty truth, there is love.
— *Thoreau, Henry David*

All great truths begin as blasphemies.
— *Shaw, George Bernard*

Though I can make my extravaganzas appear credible, I cannot make the truth appear so.
— *Shaw, George Bernard*

While you live tell the truth and shame the devil.
— *Shakespeare, William*

What is true belongs to me!
— *Seneca, Lucius Annaeus*

The more abstract the truth you want to teach, the more thoroughly you must seduce the senses to accept it.
— *Nietzsche, Friedrich*

Mystical explanations are considered deep. The truth is that they are not even superficial.
— *Nietzsche, Friedrich*

I believe that it is better to tell the truth than a lie. I believe it is better to be free than to be a slave. And I believe it is better to know than to be ignorant.
— *Mencken, Henry Louis*

It is hard to believe that a man is telling the truth when you know that you would lie if you were in his place.
— *Mencken, Henry Louis*

I never could tell a lie that anybody would doubt, nor a truth that anybody would believe.
— *Twain, Mark*

(iii) Learning

For the things we have to learn before we can do them, we learn by doing them.
— *Aristotle*

The things which hurt, instruct.
— *Franklin, Benjamin*

Studies serve for delight, for ornaments, and for ability.
— *Bacon, Francis*

Studies perfect nature and are perfected still by experience
— *Bacon, Francis*

Learning: The kind of ignorance distinguishing the studious.
— *Bierce, Ambrose*

With just enough of learning to misquote.
— *Lord Byron*

Seeing much, suffering much, and studying much, are the three pillars of learning.
— *Disraeli, Benjamin*

A university should be a place of light, of liberty, and of learning.
— *Disraeli, Benjamin*

The difference between what the most and the least learned people know is inexpressibly trivial in relation to that which is unknown.
— *Einstein, Albert*

We learn geology the morning after the earthquake.
— *Emerson, Ralph Waldo*

The years teach us much the days never knew.
— *Emerson, Ralph Waldo*

The studious class are their own victims: they are thin and pale, their feet are cold, their heads are hot, the night is without sleep, the day a fear of interruption -pallor, squalor, hunger, and egotism.
— *Emerson, Ralph Waldo*

In every man there is something wherein I may learn of him, and in that I am his pupil.
— *Emerson, Ralph Waldo*

The mind of the thoroughly well-informed man is a dreadful thing. It is like a bric-a-brac shop, all monsters and dust, with everything priced above its proper value.
— *Wilde, Oscar*

Learn of the skillful; he that teaches himself, has a fool for his master.
— *Franklin, Benjamin*

Proverbs by Subjects

He that won't be counseled can't be helped.
— *Franklin, Benjamin*

I've studied now Philosophy and Jurisprudence, Medicine - and even, alas! Theology - from end to end with labor keen; and here, poor fool with all my lore I stand, no wiser than before.
— *Goethe, Johann Wolfgang Von*

In the end we retain from our studies only that which we practically apply.
— *Goethe, Johann Wolfgang Von*

No one as ever completed their apprenticeship.
— *Goethe, Johann Wolfgang Von*

Everywhere, we learn only from those whom we love.
— *Goethe, Johann Wolfgang Von*

Their learning is like bread in a besieged town: every man gets a little, but no man gets a full meal.
— *Johnson, Samuel*

It takes a great deal of living to get a little deal of learning.
— *Ruskin, John*

That is never too often repeated, which is never sufficiently learned.
— *Seneca, Lucius Annaeus*

Never let formal education get in the way of your learning.
— *Twain, Mark*

Never learn to do anything. If you don't learn, you will always find someone else to do it for you.
— *Twain, Mark*

No man ever prayed heartily without learning something.
— *Emerson, Ralph Waldo*

— x —

10. VIRTUES

(i) Courage

Wealth lost is something lost, honor lost is something lost: Courage lost all is lost.
— *Goethe, Johann Wolfgang Von*

Be courageous. I have seen many depressions in business. Always America has emerged from these stronger and more prosperous. Be brave as your fathers before you. Have faith! Go forward!
— *Edison, Thomas Alva*

Courage consists in equality to the problem before us.

— Emerson, Ralph Waldo

When a resolute young fellow steps up to the great bully, the world, and takes him boldly by the beard, he is often surprised to find it comes off in his hand, and that it was only tied on to scare away the timid adventurers.

— Emerson, Ralph Waldo

Courage charms us, because it indicates that a man loves an idea better than all things in the world, that he is thinking neither of his bed, nor his dinner, nor his money, but will venture all to put in act the invisible thought of his mind.

— Emerson, Ralph Waldo

Half a man's wisdom goes with his courage.

— Emerson, Ralph Waldo

What a new face courage puts on everything!

— Emerson, Ralph Waldo

Whatever you do, you need courage. Whatever course you decide upon, there is always someone to tell you that you are wrong. There are always difficulties arising that tempt you to believe your critics are right. To map out a course of action and follow it to an end requires some of the same courage that a soldier needs. Peace has its victories, but it takes brave men and women to win them.

— Emerson, Ralph Waldo

A great part of courage is the courage of having done the thing before.

— Emerson, Ralph Waldo

Courage that grows from constitution often forsakes a man when he has occasion for it; courage which arises from a sense of duty acts; in a uniform manner.

— Addison, Joseph

The ideas that have lighted my way and, time after time, have given me new courage to face life cheerfully have been Kindness, Beauty, and Truth.

— Einstein, Albert

Courage is fire, and bullying is smoke.

— Disraeli, Benjamin

Courage is getting away from death by continually coming within an inch of it.

— Chesterton, Gilbert Keith

Courage is almost a contradiction in terms. It means a strong desire to live taking the form of a readiness to die.

— Chesterton, Gilbert Keith

Brave men are all vertebrates; they have their softness on the surface and their toughness in the middle.
— Chesterton, Gilbert Keith

The courage we desire and prize is not the courage to die decently, but to live manfully.
— Cartyle, Thomas

It is easy to fly into a passion... anybody can do that, but to be angry with the right person to the right extent and at the right time and in the right way... that is not easy.
— Aristotle

The ideal man bears the accidents of life with dignity and grace, making the best of circumstances.
— Aristotle

The beauty of the soul shines out when a man bears with composure one heavy mischance after another, not because he does not feel them, but because he is a man of high and heroic temper.
— Aristotle

To put it boldly, it is the attempt at a posterior reconstruction of existence by the process of conceptualization.
— Einstein, Albert

There is nothing in the world so much admired as a man who knows how to bear unhappiness with courage.
— Seneca, Lucius Annaeus

Courage is resistance to fear, mastery of fear — not absence of fear.
— Twain, Mark

It is curious that physical courage should be so common in the world, and moral courage so rare.
— Twain, Mark

I never thought much of the courage of a lion tamer. Inside the cage he is at least safe from people.
— Shaw, George Bernard

I dare to do all that may become a man: who dares do more is none.
— Shakespeare, William

That's a valiant flea that dares eat his breakfast on the lip of a lion.
— Shakespeare, William

But screw your courage to the sticking-place and we'll not fail.
— Shakespeare, William

Fortune can take away riches, but not courage.
— Seneca, Lucius Annaeus

Let us train our minds to desire what the situation demands.
— *Seneca, Lucius Annaeus*

Rest not. Life is sweeping by; go and dare before you die. Something mighty and sublime, leave behind to conquer time.
— *Goethe, Johann Wolfgang Von*

The pressure of adversity does not affect the mind of the brave man. It is more powerful than external circumstances.
— *Seneca, Lucius Annaeus*

Courage and modesty are the most unequivocal of virtues, for they are of a kind that hypocrisy cannot imitate; they too have this quality in common, that they are expressed by the same color.
— *Goethe, Johann Wolfgang Von*

Courage leads to heaven; fear leads to death.
— *Seneca, Lucius Annaeus*

Perfect courage is to do without witnesses what one would be capable of doing with the world looking on.
— *La Rochefoucauld, Francois de*

True bravery is shown by performing without witness what one might be capable of doing before all the world.
— *La Rochefoucauld, Francois de*

We can never be certain of our courage until we have faced danger.
— *La Rochefoucauld, Francois de*

Bravery has no place where it can avail nothing.
— *Johnson, Samuel*

Courage is a quality so necessary for maintaining virtue, that it is always respected, even when it is associated with vice.
— *Johnson, Samuel*

He that would be superior to external influences must first become superior to his own passions.
— *Johnson, Samuel*

It's not the size of the dog in the fight, it's the size of the fight in the dog.
— *Twain, Mark*

It is not because things are difficult that we do not dare; it is because we do not dare that they are difficult.
— *Seneca, Lucius Annaeus*

(ii) Knowledge

During the last century, and part of the one before, it was widely held that there was an unreconcilable conflict between knowledge and belief.
— Einstein, Albert

Never by reflection, but only by doing is self-knowledge possible to one.
— Goethe, Johann Wolfgang Von

God grant that not only the love of liberty but a thorough knowledge of the rights of man may pervade all the nations of the earth, so that a philosopher may set his foot anywhere on its surface and say: This is my country!
— Franklin, Benjamin

Proclaim not all thou knowest, all thou knowest, all thou hast, nor all thou cans't.
— Franklin, Beniamin

Knowledge is the only elegance.
— Emerson, Ralph Waldo

Knowledge is knowing that we cannot know.
— Emerson, Ralph Waldo

Knowledge comes by eyes always open and working hands; and there is no knowledge that is not power.
— Emerson. Ralph Waldo

Knowledge is that which, next to virtue, truly raises one person above another.
— Addison, Joseph

Of a truth, Knowledge is power, but it is a power reined by scruple, having a conscience of what must be and what may be; whereas Ignorance is a blind giant who, let him but wax unbound, would make it a sport to seize the pillars that hold up the long-wrought fabric of human good, and turn all the places of joy as dark as a buried Babylon.
— Eliot, George

More knowledge may be gained of a man's real character by a short conversation with one of his servants than from a formal and studied narrative, begun with his pedigree and ended with his funeral.
— Johnson, Samuel

Knowledge of what is does not open the door directly to what should be.
— Einstein, Albert

We don't know one-millionth of one percent about anything.
— Edison, Thomas Alva

One may understand the Cosmos, but never the ego; the self is more distant than any star.
— Chesterton, Gilbert Keith

Knowledge is the small part of ignorance that we arrange and classify.
— Bierce, Ambrose

Knowledge is power.
— Bacon, Francis

Knowledge and human power are synonymous.
— Bacon, Francis

I would have the studies elective. Scholarship is to be created not by compulsion, but by awakening a pure interest in knowledge. The wise instructor accomplishes this by opening to his pupils precisely the attractions the study has for himself. The marking is a system for schools, not for the college; for boys, not for men; and it is an ungracious work to put on a professor.
— Emerson, Ralph Waldo

Once thoroughly our own knowledge ceases to give us pleasure.
— Ruskin, John

I am not young enough to know everything.
— Wilde, Oscar

A man who carries a cat by the tail learns something he can learn in no other way.
— Twain, Mark

Between us, we cover all knowledge; he knows all that can be known and I know the rest.
— Twain, Mark

The trouble with the world is not that people know too little, but that they know so many things that ain't so.
— Twain, Mark

We have not the reverent feeling for the rainbow that a savage has, because we know how it is made. We have lost as much as we gained by prying into that matter.
— Twain, Mark

To know that we know what we know, and that we do not know what we do not know, that is true knowledge.
— Thoreau, Henry David

The greater the knowledge, the greater the doubt.
— Goethe, Johann Wolfgang Von

Own more than thou showest, speak less than thou knowest.
— Shakespeare, William

What is not fully understood is not possessed.
— *Goethe, Johann Wolfgang Von*

Our treasure lies in the beehive of our knowledge. We are perpetually on the way thither, being by nature winged insects and honey gatherers of the mind.
— *Nietzsche, Friedrich*

Knowledge always demands increase; it is like fire, which must first be kindled by some external agent, but will afterwards always propagate itself.
— *Johnson, Samuel*

Knowledge is more than equivalent to force.
— *Johnson, Samuel*

Knowledge is of two kinds: We know a subject ourselves, or we know where we can find information about it.
— *Johnson, Samuel*

Man is not weak; knowledge is more than equivalent to force.
— *Johnson, Samuel*

The next best thing to knowing something is knowing where to find it.
— *Johnson, Samuel*

There are only two kinds of people who are really fascinating- people who know absolutely everything, and people who know absolutely nothing.
— *Wilde, Oscar*

Knowledge does not come to us in details, but in flashes of light from heaven.
Thoreau, Henry David

(iii) Character

Weakness of character is the only defect which cannot be amended.
— *La Rochefoucauld, Francois de*

Judge of your natural character by what you do in dreams.
— *Emerson, Ralph Waldo*

Make the most of yourself, for that is all there is of you.
— *Emerson, Ralph Waldo*

No change of circumstances can repair a defect of character.
— *Emerson, Ralph Waldo*

People seem not to see that their opinion of the world is also a confession of character.
— *Emerson, Ralph Waldo*

That which we call character is a reserved force which acts directly by presence, and without means. It is conceived of as a certain undemonstrable force, a familiar or genius, by whose impulses the man is guided, but whose counsels he cannot impart.
— Emerson, Ralph Waldo

Gross and obscure natures, however decorated, seem impure shambles; but character gives splendor to youth, and awe to wrinkled skin and gray hairs.
— Emerson, Ralph Waldo

It is not what he had, or even what he does which expresses the worth of a man, but what he is.
— Amiel, Henri Frederic

We should be too big to take offense and too noble to give it.
— Lincoln, Abraham

Character develops itself in the stream of life.
— Goethe, Johann Wolfgang Von

Character is like a tree and reputation like its shadow. The shadow is what we think of it; the tree is the real thing.
— Lincoln, Abraham

There is no greater index of character so sure as the voice.
— Disraeli, Benjamin

Characters do not change. Opinions alter, but characters are only developed.
— Disraeli, Benjamin

Show me the man you honor, and I will know what kind of a man you are. It shows me what your ideal of manhood is, and what kind of a man you long to be.
— Carlyle, Thomas

Dignity does not consist in possessing honors, but in deserving them.
— Aristotle

Character is that which reveals moral purpose, exposing the class of things a man chooses or avoids.
— Aristotle

A character is like an acrostic or Alexandrian stanza; read it forward, backward, or across, it still spells the same thing.
— Emerson, Ralph Waldo

Character is the result of two things: Mental attitude and the way we spend our time.
— Hubbard, Elbert

To arrive at a just estimate of a renowned man's character one must judge it by the standards of his time, not ours.
— Twain, Mark

Proverbs by Subjects

We falsely attribute to men a determined character — putting together all their yesterdays — and averaging them — we presume we know them. Pity the man who has character to support — it is worse than a large family — he is the silent poor indeed.

— *Thoreau, Henry David*

The universe seems bankrupt as soon as we begin to discuss the characters of individuals.

— *Thoreau, Henry David*

Pity the man who has a character to support —it is worse than a large family — he is silent poor indeed.

— *Thoreau, Henry David*

We know but a few men, a great many coats and breeches.

— *Thoreau, Henry David*

Character is higher than intellect. A great soul will be strong to live as well as think.

— *Emerson, Ralph Waldo*

Life every man holds dear; but the dear man holds honor far more precious dear than life.

— *Shakespeare, William*

Do what you know and perception is converted into character.

— *Emerson, Ralph Waldo*

The formation of one's character ought to be everyone's chief aim.

— *Goethe, Johann Wolfgang Von*

Talents are best nurtured solitude. Character is best formed in the stormy billows of the world.

— *Goethe, Johann Wolfgang Von*

Men show their character in nothing more clearly than what they think laughable.

— *Goethe, Johann Wolfgang Von*

Character, in great and little things, means carrying through what you feel able to do.

— *Goethe, Johann Wolfgang Von*

Character is formed in the stormy billows of the world.

— *Goethe, Johann Wolfgang Von*

It is only the superficial qualities that last. Man's deeper nature is soon found out.

— *Wilde, Oscar*

The empty vessel makes the loudest sound.

— *Shakespeare, William*

(iv) Genius

We know that the nature of genius is to provide idiots with ideas twenty years later.
— *Aragon, Louis*

Neither a lofty degree of intelligence nor imagination nor both together go to the making of genius. Love, love, love, that is the soul of genius.
— *Mozart, Wolfgang Amadeus*

To believe your own thought, to believe that what is true for you in your private heart is true for all men - that is genius.
— *Emerson, Ralph Waldo*

Doing easily what others find difficult is talent; doing what is impossible for talent is genius.
— *Amiel, Henri Frederic*

There is no great genius without a mixture of madness.
— *Aristotle*

Genius is an infinite capacity for taking pains.
— *Carlyle, Thomas*

Genius, when young, is divine.
— *Disraeli, Benjamin*

Patience is a necessary ingredient of genius.
— *Disraeli, Benjamin*

His genius he was quite content in one brief sentence to define: Of inspiration one percent, of perspiration, ninety nine.
— *Edison, Thomas Alva*

Genius is one percent inspiration and ninety-nine percent perspiration.
— *Edison, Thomas Alva*

Genius at first is little more than a great capacity for receiving discipline.
— *Eliot, George*

The greatest genius is the most indebted person.
— *Emerson, Ralph Waldo*

Coffee is good for talent, but genius wants prayer.
— *Emerson, Ralph Waldo*

In every work of genius we recognize our own rejected thoughts; they come back to us with a certain alienated majesty.
— *Emerson, Ralph Waldo*

To do easily what is difficult for others is the mark of talent. To do what is impossible for talent is the mark of genius.
— *Amiel, Henri Frederic*

Proverbs by Subjects

The hearing ear is always found close to the speaking tongue; and no genius can long or often utter anything which is not invited and gladly entertained by men around him.
— *Emerson, Ralph Waldo*

The public is wonderfully tolerant. It forgives everything except genius.
— *Wilde, Oscar*

Only an inventor knows how to borrow, and every man is or should be an inventor.
— *Emerson, Ralph Waldo*

A man of genius is privileged only as far as he is genius. His dullness is as insupportable as any other dullness.
— *Emerson, Ralph Waldo*

When Nature has work to be done, she creates a genius to do it.
— *Emerson, Ralph Waldo*

Hide not your talents. They for use were made. What's a sundial in the shade.
— *Franklin, Benjamin*

Genius without education is like silver in the mine.
— *Franklin, Benjamin*

The first and last thing required of genius is, love of the truth.
— *Goethe, Johann Wolfgang Von*

The greatest genius will never be worth much if he pretends to draw exclusively from his own resources.
— *Goethe, Johann Wolfgang Von*

Towering genius disdains a beaten path.
— *Lincoln, Abraham*

Thousands of geniuses live and die undiscovered, either by themselves or by others.
— *Twain, Mark*

I have nothing to declare except my genius.
— *Wilde, Oscar*

Genius lasts longer than Beauty. That accounts for the fact that we all take such pains to over-educate ourselves.
— *Wilde, Oscar*

I put all my genius into my life; I put only my talent into my works.
— *Wilde, Oscar*

Accept your genius and say what you think.
— *Emerson. Ralph Waldo*

(v) Wisdom

There is more wisdom in your body than in your deepest philosophy.
— *Nietzsche, Friedrich*

Who is the wisest man? He who neither knows or wishes for anything else than what happens.
— *Goethe, Johann Wolfgang Von*

Silence is the sleep that nourishes wisdom.
— *Bacon, Francis*

It is characteristic of wisdom not to do desperate things.
— *Thoreau, Henry David*

As it is the characteristic of great wits to say much in few words, so small wits seem to have the gift of speaking much and saying nothing.
— *La Rochefoucauld, Francois de*

Where sense is wanting, everything is wanting.
— *Franklin, Benjamin*

The doors of wisdom are never shut.
— *Franklin, Benjamin*

Let us be poised, and wise, and our own, today.
— *Emerson, Ralph Waldo*

Life is a festival only to the wise.
— *Emerson, Ralph Waldo*

Great men are the commissioned guides of mankind, who rule their fellows because they are wiser.
— *Carlyle, Thomas*

He is no wise man who will quit a certainty for an uncertainty.
— *Johnson, Samuel*

The greatest event for the world is the arrival of a new and wise person.
— *Carlyle, Thomas*

There is a time when a man distinguishes the idea of felicity from the idea of wealth; it is the beginning of wisdom.
— *Emerson, Ralph Waldo*

Wisdom is like electricity. There is no permanently wise man, but men capable of wisdom, who, being put into certain company, or other favorable conditions, become wise for a short time, as glasses rubbed acquire electric power for a while.
— *Emerson, Ralph Waldo*

Mixing one's wines may be a mistake, but old and new wisdom mix admirably.
— *Brecht, Bertolt*

There is a difference between happiness and wisdom: he that thinks himself the happiest man is really so; but he that

thinks himself the wisest is generally the greatest fool.
— Bacon, Francis

Raphael paints wisdom; Handel sings it, Phidias carves it, Shakespeare writes it, Wren builds it, Columbus sails it, Luther preaches it, Washington arms it, Watt mechanizes it.
— Emerson, Ralph Waldo

This is the highest wisdom that I own; freedom and life are earned by those alone who conquer them each day anew.
— Goethe, Johann Wolfgang Von

A man never reaches that dizzy height of wisdom that he can no longer be lead by the nose.
— Twain, Mark

It's the height of folly to want to be the only wise one.
— La Rochefoucauld, Francois de

It is more easy to be wise for others than for ourselves.
— La Rochefoucauld, Francois de

It is great folly to wish to be wise all alone.
— La Rochefoucauld, Francois de

No matter how long he lives, no man ever becomes as wise as the average woman of forty-eight.
— Mencken, Henry Louis

The growth of wisdom may be gauged exactly by the diminution of ill temper.
— Nietzsche, Friedrich

Does wisdom perhaps appear on the earth as a raven which is inspired by the smell of carrion?
— Nietzsche, Friedrich

Wisdom does not show itself so much in precept as in life — in firmness of mind and a mastery of appetite. It teaches us to do as well as to talk; and to make our words and actions all of a color.
— Seneca, Lucius Annaeus

So wise so young, they say, do never live long.
— Shakespeare, William

To be wise and love exceeds man's might.
— Shakespeare, William

The only man I know who behaves sensibly is my tailor; he takes my measurements anew each time he sees me. The rest go on with their old measurements and expect me to fit them.
— Shaw, George Bernard

Wisdom is found only in truth.
— Goethe, Johann Wolfgang Von